# Inequalities in the Teaching Profession

D1187970

# Inequalities in the Teaching Profession

## A Global Perspective

Edited by

Marie-Pierre Moreau
*Reader in Education, University of Roehampton, UK*

First published 2014 by
PALGRAVE MACMILLAN

Palgrave Macmillan in the UK is an imprint of Macmillan Publishers Limited, registered in England, company number 785998, of Houndmills, Basingstoke, Hampshire RG21 6XS.

Palgrave Macmillan in the US is a division of St Martin's Press LLC, 175 Fifth Avenue, New York, NY 10010.

Palgrave Macmillan is the global academic imprint of the above companies and has companies and representatives throughout the world.

Palgrave® and Macmillan® are registered trademarks in the United States, the United Kingdom, Europe and other countries.

ISBN 978–1–137–32859–5

This book is printed on paper suitable for recycling and made from fully managed and sustained forest sources. Logging, pulping and manufacturing processes are expected to conform to the environmental regulations of the country of origin.

A catalogue record for this book is available from the British Library.

A catalog record for this book is available from the Library of Congress.

# Contents

# Acknowledgements

A number of people have helped me to progress from the initial book idea to the final manuscript. I would like to acknowledge the support of my colleagues at the University of Bedfordshire, where I was based during the course of this project. In particular, I am very much indebted to Annika Coughlin for endorsing the role of a critical friend and for reading and commenting on various aspects of this volume. Thank you, Annika. I am also grateful to Heather Mendick, Brunel University, for commenting on some of the material included in this volume and for providing me with some much-needed advice over the years. The conversations I have had during the course of my PhD with Nicky Le Feuvre (Université de Lausanne), Merryn Hutchings and Lyn Thomas (both previously at London Metropolitan University) still resonate and shape the way I think about equality issues – thank you. I am grateful to Andrew James, my editor at Palgrave Macmillan, for his enthusiasm about this project and for 'making it happen'. As always, Julien and Nina Malzac deserve some special thanks for their love and support, and so do my extended family and friends. Last but not least, I would like to thank the book's contributors – I have been incredibly lucky to work with a bunch of such capable and generous people.

# Contributors

**Anthony L. Brown** is Associate Professor of Curriculum and Instruction and Fellow in the Lawrence & Stel Marie Lowman College of Education Endowed Excellence Fund at the University of Texas at Austin. He is also affiliated faculty in the area of Cultural Studies in Education at the John Warfield Center of African and African American Studies. He received his BA and MA in Political Science from California State University, Long Beach, and received his PhD from the University of Wisconsin–Madison. Overall, his work pursues a theoretical argument, which suggests that the examination of the historical and racial constructions of African Americans in social sciences and educational literature, popular discourse and curriculum is vital to making sense of how questions are raised and how educational and curricular reforms are pursued for African American students in the present. His work has been published in *Teachers College Record, Harvard Educational Review, Race Ethnicity and Education* and the *Journal of Education Policy*.

**Keffrelyn D. Brown** is Associate Professor in the Department of Curriculum and Instruction and Fellow in the Lawrence & Stel Marie Lowman College of Education Endowed Excellence Fund at the University of Texas at Austin. She holds a primary appointment in the Cultural Studies in Education area. Keffrelyn is a former elementary and middle school teacher, school administrator and curriculum developer. Her research and teaching interests concern the sociocultural knowledge of teaching, multicultural teacher education and educational discourses related to African American students. She has published numerous journal articles, book chapters and other educational texts. She serves on the editorial boards for *Teachers College Record, Race Ethnicity and Education, Teaching and Teacher Education* and *Urban Education*.

**Anita K. W. Chan** is Associate Professor in the Department of Social Sciences, Hong Kong Institute of Education. She has deep interests in gender issues in the field of education and family studies. Her research covers the following topics: life history of school principals, cultural constructions of motherhood and childhood in parenting magazines, family changes and experiences and identities of cross-border students.

Her publications have appeared in journals such as *Gender and Education, History of Education, Equal Opportunities International, Families, Relationships and Societies* and *Gender Equity Education Quarterly*. She is also the co-editor of the following books: *Gendering Hong Kong Society: A Reader* (2004), *The Making of Gender Identities: Education & Personal Growth* (2012) and *Gender Perspectives in Education: Empirical Research into Schooling Processes* (2012).

**Tania Ferfolja** is Senior Lecturer in the School of Education at the University of Western Sydney, Australia. She teaches and researches in the areas of social justice and equity in education. Her research interests focus on Lesbian, Gay, Bisexual, Transgender, Queer and Intersex (LGBTQI) issues in education, particularly in relation to the intersections of subjectivities with school cultures, policies and practices. She has written extensively on the working lives and experiences of sexually diverse teachers, and her work has been published internationally. She is also the lead author of *Crossing Borders: African Refugees, Teachers and Schools* (2011) and is a co-editor of *From Here to Diversity: The Social Impact of Lesbian and Gay Issues in Education in Australia and New Zealand* (2002).

**June A. Gordon** is Professor of Education at the University of California, Santa Cruz. She received her BA in East Asian Studies from Stanford University and her PhD in Educational Leadership and Policy Studies from the University of Washington. She served as Visiting Research Professor at the University of Tokyo in 2002–2003 and received a Japan Foundation Research Fellowship in 2006. Her research explores how economics, culture and politics impact educational options and opportunities for young people. She has conducted research in a variety of countries, including the United States, Japan, China, Great Britain, India and Bhutan. Her work is also informed by visits to Myanmar, Iran, Vietnam, Cambodia, Laos and Indonesia, as well as various parts of Latin America, Europe and Africa. She has published four books, including *Challenges to Japanese Education: Economics, Reform and Human Rights; Japan's Outcaste Youth: Education for Liberation; Beyond the Classroom Walls: Ethnographic Inquiry as Pedagogy;* and *The Color of Teaching,* as well as numerous articles and chapters. Currently she is exploring ways in which Asian immigration is influencing American education.

**Elina Lahelma** is Professor of Education at the University of Helsinki, Finland. Her fields of research are sociology of education and gender studies in education. She has conducted ethnographic studies in secondary schools, longitudinal life historical studies of young people's transitions and documentary analysis focusing on gender and differences in education. She is interested in the construction of gender, nationality, difference and processes of inclusion and exclusion in education. She has published extensively in Finland and internationally. She is also leader of the Cultural and Feminist Studies in Education research community at the University of Helsinki. She has directed several research projects funded by the Academy of Finland and the Finnish Ministry of Education. She is a senior member of the Nordic Centre of Excellence 'Justice through Education in the Nordic Countries' (2013–2017).

**Jukka Lehtonen** is Professor Adjunct of the Sociology of Education at the University of Helsinki, Finland. His work specialises in gender, sexuality and youth studies. He has conducted various research projects on sexual and gender diversity in the contexts of education, work and social work and health care. His PhD thesis (2003) explored heteronormativity in schools. He has directed a range of research projects about gender and sexuality, funded by the European Social Fund, the Finnish Ministry of Labour and the Academy of Finland. His current research focuses on non-heterosexual and transgender youth in upper secondary education, including a study of LGBT youth work in Finland and South Africa (2013–2016, funded by the Academy of Finland).

**Christine Mallozzi** is Assistant Professor of Literacy Education in the Curriculum and Instruction Department at the University of Kentucky, USA. She was awarded the Carol J. Fisher Award for Excellence in Research from the University of Georgia. Dr. Mallozzi's research interests include gender and teacher education, middle grades reading education, feminist theories and discourse analysis. Her work involves studies of women teachers' bodies and gender issues among teachers.

**Wayne J. Martino** is Professor of Education in the Faculty of Education at Western University, Canada. Previously, he taught in the School of Education at Murdoch University, Perth, Western Australia. His research interests are in the fields of gender equity, boys' education, masculinities, minority underachievement and queer and transgender studies in education. He has published in a range of international refereed journals and serves on several editorial boards. His books include *So What's a Boy? Addressing Issues of Masculinity and Schooling* (with Maria Pallotta-Chiarolli, 2003), *'Being Normal Is the Only Way to Be'*: *Adolescent Perspectives on Gender and School* (with Maria Pallotta-Chiarolli, 2005), *Gendered Outcasts and Sexual Outlaws: Sexual Oppression and Gender Hierarchies in Queer Men's Lives* (with Christopher Kendall, 2006), *Boys and Schooling: Beyond Structural Reform* (with Bob Lingard and Martin Mills, 2009), *The Problem with Boys' Education: Beyond the Backlash* (with Michael Kehler and Marcus Weaver-Hightower, 2009), *Gender, Race and the Politics of Role Modelling: The Influence of Male Teachers* (with Goli Rezai-Rashti, 2012) and *Canadian Men and Masculinities* (with Christopher Greig, 2012). His most recent book is titled *Globalizing Educational Accountabilities: Testing Regimes and Rescaling Governance* (co-authored with Bob Lingard, Goli Rezai-Rashti and Sam Sellar, 2014).

**Marie-Pierre Moreau** is Reader in Education at the University of Roehampton, UK. Her research is at the nexus of education, work and equality issues, with particular reference to gender. She has published many articles in international refereed journals, including in *Gender and Education, Gender Work and Organisation, Discourse: Studies in the Cultural Politics of Education, Studies in Higher Education, Journal of Education Policy, Cambridge Journal of Education* and *British Journal of Sociology of Education*. Her first book, *Les Enseignants et Le Genre: Les inégalités hommes-femmes dans l'enseignement du second degré en France et en Angleterre* (2011), was a comparative study of gender inequalities in the teaching profession in England and France. She serves on several editorial boards and is an elected Executive Member of the Gender and Education Association.

**Tarja Palmu** is Adjunct Professor in Education. She works as a university researcher in the Department of Behavioral Sciences at the University of Helsinki. Her research interests are focused on gender and education in the field of life history and ethnographic studies. Currently she works on a research project entitled 'Citizenship, Agency and Difference in Upper Secondary Education' (funded by Academy of Finland, 2010–2013), led by Professor Elina Lahelma.

**Ninetta Santoro** has recently taken up a Chair in Education at the University of Strathclyde in Scotland, having previously been a Professor of Education and Head of the School of Teacher Education at Charles Sturt University. She has almost 20 years' experience in the preparation of teachers for multi-ethnic contexts. Her research draws on post-structuralist theories to examine how learner and teacher identities are constructed and taken up in education. Her work falls into three interrelated main areas: teacher ethnicity and race and how these positionings shape pedagogy and practice; teacher education for ethnically and racially diverse contexts; and culturally responsive pedagogy. Professor Santoro has published widely in the areas of race and ethnicity, teacher education and qualitative research methodologies. She has been a co-editor of the *Asia-Pacific Journal of Teacher Education* since 2008.

**Jill Sperandio** is Associate Professor of Education in the College of Education at Lehigh University in Pennsylvania, where she currently teaches graduate students seeking leadership positions in schools. Her professional career has spanned all aspects of education, as school teacher and administrator, teacher trainer, program evaluator and college lecturer, and she has lived and worked in over ten countries throughout the world. She received her doctorate from the University of Chicago with a study of girls' access to secondary education in Uganda. Her research interests continue to focus on issues of gender in education, including issues of social justice and women's access to school leadership in both national and international contexts, and she has published widely. She most recently completed a study of women in the superintendency in Pennsylvania.

**Nicky Watts** is Associate Lecturer in Teacher Education at Sheffield Hallam University. She has worked in primary education for 25 years. Her areas of interest include provision for children with special educational needs and the impact of digital technologies in educational settings. She has recently completed a doctoral study on the perceptions of older female primary school teachers in England. This experience has opened her eyes to the issues surrounding intergenerational fairness in our society.

# Part I

# Mapping and Understanding Inequalities in the Teaching Profession

# 1
# Introduction: Theorising and Mapping Inequalities in the Teaching Profession

*Marie-Pierre Moreau*

## Inequalities in the teaching profession, the *parent pauvre* of education research?

Since the 1970s, equality issues in education have generated a wealth of research in many regions of the world. This extensive corpus has shed light on how education contributes to the formation of learners' identities and on how social class, gender, ethnicity and other identity markers play out in this process (see, for example, Archer and Francis, 2007; Gillborn, 2008; Martino and Meyenn, 2001; Mills, 2003; Modood, 2003; Modood and Shiner, 2002; Moss, 2007; Reay, 2002; Skelton and Francis, 2003; Spender, 1982; Willis, 1977). Crucially for governments, groups and individuals with a concern for social justice, this work has shown that education can open avenues towards social change (Bowles, 1983; hooks, 1994), yet simultaneously represents a site where social divides reproduce (Bourdieu and Passeron, 1970).

However, schools and other education settings do not solely represent a site for learning: they provide employment opportunities to a range of occupational and professional groups, including school teachers, the focus of this volume. Compared with learners, teachers appear to be the *parent pauvre* of research and policy intervention addressing social justice issues in education. The relative wealth of studies exploring the relationship between teachers' and students' identities, including the way teachers contribute to the production of gendered, raced and classed identities among learners (Allard, 2004; Causey et al., 2000; Echols and Stader, 2002; Kannen and Acker, 2008; Olmedo, 1997; Walkerdine et al., 2001), has not been matched by a similar amount of research on the effects of social structures and school cultures on teachers' identities.

3

In relation to this point, Allard and Santoro (2006) argue that, 'Too often, the focus is on developing student teachers' understandings of how gender, ethnicity, "race" and class shape *learner* identities but how these *also* shape *teachers'* identities is rarely explored' (p. 116, emphasis in original).

While Allard and Santoro's comment was made in relation to research, their point finds particular resonance in relation to policy. When policymakers have been concerned with identity and equality issues in the teaching profession, such concern has usually been driven by instrumental motives, that is, the need to understand how the composition of the teaching body affects students in relation to their academic performance, behaviour or identity formation, rather than by some interest in teachers *per se*. In that respect, the debate on 'boys' underachievement', which has been ongoing in a range of countries since the late 1980s (for example, in Australia, Canada, Ireland, New Zealand, the UK and the United States), provides a striking illustration. In these countries, concerns for bringing more male teachers, in particular Black male teachers, in the profession have been driven by the view encapsulated in government reports and policy texts that this will automatically bring benefits for boys, while simultaneously reviving the status of the profession through its statistical and normative 'masculinisation' (see, for example, Canadian Teachers' Federation, 2002; DfEE, 1998; Education Queensland, 2002). Such views have been profusely criticised by feminist researchers, who have highlighted the lack of empirical evidence and the flawed assumptions undergirding this argument (Epstein et al., 1998; Francis, 1999; Francis and Skelton, 2005; Hutchings, 2002; Hutchings et al., 2008; Moreau, 2011b). In addition, it has been noted that this policy focus usually disregards the issues faced by women and minority ethnic teachers (such as access to the most rewarded and prestigious segments of the profession and experiences of sexist/racist abuse in and out of the classroom) or even compounds these, for example when women teachers are blamed for 'feminising' boys and hindering their academic performance (Skelton, 2002).

While there may be a lack of interest for inequalities in the teaching profession, one would be mistaken, however, to conclude that there is an absence of research activity in this area, as evidenced by the original contributions gathered in this volume. Indeed, researchers have explored how teaching offers a range of opportunities to individuals from a range of backgrounds, and how these opportunities are constrained by processes of exclusion and marginalisation which permeate national, local and school cultures. While this book focuses on inequalities based on identity markers such as race, gender and class, it does acknowledge that power relationships take other forms. For example, school managers usually have considerably more power than classroom teachers (Blase and Blase, 2002; Coleman, 2002). Some educational institutions and subjects are more valued than others, often resulting in a hierarchy of teachers, based on whom and what they teach (Chapter 2; Palheta, 2011; Richards and Acker, 2006; Santee Siskin and Warren Little, 1995). In particular, secondary school teaching usually confers higher status than primary teaching (Chapter 3). These divides, however, often reflect the broader power relationships at play in society, with individuals belonging to dominated groups tending to concentrate in the segments of the teaching profession associated with the lower levels of financial and symbolic capitals.

## The development of a feminist sociology of women teachers

From the 1980s onwards, second- and third-wave feminists have played a key role in documenting the experiences of women teachers. Much of this work has explored how social expectations of women constrained the opportunity for them to enter the teaching profession during the 19th and 20th centuries (for example, Acker, 1989, 1994, 1999; Brehmer, 1980; Clifford, 1981; Cortina and San Román, 2006; De Lyon and Widdowson Migniuolo, 1989; Grumet, 1988; Hoffman, 1981Markowitz, 1993; Miller, 1996; Prentice and Theobald, 1991; Rogers and van Essen, 2003; Schmuck, 1980; Tamboukou, 2003).

While there had been some earlier work on women teachers, this scholarship has developed on an unprecedented scale and has been associated with a paradigm shift, departing from a sociology of education, work and the professions which either ignored women, blamed their 'less successful' careers through a 'deficit' discourse or correlated their presence with the decline of the status of the profession (see, for example, Etzioni, 1969). This has led to studies exploring the cultural association of women with children and care (Beatty, 1990; Chan, 2004; Chapter 3) or what Gannerud has described as 'a long-lasting appreciation of the relationship between teaching as "women's work" and related to mothering, where the positioning of women close to children is both normal (needing no analysis) and acceptable (needing no critique)' (2001, p. 61).

While it is indeed the case that, in many countries, the majority of school teachers are women (Eurydice, 2013; UNESCO, 2010), their proportion varies significantly across subjects, phases and levels of responsibility (Hutchings, 2002), as well as across countries and periods of time. As noted by Acker (1994), 'The relative proportions of men and women, of single women and married women, of female head teachers and male head teachers, have all varied over time in response to government policies, wars, population trends, social attitudes and economic circumstances' (p. 83). Other work has concentrated on the social construction of teaching as a suitable occupation for some women, and on how this has evolved over time. In particular, some of this literature recalls how, in some countries, the figure of the 'spinster' teacher became increasingly vilified and pathologised between the two world wars, leading the way to an image of teaching as a profession suitable for married women, who had previously been excluded from the profession due to the 'marriage bar' or to implicit social norms which condemned their participation in the teaching profession (Cacouault, 1984; Cacouault-Bitaud, 1999; Oram, 1989; Schroeder, 1991).

Other feminist scholars have concentrated on providing explanations of the under-representation of women in the most prestigious and rewarded segments of the teaching labour market (Eurydice, 2013), with many focusing on the so-called glass ceiling (Wirth, 2001). As well as critically exploring the cultural link between leadership and masculinity (Mahony et al., 2004), these studies have considered how headteachers' and governors' prejudiced attitudes towards women, national welfare policies, teachers' working conditions and the gendered division of domestic and care work hinder the progression of women teachers on the career ladder (Coleman, 2002; Moreau, 2011a; Moreau et al., 2007, 2008).

Some of the most recent work in this area, often informed by a feminist post-structuralist perspective, has focused on the regimes of surveillance to which women teachers are subjected, both inside and outside the classroom. In contrast with earlier feminist work, which had emphasised how the opportunities offered to this group are constrained by social contexts, this scholarship tends to foreground women teachers' agency and resistance, as argued by Essen and Rogers (2003) and as illustrated by the work of Tamboukou in the UK (2003) and Mallozzi in the United States (2012; see also Chapter 6).

## Post-colonial and feminist theories and the development of a scholarship on Black and minority ethnic teachers

During the 1980s and 1990s, a scholarship informed by post-colonial and critical race theories explored the lives of Black and minority ethnic teachers, including barriers to entry in the profession and experiences of racism for practising teachers (Foster, 1998; Osler, 1997; Troyna, 1994).

The implicit association between femininity and Whiteness which underpinned many studies of women teachers became challenged by Black feminists (for example, Hills-Collins, 1990), who called for the redefinition of feminist frameworks to reflect the experiences of Black and minority ethnic women and, more generally, for a more intersectional approach to social structures of power (Crenshaw, 1989). It led to a range of studies informing the experiences of Black and minority ethnic women teachers (Bangar and McDermott, 1989; Casey, 1993; Henry, 1995). Only recently has some similar work on Black and minority ethnic men teachers emerged (Brown, 2009, 2011; Lewis, 2006; Lynn, 2006; see also Chapter 10).

The existing literature on teachers and race comes predominantly from the United States, as well as, to a lesser extent, from the UK and Canada. In the United States, as recalled in Brown (2012), earlier theorisation of Black teachers goes back to the 19th century. Some of these accounts discuss the contribution of Black teachers, with some emphasising the benefits of providing Black teachers to the Black community and others questioning the assumption that all Black teachers are automatically in a position to provide a valuable experience to Black students (see, for example, Blackshear, [1902] 1969; Woodson, [1933] 2000) – a debate which remains vivid to this day.

The studies of teachers and race which emerged in the 1980s and 1990s challenged earlier discourses which had blamed and pathologised Black communities, often through a psychological lens (Hannerz, 1970; Moynihan, 1967). This work explored Black teachers' pedagogy and how this and their wider experiences were shaped by politics of race (Foster, 1991, 1998; Howard, 2001; King 1991; Ladson-Billings 1994; Osler, 1997). While the perceived need for attracting more Black (male) teachers to the profession has a long history in the United States, this debate was further reignited by the election of Barack Obama to the US presidency, with the introduction of a nationwide campaign to increase the presence of Black men in schools (Williamson, 2011, in Brown, 2012). Policies concerned with the racial diversity and representativeness of the teaching profession have also emerged in other regions of the world. In the UK, the government and a number of high-profile politicians have made calls for attracting more Black and minority ethnic teachers, particularly men, in the profession (see, for example, Abbott, 2002; DfEE, 1998). In Australia, a range of initiatives have been implemented over the past 40 years to increase the numbers of Indigenous teachers in schools (see Chapter 4).

While most authors concur in thinking that the attraction of Black and minority ethnic teachers to the profession represents a cause for celebration, the rationale underpinning the perceived 'need' for Black (male) teachers has attracted a number of criticisms. In particular, it has been argued that constructions of the Black male teacher as 'the ideal pedagogue and role model for the Black male student' and 'the central agent of social change for Black male students' feed into a wider discourse which essentialises race and gender and constructs Black teachers as a homogeneous group (Brown, 2012, p. 297). By presenting the Black teacher as a 'saviour', it is also implicitly assumed that Black children need 'to be saved' and Black communities need to be 'fixed' (Brown, 2012; see also Chapter 10). This discourse 'reifies problematic raced and gendered stereotypes that privilege the physical capacities of African American men, rather than their mental and pedagogical capacities to work with Black male students' (Brown, 2012, p. 311). Also problematic is the fact that Black women and Black girls are usually absent from this policy intervention. Similar constructions of Black and minority ethnic teachers are not unheard of in other countries. In the UK, the call for more Black teachers has sometimes been problematically justified by the need to tackle 'gang violence' (Johnson, 2007, in Callender, 2012) although there is evidence that Black and minority ethnic teachers do not necessarily envision their role in those terms, nor see themselves as 'cultural experts' (Basit and Santoro, 2011).

Other research on this group has specifically focused on barriers to entry in the profession, and retention issues, for example, pointing to discrepancies between the composition of the teaching workforce and the student population, to the difficulties faced by some Black and minority ethnic teachers in finding work in schools and to their commonplace allocation to schools which are difficult to staff (Callender, 2012; DCSF, 2008; Maylor et al., 2006; Santoro et al., 2011), although there are major differences across countries and ethnic groups. Other studies have highlighted experiences of racism for practising Black and minority ethnic teachers. For example, Foster (1993) has observed that Black teachers 'often report feeling alienated from the school and its culture, outside collegial and friendship groups' (p. 103). Some of this work also highlights the resistance of predominantly White communities to this group (Casey, 1993; Foster, 1998) and how their credentials and skills are questioned by parents and colleagues (Carrington and Tomlin, 2000; Osler, 1997; Siraj-Blatchford, 1991). Other work has shown that Black and minority ethnic teachers can be disadvantaged in achieving leadership roles (Hargreaves, 2011; Powney et al., 2003). While evidence of the significance of religion in teachers' lives remains scarce, Black and minority ethnic teachers from religious minorities can experience multiple prejudices, particularly Islamophobia in the case of Muslim teachers living in the West (Osler, 1997, 2003). However, not all minority ethnic groups have been given the same level of attention (see Chapter 4). In addition, there has been limited research problematising the experiences of White majority teachers (in countries where they represent the majority) – something which may be seen as part of a discourse in which Whiteness constitutes the norm and remains invisible.

## Emerging voices: Masculinities and sexual minorities in the teaching profession

There is not a great tradition of researching the experiences of men and of sexual minorities in teaching. Until recently, masculinity was left unproblematised and heterosexuality was assumed to be the norm. However, research on this group has considerably taken off during the first decade of the 21st century, as exemplified by a range of publications exploring the experiences of men and of lesbian, gay, bisexual and transgender (LGBT) teachers, as well as the related construction of teaching through a heteronormative matrix (see, for example, Cushman, 2008; Ferfolja, 2007, 2008; McCarthy, 2003; Rudoe, 2010).

Recognising, as this volume does, 'the privileged position from which men operate within the existing gender order' (Mills et al., 2004, p. 359) and, in particular, the 'glass escalator' (Williams, 1992) which benefit many men teachers does not imply that the study of masculinities is irrelevant to the study of inequalities in the teaching profession: first, gender is relational; second, men play a central role in the reproduction of inequalities; third, most men will experience domination during their lifetime, because they do not subscribe to a hegemonic type of masculinity or because of their 'other' identities, for example, in relation to their ethnic or class background. In particular, where and when teaching is constructed as a 'caring' occupation, men's decision to teach has been questioned. In the case of men working in early-years and primary school settings, a level of education at which they are under-represented (DCSF, 2008), this career choice can be perceived as 'unnatural' (Ashley and Lee, 2003; Cameron et al., 1999) and their motives questioned (King, 2000; Mills et al., 2004; Murray, 1996; Smedley, 1998, 2007), even leading in some instances to accusations of paedophilia (Berrill and Martino, 2002). As recalled by Mills and colleagues (2004), teaching young children 'is constructed within patriarchal societies as women's work and is devalued. The consequence of this is that men who want to teach young children risk being positioned as deviant, abnormal or lacking. That is, they are at risk of being seen as gay, "effeminate" or a paedophile' (pp. 360–1).

While there is a broadly consensual view among feminist scholars that men should take more responsibility in teaching children, this literature also invites some critical examination of the policy call for 'more men' and of its underlying tropes (Mills et al., 2004). Some of this work also highlights how men teachers can contribute to reinforcing school regimes which are misogynistic and homophobic and argues that the risk that some men pose to children in educational settings should not be trivialised (Cameron et al., 1999; Francis and Skelton, 2001b; King, 2000; Mills et al., 2004).

This leads to a related point, which is the place and treatment of sexual minority groups in teaching. As noted above, work questioning the construction of teaching through a heteronormative matrix has expanded in the recent period (Cushman, 2008; Ferfolja, 2007, 2008; McCarthy, 2003; Rudoe, 2010). This literature highlights how schools regulate students' and teachers' gender and sexual identities and the consequences of working within heterosexist organisations for non-heterosexual teachers (Epstein and Johnson, 1998). It shows that, due to their sexual orientation, some non-heterosexual teachers face abuse and harassment inside and outside the classroom (Chapter 7; Lahelma, 2002; Lehtonen, 2004). As a result, LGBT teachers tend to regulate and monitor their own behaviour and tell stories that allow their identification with heterosexuality, something which can further isolate and marginalise them in the workplace (Epstein and Johnson, 1998; Faderman, 1991; Harbeck, 1991; Lehtonen, 2003).

## Silenced voices: Disability, social class and age

The level of attention given to equality issues in the teaching profession varies considerably depending on which type of equality is considered. Some groups have only attracted limited research and policy interest. While there is evidence that disabled people suffer a range of barriers and prejudice (DAA, 1998), disabled teachers have remained broadly invisible, and research about this group tends to focus on those teaching in the post-compulsory sector, often, though not always, in the form of reflective pieces based on the author's experience of disability (Anderson, 2006; Campbell, 2009; Ferri et al., 2005; Vogel and Sharoni,

2011). While this work provides in-depth insights into the way disability plays out in educational settings, the blatant lack of funding in this area hinders the capacity to gain a broader view of the problems faced by disabled teachers, let alone to engage with the diversity of this group. Equality issues based on class and age have met a similar fate, with the experiences of teachers who identify as working class and of mature teachers remaining predominantly invisible in research. Yet the scarce scholarship in this area shows that the experiences of these groups are far from being unproblematic (see, for example, George and Maguire, 1998; Maguire, 2001; see also Chapter 5). Studies looking at teaching from a social class perspective have usually focused on the class position of teachers as a profession (for example, Carter, 1997; Ozga and Lawn, 1981; Wright, 1979), rather than on teachers' classed subjectivities, maybe because social class is often perceived as attached to occupation and, since they share the same occupation, teachers are assumed to occupy the same class position. In these studies, a contentious point relates to whether teaching should be regarded as a middle-class occupation, with a professional status, or not. Yet, as argued by Maguire (2005), teachers' classed subjectivities do not simply derive from the status of the profession. Her own research has shown how feelings of being an 'outsider' and 'not fitting in' can last, even when individuals enter a profession considered (at least in some contexts) as 'middle class'. Others have also analysed how the dynamics of class identity play out in school settings, for example, how teachers working in urban disadvantaged schools can be constructed as outsiders by students and their families and how members of the local communities who become part of the local school workforce can be viewed as 'selling out' (Gordon, 2003; see also Chapter 2).

The scarce literature exploring the age-related issues faced by teachers highlights how mature teachers can struggle to get jobs and promotion after a certain age (particularly for women 'returners') (Moreau, 2011a). For example, in England, pressure for schools to cut on expenditure means they favour the recruitment of a younger, 'cheaper' workforce (Chapter 5). The experiences of mature teachers are shaped by institutional ageism (Taylor and Walker, 1998). It has been shown that they are often seen by their line managers as unable to adapt in an environment which has drastically changed over the past 40 years (NASUWT, 2010). As argued by Watts (Chapter 5), 'older' age and life experience can be regarded as a disadvantage and a liability rather than as a resource, particularly in the case of mature women teachers – something that may reflect 'the double standard of ageing' (Sontag, 1978). Some other work has drawn attention to the feelings of invisibility that older teachers can experience in the workplace. George and Maguire (1998), in particular, have looked at how discourses of ageism and sexism in education work together to affect 'older' women student teachers, who, as a result, can feel isolated and rendered invisible by students and staff alike.

## The theoretical approach underpinning this volume

Studies of the teaching profession have been underpinned by a range of theoretical perspectives, as already alluded to in this short overview. A prevailing approach has explored teachers' professional lives in isolation, constructing teachers as disembodied selves. This analytical framework usually excludes gender, race, class, caring responsibilities and other identity markers or, at best, conceptualises these as variables, enabling the researcher to disaggregate the data by subgroup (see, for example, Hirschhorn, 1993; Hüberman, 1989). This approach often leaves the wider theoretical frameworks untouched, and teacher professionalism remains conflated with Whiteness, middle-classness, masculinity and heterosexuality, although constructions of the 'ideal' teacher vary across contexts.

Other work has engaged with issues of identity and equality (although without necessarily drawing on this rhetoric) through a theoretical lens underpinned by a 'deficit' or 'trait' perspective (Morgan et al., 1983). On a micro-social level, the exclusion of some groups from teaching or the subordinated position they occupy has been explained and, sometimes, justified by their alleged 'lacks' – lack of competence, lack of aspiration and lack of time due to other commitments, as noted in the literature (for example, Boulton and Coldron, 1998; Moreau et al., 2008). On a meso-social (that is, school sector) level, this deficit approach is illustrated by studies linking the entry of minority/dominated groups in the profession and the decline of its status. Acker (1994), for example, recalls how sociologists of the profession have linked both aspects and, in some cases, established a causal relationship between the feminisation of a profession and its status (see, for example, Simpson and Simpson, 1969, in Acker, 1994). Some researchers have criticised this approach and emphasised the need for more nuanced and sophisticated accounts of the relationship between the status of a profession and its composition (Le Feuvre, 1999). In particular, Sperandio (Chapter 3) shows that the link between the feminisation of the teaching profession and its status is much more complex than being a single, unilateral, causal relationship and reminds us that in some countries the high social status of teaching is associated with a high level of feminisation of the profession.

The cultural turn that took place in the sociology of education in the 1970s offered some more complex conceptualisations of equality matters, through a broader cultural angle moving away from older studies with a narrower quantitative concern for pupil performance or teacher roles (Francis and Skelton, 2008). This literature, with its focus on the way schools and teachers contribute to the (re)production of gender, class and race regimes, brought some fundamental insights into the way teachers' practices and views can contribute to the production of inequalities. Yet the criticality of these studies in showing teachers' implications in this process has not been matched by some equivalent concern for the way they are positioned within school discourses of gender, race and class, nor did it always consider the way teachers resisted policy incentives and eschewed their positioning as 'helpless agents' (Ball and Goodson, 1985, p. 7).

In contrast, since the 1980s, some authors have called for approaches taking into account the influence of social structures on the experiences and aspirations of teachers, to understand the difficulties they face in entering and progressing through the profession. This work has rejected deficit and essentialist discourses and has shed light on how teachers' trajectories and experiences are compounded by socio-historical contexts and by social relations of gender, race and other identity markers. These studies have favoured an approach which has evidenced how recruitment and promotion criteria and school cultures favour White, heterosexual men (Blackmore, 1999; Boulton and Coldron, 1998; De Lyon and Widdowson Migniuolo, 1989; Krüger, 1996; Ozga, 1993; Scase and Goffee, 1989; Shakeshaft, 1989). This approach has been particularly fruitful in generating studies which foreground issues of equality and identity, for example, by producing detailed and informative accounts of the way discourses of teachers and teacher professionalism are gendered (Gannerud, 2001; Skelton, 2002), raced (Brown, 2012; Foster, 1998) and classed (Maguire, 2001, 2005). Thanks to its focus on teachers' perspectives, this approach also favours an understanding of how teachers' lives are shaped by these discourses, yet simultaneously recognises teachers' ability to resist the discourses and norms which prevail in a given context. While the uniqueness of each chapter in theoretical terms is acknowledged, the contributions gathered in this volume share this conceptual perspective.

## Researching equality issues in the teaching profession: A timely endeavour

The pursuit of research on equality issues in the teaching profession appears timely. First, teachers' identities and working environment have substantially transformed over the past 30 years. The introduction of new public management principles to the school sector in many parts of the world has increased the autonomy of schools and, in some cases, resulted in the emergence of a 'quasi market' (Glennerster, 1991). This phenomenon has been associated with the weakening of the contractual agreements in place, resulting in an increased differentiation of the school sector, including in terms of teachers' working conditions and environment. Since the late 1980s, teachers have also been subjected to neoliberal discourses of managerialism and regimes of surveillance and accountability, which have led to the redefinition of what it means to be a teacher (Mahony and Hextall, 2000; Malet and Brisard, 2005). It is sometimes claimed that, because of these changes, the teacher's professionalism is now more than ever conflated with Whiteness, middle-classness and heterosexual hegemonic masculinity (Mahony et al., 2004), although the precise characteristics of what constitutes a 'good teacher' vary across contexts, as evidenced in this volume.

Second, following the rise of the civil rights movement in the 1960s and 1970s and the subsequent establishment in the West of an abundant, yet not always effective, legislation addressing inequalities (Mazur, 1995), conceptions of equality have shifted (Arnot and Mac an Ghaill, 2006). The salience of equality issues in policy and research narratives rises and falls, with some considerable variations depending on the socio-historical context. In the neoliberal understanding of equality characteristic of late modern societies, people's position in society has been increasingly explained through the rhetoric of choice and individualisation, which plays down the influence of social structures (Beck, 1992; Beck and Beck-Gernsheim, 2002; Giddens, 1984, 1991). The view that inequalities and power relations have been erased or even in some instances inverted has grown in popularity over the years, with groups once thought of as dominated now thought to be in a position of domination – something described by feminist authors as a 'backlash' (Faludi, 1991) and challenged by this volume.

In the current climate of financial austerity, this ideological shift has not been innocuous. In many countries, it has translated into significant cuts to equality provision which have been described as particularly damaging to children, women and other dominated groups (David, 2010; Ortiz et al., 2011; Women's Budget Group, 2012). In policy discourses, becoming a teacher has somewhat been taken out of its structural context and been re-fashioned as a project of the neoliberal self. Yet, despite this rhetoric and policy shift, this volume and other research highlight how these groups continue to experience domination, including, in the case of teaching, in the form of barriers to entry in the profession, difficulties in accessing the most prestigious and rewarded positions, harassment/bullying and feelings of 'not belonging'. While gender, race and class continue to retain some centrality in policy discourses, they are not thought of as equality matters but as *attributes*. In other terms, the power differential which characterises, for example, gender, race and social class relations has become negated or inverted, and these have been redefined as mere characteristics. This discourse of individualisation often has essentialist undertones as those sharing certain attributes are assumed to share similar qualities and to be better suited for the teaching of students from a similar background.

Altogether, these social and political changes, which operate on a material and discursive level, provide an important rationale for this book's focus on equality issues in the teaching profession, especially as little remains known about the way they affect teachers from various backgrounds in the early 21st century.

## Content and structure of the present volume

Drawing on what could be broadly described as a theorisation of equality and identity informed by social constructivist (Burr, 1995), feminist (Crompton, 1999; Francis and Skelton, 2001a) and post-colonial theories (Bhabha, 1990; Hall, 2000), this volume explores equality issues in the teaching profession and scrutinises a common view of teaching as inclusive and egalitarian (that is, as open and offering the same opportunities to all). The ways identity markers such as gender, social class, ethnicity, sexual orientation and age 'intersect' (Crenshaw, 1989; McCall, 2005; Valentine, 2007) and play out in relation to teachers' entry to the profession, to their career progression and to their wider professional and 'private' experiences are considered, although there are obvious limits to how comprehensive this collection can be.

A range of institutional and national contexts are covered (including Australia, Bangladesh, Bhutan, Canada, China, Finland, Japan, Uganda, the UK and the United States). This coverage adds a cross-national comparative dimension to this volume, of heuristic value to the study of identity and equality matters. Indeed, through biological essentialist and social differentialist discourses (Moreau, 2011a), identity markers such as gender, race and class are often constructed as permanent attributes or identity features, as encapsulated in the widespread use of formulas such as 'boys will be boys' (in Anglo-Saxon countries) or '*l'éternel féminin*' (in French-speaking ones). On the contrary, comparison, particularly cross-national comparison, questions views of identity and equality matters as natural and fixed by highlighting the variability of, for example, gender, race and class arrangements across contexts (Moreau, 2011a). In doing so, this comparative lens facilitates an understanding of inequalities as socially constructed and helps to conceive a different future, including one in which relationships between different groups may be fairer.

*Inequalities in the Teaching Profession* is organised into three parts. Part 1 (Mapping and Understanding Inequalities in the Teaching Profession) adopts a broad perspective by providing a conceptual framework and approaching the study of inequalities in the teaching profession primarily through a macro-social lens. Chapter 1 is my attempt to establish which voices and perspectives are heard or silenced in the study of inequalities in the teaching profession and to spell out the theoretical perspective which underpins the work presented in this volume. In Chapter 2, June A. Gordon considers how teachers working with marginalised populations become stigmatised through their association with these students, in a range of countries which all advocate a meritocratic form of educational access and progress to careers in teaching (including Japan, the UK, the United States, China and Bhutan). She highlights how policies and practices can block the selection and retention of teachers willing to work with marginalised youth, as well as the tensions and contradictions experienced by teachers themselves. In Chapter 3, Jill Sperandio explores the status of women teachers in different societies, with specific reference to Uganda and Bangladesh. She shows that, while the preponderance of women in the teaching profession is associated in certain contexts with its low status, this is not always the case, and the relationship between the 'feminisation' of teaching and its status appears complex.

Part II (Teachers, Equality and Identities) is located at a more micro-social and experiential level. This section foregrounds teaching subjectivities while acknowledging how teachers' lives unfold against institutional and national backgrounds which are more or less supportive of different groups. In Chapter 4, Ninetta Santoro asks who counts as a 'real' teacher in the contemporary context of Australia. In recent years, there has been a drive in this particular country to diversify the teaching profession and, in particular, to increase the numbers of Indigenous teachers. Yet, drawing on post-colonial theories, she shows how historical and contemporary constructions of Indigenous peoples position them as 'unteacherly' and work to marginalise them within the profession. In Chapter 5, Nicky Watts offers an insight into the life experiences of a group which remains, to this day, very much underresearched: female veteran teachers. Her piece shows the extent of ageist stereotypes to which this group is subjected in the UK context, including through their construction as 'grumpy old teachers'. The two following chapters in Part II move to issues relating to the regulation of teachers' bodies and sexualities. In Chapter 6, Christine Mallozzi provides a sociohistorical account of how, in the United States, women teachers' lives and, in particular, bodies have been subjected to a high level of surveillance. As a result, women teachers' suitability to enter and remain in the profession has been and continues to be constrained by their self-presentation and behaviour, in and out of the classroom. In Chapter 7, Jukka Lehtonen, Tarja Palmu and Elina Lahelma explore the effects of the heteronormative culture that predominates in Finnish schools. Drawing on a range of data sets, they show how teachers contribute to and negotiate schools' regimes of sexuality, with specific reference to the experiences of gay and lesbian teachers.

Part III (Understanding Social Divides and Moving Towards Social Change) simultaneously embraces issues of social reproduction and social change, and their relationship with educational policies. Chapter 8 and Chapter 9 both question the meaning of equality in this profession as they look at groups of teachers who may be formally 'included' and even seen as professionally successful, yet remain to some extent marginalised. In Chapter 8, Tania Ferfolja shows how, in the case of lesbian and gay teachers living in the multicultural Sydney metropole, inclusiveness in the sense of access to the profession does not mean equal treatment, in the context of school regimes which are prevailingly homophobic. In Chapter 9, Anita K. W. Chan explores the work narratives of women primary school principals in Hong Kong and shows that, while women principals have been benefiting from the opportunities which have opened to women in the past decades, their experiences are not unproblematic from a gender perspective and that they often draw on stereotypical gender scripts and discourses when narrating their professional and personal experiences. Chapter 10 and Chapter 11 concentrate on education policies and on the discourses underpinning these, with particular reference to role model theories.

In Chapter 10, Anthony L. Brown and Keffrelyn Brown examine the racial politics and public discourse of African American male teachers in the US context. They provide a comprehensive account of how this group has been constructed as responsible for many of the issues faced by Black communities in general and Black boys in particular, while also being constructed, problematically, as their potential 'saviours'. Finally, in Chapter 11, Wayne Martino addresses the limits of gender- and race-based role modelling as a policy frame and grid of intelligibility for addressing equality issues in the teaching profession. Using the Ontario context as an example, he argues that policy narratives and discourses about male teacher shortage remain framed by neoconservative ideals which are not supported by empirical evidence and can compound equality issues.

## References

Abbott, D. (2002) Teachers are failing Black boys. *Observer*. https://www.guardian.co.uk/racism/Story/0,,628494,00.html (Accessed online: 5 July 2012).

Acker, S. (ed.) (1989) *Teachers, gender and careers* (New York and London: Falmer Press).

Acker, S. (1994) *Gendered education: Sociological reflections on women, teaching and feminism* (Buckingham: Open University Press).

Acker, S. (1999) *The realities of teachers' work: Never a dull moment* (London: Cassell).

Allard, A. (2004) 'Speaking of gender: Teachers' metaphorical constructs of male and female students', *Gender and Education*, 16(3), 347–63.

Allard, A. and Santoro, N. (2006) 'Troubling identities: Teacher education students' constructions of class and ethnicity', *Cambridge Journal of Education*, 36(1), 115–29.

Anderson, R. (2006) 'Teaching (with) disability: Pedagogies of lived experience', *Review of Education, Pedagogy and Cultural Studies*, 28(3/4), 367–79.

Archer, L. and Francis, B. (2007) *Understanding minority ethnic achievement: Race, gender, class and 'success'* (London: Routledge).

Arnot, M. and Mac an Ghaill, M. (2006) '(Re)contextualising gender studies in education', in M. Arnot and M. Mac an Ghaill (eds.) *The RoutledgeFalmer reader in gender and education* (Abingdon: Routledge).

Ashley, M. and Lee, J. 2003. *Women teaching boys: Caring and working in the primary schools* (Stoke-on-Trent: Trentham Books).

Ball, S. J. and Goodson, I. F. (eds.) (1985) *Teachers' lives and careers* (London: RoutledgeFalmer).

Bangar, S. and McDermott, J. (1989) 'Black women speak', in H. De Lyon and F. Widdowson Migniuolo (eds.) *Women teachers: Issues and experiences* (Milton Keynes: Open University Press).

Basit, T. and Santoro, N. (2011) 'Playing the role of "cultural expert": Teachers of ethnic difference in Britain and Australia', *Oxford Review of Education*, 37(1), 37–52.

Beatty, B. (1990) ' "A vocation from on high": Kindergarten teaching as an occupation for women in turn-of-the century America', in J. Antler and S. Biklen (eds.) *Changing education: Women as radicals and conservators* (Albany, NY: State University of New York Press).

Beck, U. (1992) *Risk society* (London: Sage).

Beck, U. and Beck-Gernsheim, E. (2002) *Individualization: Institutionalized individualism and its social and political consequences* (Cambridge, UK: Polity).

Berrill, D. and Martino, W. (2002) 'Pedophiles and deviants: Exploring issues of sexuality, masculinity and normalization in male teacher candidates' lives', in R. Kissen (ed.) *Waiting for Benjamin: Sexuality, curriculum and schooling* (Boulder, CO: Rowan & Littlefield).

Bhabha, H. (1990) *Nation and narration* (London: Routledge).

Blackmore, G. (1999) *Troubling women: Feminism, leadership and educational change* (Milton Keynes: Open University Press).

Blackshear, E. (1969 [1902]) 'What is the Negro teacher doing in the matter of uplifting the race?', in D. Wallace Kulp (ed.) *Twentieth century Negro literature* (New York: Arno).

Blase, J. and Blase, J. (2002). *Breaking the silence: Overcoming the problem of principal mistreatment of teachers* (Thousand Oaks, CA: Corwin).

Boulton, P. and Coldron, J. (1998) 'Why women teachers say "stuff it" to promotion: A failure of equal opportunities', *Gender and Education*, 10(2), 149–61.

Bourdieu, P. and Passeron, J. C. (1970) *La reproduction: Eléments d'une théorie du système d'enseignement* (Paris: Les Editions de Minuit).

Bowles, G. (1983) 'Is women's studies an academic discipline?', in G. Bowles and R. Duelli-Klein (eds.) *Theories of women's studies* (Berkeley: University of California Press).

Brehmer, I. (1980) *Lehrerinnen: Zur Geschichte eines Frauenberufes. Texte aus dem Lehrerinnenalltag* (Munich, Vienna and Baltimore, MD: Urban & Schwarzenberg).

Brown, A. L. (2009) ' "O brotha where art thou?" Examining the ideological discourses of African American male teachers working with African American male students', *Race Ethnicity and Education*, 12(4), 473–93.

Brown, A. L. (2011) 'Pedagogies of experience: A case of the African American male teacher', *Teaching Education*, 22(4), 363–76.

Brown, A. L. (2012) 'On human kinds and role models: A critical discussion about the African American male teacher', *Educational Studies: Journal of the American Educational Studies Association*, 48(3), 296–315.

Burr, V. (1995) *An introduction to social constructionism* (London: Routledge).

Cacouault, M. (1984) 'Diplôme et célibat. Les femmes professeurs de lycée entre les deux guerres', in A. Farge and C. Klapisch-Zuber (eds.) *Madame ou Mademoiselle* (Paris: Montalba).

Cacouault-Bitaud, M. (1999) 'Professeur du secondaire: Une profession féminine? Eléments pour une approche socio-historique', *Genèses*, 36, 92–115.

Callender, C. (2012) *BAME men in teaching: Identity construction(s) on the way to (and beyond) QTS*. Paper presented at the Teaching Cultures ESRC seminar, 24 October (London: National Union of Teachers).

Cameron, C., Moss, P. and Owen, C. (1999) *Men in the nursery, gender and caring work* (London: Paul Chapman).

Campbell, F. K. (2009) 'Having a career in disability studies without even becoming disabled! The strains of the disabled teaching body', *International Journal of Inclusive Education*, 13(7), 713–25.

Canadian Teachers' Federation (2002) *On teacher retention* (Ottawa, ON: CTF).

Carrington, B. and Tomlin, R. (2000) 'Towards a more inclusive profession: Teacher recruitment and ethnicity', *European Journal of Teacher Education*, 23(2), 139–57.

Carter, B. (1997) 'The restructuring of teaching and the restructuring of class', *British Journal of Sociology of Education*, 18(2), 201–15.

Casey, K. (1993) *I answer with my life* (New York: Routledge).

Causey, V., Thomas, C. and Armento, B. (2000) 'Cultural diversity is basically a foreign term to me: The challenges of diversity for preservice teacher education', *Teaching and Teacher Education*, 16(1), 33–45.

Chan, A. K. (2004) 'Gender, school management and educational reforms: A case study of a primary school in Hong Kong', *Gender and Education*, 16(4), 491–510.

Clifford, G. (1981) 'Eve: Redeemed by education and teaching school', *History of Education Quarterly*, 21, 479–91.

Coleman, M. (2002) *Women as headteachers: Striking a balance* (Stoke-on-Trent: Trentham Books).

Cortina, R. and San Román, S. (eds.) (2006) *Women and teaching: Global perspectives on the feminization of a profession* (New York: Palgrave).

Crenshaw, K. (1989) 'Demarginalizing the intersection of race and sex', *University of Chicago Legal Forum*, 129, 139–67.

Crompton, R. (ed.) (1999) *Restructuring gender relations and employment: The decline of the male breadwinner* (Oxford: Oxford University Press).

Cushman, P. (2008) 'So what exactly do you want? What principals mean when they say "male role model" ', *Gender and Education*, 20(2), 123–36.

DAA (1998) *Are disabled people included?* (London: Disability Awareness in Action).

David, M. (2010) *Browne Report + the White Paper = A Murky Outlook for Educational Equality.* http://www.genderandeducation.com/wp-content/uploads/2011/01/GEA_Policy_Report_October_December_20101.pdf (Accessed online: 1 December 2011).

DCSF (2008) School workforce in England (including local authority level figures) January 2008 revised September 2008. www.dcsf.gov.uk/cgi-bin/rsgateway/search.pl?cat=1&subcat=1_2_5&q1=Search (Accessed online: 15 September 2011).

De Lyon, H. and Widdowson Migniuolo, F. (1989) *Women teachers: Issues and experiences* (Milton Keynes: Open University Press).

DfEE (1998) *Green paper 'Teachers: Meeting the challenge of change'* (London: DfEE).

Echols, C. and Stader, D. (2002) 'Education majors' attitudes about diversity', *Education Leadership Review*, 3(2), 1–7.

Education Queensland (2002) *Male teachers' strategy: Strategic plan for the attraction, recruitment and retention of male teachers in Queensland State schools 2002–2005* (Brisbane: Queensland Government).

Epstein, D., Elwood, J., Hey, V. and Maw, J. (eds.) (1998) *Failing boys? Issues in gender and underachievement* (Buckingham: Open University Press).

Epstein, D. and Johnson, R. (1998) *Schooling sexualities* (Buckingham and Philadelphia: Open University Press).

Etzioni, A (ed.) (1969) *The semi-professions and their occupations: Teachers, nurses and social workers* (New York: Free Press).

Eurydice (2013) *Key data on teachers and school leaders in Europe. 2013 Edition. Eurydice Report* (Luxembourg: Publications Office of the European Union).

Faderman, L. (1991) *Odd girls and twilight lovers: A history of lesbian life in twentieth-century America* (New York: Columbia University Press).

Faludi, S. (1991) *Backlash: The undeclared war against American women* (New York: Crown).

Ferfolja, T. (2007) 'Teacher negotiations of sexual subjectivities', *Gender and Education*, 19(5), 569–86.

Ferfolja, T. (2008) 'Discourses that silence: Teachers and anti-lesbian harassment', *Discourse: Studies in the Cultural Politics of Education*, 29(1), 107–19.

Ferri, B. A., Connor, D. J., Solis, S., Valle, J. and Volpitta, D. (2005) 'Teachers with LD: Ongoing negotiations with discourses of disability', *Journal of Learning Disabilities*, 38(1), 62–78.

Foster, M. (1991) 'The politics of race: Through African American teacher's eyes', *Journal of Education*, 172(3), 123–41.

Foster, M. (1993) 'Othermothers: Exploring the educational philosophy of Black American women teachers', in M. Arnot and K. Weiler (eds.) *Feminism and social justice in education: International perspectives* (Washington, DC: Falmer Press).

Foster, M. (1998) *Black teachers on teaching* (New York: The New Press).

Francis, B. (1999) 'Modernist reductionism or post-structuralist relativism: Can we move on? An evaluation of the arguments in relation to feminist educational research', *Gender and Education*, 11(4), 381–93.

Francis, B. and Skelton, C. (2001a) *Investigating gender: Contemporary perspectives in education* (Buckingham: Open University Press).

Francis, B. and Skelton, C. (2001b) 'Men teachers and the construction of heterosexual masculinity in the classroom', *Sex Education*, 1(1), 9–21.

Francis, B. and Skelton, C. (2005) *Reassessing gender and achievement* (London: RoutledgeFalmer).

Francis, B. and Skelton, C. (2008) 'Introduction to Special Issue on Teacher Identities', *Pedagogy Culture and Society*, 16(1), 1–6.

Gannerud, E. (2001) 'A gender perspective on the work and lives of women primary school teachers', *Scandinavian Journal of Educational Research*, 45(1), 55–70.

George, R. and Maguire, M. (1998) 'Older women training to teach', *Gender and Education*, 10(4), 417–30.

Giddens, A. (1984) *The constitution of society. Outline of the theory of structuration* (Cambridge, UK: Polity).

Giddens, A. (1991) *Modernity and self identity* (Cambridge, UK: Polity).

Gillborn, D. (2008) *Racism and education: Coincidence or conspiracy?* (London: Routledge).

Glennerster, H. (1991) 'Quasi-markets for education?', *Economic Journal*, 101, 1268–76.

Gordon, J. A. (2003) 'A shoelace left untied: Teachers confront class and ethnicity in a city of northern England', *Urban Review*, 35(3), 191–215.

Grumet, M. R. (1988) *Bitter milk. Women and teaching* (Amherst: University of Massachusetts Press).

Hall, S. (2000) 'Old and new identities, old and new ethnicities', in L. Black and J. Solomos (eds.) *Theories of race and racism* (New York: Routledge).

Hannerz, U. (1970) 'Another look at lower-class Black culture', in L. Rainwater (ed.) *Soul* (New York: Aldine).

Harbeck, K. (ed.) (1991) *Coming out of the classroom closet* (New York and London: Harrington Park Press).

Hargreaves, L. (2011) 'The status of minority ethnic teachers in England: Institutional racism in the staffroom', *Dedica. Revista de Educaçao e Humanidades*, 1 (March), 37–52.

Henry, A. (1995) 'Growing up Black, female, and working class: A teacher's narrative', *Anthropology and Education Quarterly*, 26(3), 279–305.

Hills-Collins, P. (1990) *Black feminist thought: Knowledge, consciousness, and the politics of empowerment* (Boston: UnwinHyman).

Hirschhorn, M. (1993) *L'ère des enseignants* (Paris: Presses Universitaires de France).

Hoffman, N. (ed.) (1981) *Women's 'true' profession: Voices from the history of teaching* (Old Westbury, NY: Feminist Press).

hooks, B. (1994) *Teaching to transgress: Education as the practice of freedom* (New York: Routledge).

Howard, T. (2001) 'Powerful pedagogy for African American students: A case of four teachers', *Urban Education*, 36, 179–202.

Hu¨berman, M. (1989) *La vie des enseignants* (Lausanne: Delachaux et Niestlé).

Hutchings, M. (2002) 'A representative profession? Gender issues', in M. Johnson and J. Hallgarten (eds.) *From victims of change to agents of change: The future of the teaching profession* (London: ippr).

Hutchings, M., Skelton, C., Francis, B., Carrington, B., Read, B. and Hall, I. (2008) 'Nice and kind, smart and funny: What children like and want to emulate in their teachers', *Oxford Review of Education*, 34(2), 135–57.

Kannen, V. and Acker, S. (2008) 'Identity "issues" and pedagogical silences: Exploring teaching dilemmas in the northern Ontario kindergarten classroom', *Pedagogy, Culture and Society*, 16(1), 25–41.

King, J. (1991) 'Unfinished business: Black student alienation and Black teachers' emancipatory pedagogy', in M. Foster (ed.) *Readings on equal education, Volume 11: Qualitative investigations into schools and schooling* (New York: AMS).

King, J. (2000) 'The problem(s) of men in early education', in N. Lesko (ed.) *Masculinities at school* (Thousand Oaks, CA: Sage).

Krüger, M. (1996) 'Gender issues in school headship: Quality versus power?', *European Journal of Education*, 31(4), 447–461.

Ladson-Billings, G. (1994) *The dreamkeepers: Successful teachers of African American children* (San Francisco: Jossey-Bass).

Lahelma, E. (2002) 'Sexual name-calling of teachers – Challenging the power relations', in J. Lehtonen (ed.) *Sexual and gender minorities at work* (Helsinki: Stakes).

Le Feuvre, N. (1999) 'Gender, occupational feminization and reflexivity: A cross-national perspective', in R. Crompton (ed.) *Restructuring gender relations and employment: The decline of the male breadwinner* (Oxford: Oxford University Press).

Lehtonen, J. (2003) *Seksuaalisuus ja sukupuoli koulussa* (Sexuality and gender at school) (Helsinki: Yliopistopaino and Nuorisotutkimusverkosto).

Lehtonen, J. (2004) 'Lesbian, gay, and bisexual teachers: Invisible in the mind of the students?', in J. Lehtonen and K. Mustola (eds.) *Straight people don't tell, do they? Negotiating the boundaries of sexuality and gender at work* (Helsinki: Ministry of Labour).

Lewis, C. (2006) 'African American male teachers in public schools: An examination of three urban districts', *Teachers College*, 108(2), 224–45.

Lynn, M. (2006) 'Dancing between two worlds: A portrait of the life of a Black male teacher in south central LA', *International Journal of Qualitative Studies in Education*, 19(2), 221–4.

Maguire, M. (2001) 'The cultural formation of teachers' class consciousness', *Journal of Education Policy*, 16(4), 315–31.

Maguire, M. (2005) ' "Not footprints behind but footsteps forward": Working class women who teach', *Gender and Education*, 17(1), 3–18.

Mahony, P. and Hextall, I. (2000) *Reconstructing teaching: Standards, performance and accountability* (London: RoutledgeFalmer).

Mahony, P., Hextall, I. and Menter, I. (2004). 'Threshold assessment and performance management: Modernizing or masculinizing teaching in England?', *Gender and Education*, 16(2), 131–49.

Malet, R. and Brisard, E. (eds.) (2005) *Modernisation de l'école et contextes culturels: Des politiques aux pratiques en France et en Grande-Bretagne* (Paris: L'Harmattan).

Mallozzi, C. (2012) 'Cultural models of bodily images of women teachers', *Societies*, 2, 252–69.

Markowitz, R. (1993) *My daughter the teacher: Jewish teachers in New York City schools* (New Brunswick, NJ: Rutgers University Press).

Martino, W. and Meyenn, B. (eds.) (2001) *What about the boys? Issues of masculinity in schools* (Buckingham: Open University Press).

Maylor, U., Ross, A., Rollock, N. and Williams, K. (2006) *Black teachers in London report 2005* (London: Greater London Authority).

Mazur, A. (1995) 'Strong state and symbolic reform: The ministère des droits de la femme in France', in A. Mazur and D. McBride Stetson (eds.) *Comparative state feminism* (Thousand Oaks, CA: Sage).

McCall, L. (2005) 'The complexity of intersectionality', *Signs*, 30(3), 1771–800.

McCarthy, L. (2003) 'Wearing my identity: A transgender teacher in the classroom', *Equity and Excellence in Education*, 36(2), 170–83.

Miller, J. (1996) *School for women* (London: Virago).

Mills, M., Martino, W. and Lingard, B. (2004) 'Attracting, recruiting and retaining male teachers: Policy issues in the male teacher debate', *British Journal of Sociology of Education*, 25(3), 355–69.

Mills, M. D. (2003) 'Shaping the boys' agenda: The backlash blockbusters', *International Journal of Inclusive Education*, 7(1), 57–73.

Modood, T. (2003) Ethnic differentials in educational performance, in D. Mason (ed.) *Explaining ethnic differences* (Cambridge, UK: ESRC and Polity).

Modood, T. and Shiner, M. (2002) 'Help or hindrance? Higher education and the route to ethnic equality', *British Journal of Sociology of Education*, 23(2), 209–32.

Moreau, M. P. (2011a) *Les enseignants et le genre: Les inégalités hommes-femmes dans l'enseignement du second degré en France et en Angleterre* (Paris: Presses Universitaires de France).

Moreau, M. P. (2011b) 'The societal construction of "boys' underachievement" in educational policies: A cross-national comparison', *Journal of Education Policy*, 26(2), 161–80.

Moreau, M. P., Osgood, J. and Halsall, A. (2007) 'Making sense of the glass ceiling: An exploration of women teachers' discourses', *Gender and Education*, 19(2), 237–53.

Moreau, M. P., Osgood, J. and Halsall, A. (2008) 'Equal opportunities policies in English schools: Towards greater gender equality in the teaching workforce?', *Gender, Work and Organization*, 15(6), 553–78.

Morgan, C., Hall, V. and Mackay, H. (1983). *The selection of secondary school heads* (Milton Keynes: Open University Press).

Moss, G. (2007) *Literacy and gender: Researching texts, contexts and readers* (London: Routledge).

Moynihan, P. (1967) 'The Negro family: The case for national action', in R. Rainwater and W. Yancey (eds.) *The Moynihan report and politics of controversy* (Cambridge, MA: MIT Press).

Murray, S. (1996) ' "We all love Charles": Men in childcare and the social construction of gender', *Gender and Society*, 10, 368–85.

NASUWT (2010) *No experience necessary? A survey of the experience of age discrimination of older teachers in the UK* (Birmingham: NASUWT).

Olmedo, I. (1997) 'Challenging old assumptions: Preparing teachers for inner city schools', *Teaching and Teacher Education*, 13(3), 245–58.

Oram, A. (1989) 'A master should not serve under a mistress: Women and men teachers 1900–1970', in Acker, S. (ed.) *Teachers, gender and careers* (London: Falmer Press).

Ortiz, I., Chai, J. and Cummins, M. (2011) *Austerity measures threaten children and poor households: Recent evidence in public expenditures from 128 Developing Countries*. Social and Economic Policy Working Paper (New York: UNICEF).

Osler, A. (1997) *Education and careers of Black teachers: Changing identities, changing lives* (Buckingham: Open University Press).

Osler, A. (2003) 'Muslim women teachers: Life histories, identities and citizenship', in H. Jawad and T. Benn (eds.) *Muslim women in the United Kingdom and beyond: Images and experiences* (Leiden and Boston: Brill).

Ozga, J. (1993) *Women in educational management* (Milton Keynes, UK: Open University Press).

Ozga, J. and Lawn, M. (1981) *Teachers' professionalism and class: A study of organized teachers* (London: Falmer Press).

Palheta, U. (2011) 'Enseignement professionnel et classes populaires: comment s'orientent les élèves "orientés" ', *Revue Française de Pédagogie*, 175(2), 59–72.

Powney, J., Wilson, V., Hall, S., Davidson, J., Kirk, S., Edward, S. and Mirza, S. F. (2003) *Teachers' careers: The impact of age, disability, ethnicity, gender and sexual orientation* (London: DfES).

Prentice, A. L. and Theobald, M. R. (1991) *Women who taught: Perspectives on the history of women and teaching* (Toronto: University of Toronto Press).

Reay, D. (2002) 'Shaun's story: Troubling discourses of White working class masculinities', *Gender and Education*, 14(3), 221–34.

Richards, E. and Acker, S. (2006) 'Collegiality and gender in elementary school teachers' workplace cultures: A tale of two projects', in Cortina, R. and San Román, S. (eds.) *Women and teaching: Global perspectives on the feminization of a profession* (New York: Palgrave).

Rudoe, N. (2010) 'Lesbian teachers' identity, power and the public/private boundary', *Sex Education*, 10(1), 23–36.

Santee Siskin, L. and Warren Little, J. (eds.) (1995) *The subjects in question: Departmental organization and the high school* (New York: Teachers College Press).

Santoro, N., Reid, J., Crawford, L. and Simpson, L. (2011) 'Teaching Indigenous children: Listening to and learning from Indigenous teachers', *Australian Journal of Teacher Education*, 36(10), 65–76.

Scase, R. and Goffee, R. (1989) *Reluctant managers: Their work and lifestyles* (London: Unwin Hyman).

Schmuck, P. (ed.) (1980) *Women educators. Employees of schools in Western countries* (New York: New York State University Press).

Schroeder, H. (1991) 'Die "verkümmerte" und "verbitterte" Lehrerin. Die Debatte um das Lehrerinnenzölibat in der ersten Frauenbewegung', in M. Horstkemper and L. Wagner-Winterhager (eds.), *Mädchen und Jungen – Männer und Frauen in der Schule* (Weinheim: Beltz Verlag).

Shakeshaft, C. (1989) *Women in educational administration* (Newbury Park: Sage).

Siraj-Blatchford, I. (1991) 'A study of Black students' perceptions of racism in initial teacher education', *British Educational Research Journal*, 17(1), 35–50.

Skelton, C. (2002) 'The "feminisation of schooling" or "re-masculinising" primary education', *International Studies in Sociology of Education*, 12(1), 77–96.

Skelton, C. and Francis, B. (eds.) (2003) *Boys and girls in the primary classroom* (Maidenhead: Open University Press).

Smedley, S. (1998) 'Perspectives on male primary teachers', *Changing English*, 5, 147–59.

Smedley, S. (2007) 'Learning to be a primary school teacher: Reading one man's story', *Gender and Education*, 19(3), 369–385.

Sontag, S. (1978) 'The double standard of ageing', *Saturday Review*, 23 September.

Spender, D. (1982) *Invisible women* (London: Writers and Readers Co-operative).

Tamboukou, M. (2003) *Women, education and the self: A Foucauldian perspective* (Basingstoke and New York: Palgrave Macmillan).

Taylor, P. and Walker, A. (1998) 'Policies and practices towards older workers: A framework for comparative research', *Human Resource Management Journal*, 8(3), 61–76.

Troyna, B. (1994) 'The "everyday world" of teachers: Deracialised discourses in the sociology of teachers and the teaching profession', *British Journal of Sociology of Education*, 15(3), 325–39.

UNESCO (2010) *Country case studies in early childhood care and education in selected sub-Saharan countries 2007/8: Some key teacher issues and policy recommendations. A summary report* (Addis Ababa: UNESCO).

Valentine, G. (2007). 'Theorizing and researching intersectionality: A challenge for feminist geography', *Professional Geographer*, 59(1), 10–21.

van Essen, M. and Rogers, R. (2003) 'Ecrire l'histoire des enseignantes', *Histoire de l'Education*, 98, 5–35.

Vogel, G. and Sharoni, V. (2011) ' "My success as a teacher amazes me each and every day" – Perspectives of teachers with learning disabilities', *International Journal of Inclusive Education*, 15(5), 479–95.

Walkerdine, V., Lucey, H. and Melody, J. (2001) *Growing up girl: Psychosocial explorations of gender and class* (Basingstoke: Palgrave).

Williams, C. (1992) 'The glass escalator: Hidden advantages for men in the female professions', *Social Problems*, 39, 253–67.

Willis, P. (1977) *Learning to labour: Why working class kids get working class jobs* (Farnborough: Saxon House).

Wirth, L. (2001) *Breaking through the glass ceiling: Women in management* (Geneva: International Labour Organization).

Women's Budget Group (2012) *Autumn financial statement – Uncaring and unequal.* http://www.genderandeducation.com/issues/wbg-2/ (Accessed online: 4 July 2013).

Woodson, C. G. (2000 [1933]) *The mis-education of the Negro* (Chicago, IL: African American Images).

Wright, E. O. (1979) *Class structure and income determination* (New York: Academic Press).

# 2

# A Global Concern: Creating a Diverse Teaching Force for Marginalised Communities – In Japan, the UK, the United States, China and Bhutan

*June A. Gordon*

## Introduction

Teachers who work with marginalised populations tend to become stigmatised through their association with their students. If they themselves are not a member of the marginalised group whom they teach, there is a tendency for the teachers to be viewed as 'outsiders' even when they share the same ethnicity, religion and/or language. The conditions that marginalise individuals are often beyond their control and yet this awareness is seldom embraced by those who are asked to work with them. Ironically, the desire to distinguish oneself from those who are marginalised is often greatest when the 'server' and the client have the most in common and the server sees the potential for slippage into marginalisation. In this chapter I hope to explore this thesis from a range of international perspectives as it pertains to teachers in five countries: Japan, the UK, the United States, China and Bhutan.

Drawing on research conducted over the last 20 years, I will try to demonstrate two points: (1) how blatant policies and subtle practices have blocked the selection and retention of teachers who are willing to work with marginalised youth; and (2) how teachers who share a common heritage with youth on the margins have attempted to distance themselves from their origins. The five nations discussed here all advocate a meritocratic form of educational access and progress, which is said to provide successful schooling for all children and, presumably, the choice of teaching as a profession. And yet, upon closer scrutiny, each nation places limits on not only who is able to enter the teaching profession but who perseveres. Patterns of discrimination and inequity are specific to each culture and need to be understood within those contexts. Conclusions about the fairness or justness of these various examples should be held in abeyance as each comes with a historical context, which can only be briefly developed in a short chapter. Given this limitation, I begin this piece with Japan, followed by shorter sections on the other four countries as the discussion of what constitutes marginalisation shifts from caste to class, race, region and labour.

## Positionality

I come into this work as a second-generation immigrant to the United States whose extended family continues to live in the North of England in low-income government-subsidised housing in an area known for its violence and lack of interest in education. The area has the lowest higher education attendance rate in the UK. Due to post-war employment discrimination against my Irish father, my parents moved to the United States, where I was raised in a predominantly African American community. Post-secondary education took me to Stanford University on a scholarship. From there I accepted a volunteer teaching post in Asia at age 19 in lieu of quitting for the second time. Living and teaching in both Taiwan and Japan exposed me to yet other ways of viewing the world. With parents who had never attended school beyond ages 13 and 14 and relatives who viewed educated people with distrust, my transformation into a scholar was a difficult road filled with class betrayal. However, having a father who had served as a foot soldier in India and a brother who had died soon after a return from Asian travels at age 19, I could not ignore my own transnational experiences as well as those of my family, all of which led to an uneasy relationship with the educators intent on my schooling. Once I launched an academic career, the focus of my research naturally found its way to exploring the political and cultural contexts of variation amongst countries to which I had been exposed and issues of access and success in education. Teachers became one of the main sources of my inquiry as I attempted to determine not only the background of teachers in 'difficult' schools but also how they viewed their clientele, how they were viewed and how their work had led to their own marginalisation within the profession (Gordon, 2000a).

# Japan

## Some contextual elements

Unlike many other modern nations, Japan views itself as a homogeneous country, free of class and ethnic distinctions, where societal norms are known to all and the maintenance of those norms is expected of those who participate in Japanese society, regardless of country of origin (Befu, 2001). Such conformity provides a degree of comfort as shared expectations are assumed and outward formality masks what differences lie beneath. Teachers as the conveyors of culture serve an essential function in socialising children not only to standards of performance and identity but also to their position within society (Okano and Tsuchiya, 1999). While Japan claims to have an egalitarian educational system whereby all students have the freedom to compete, after having partaken of a common curriculum and passed common exams, the reality is that the context in which a child is raised, and the prejudices that arise as a result, make the playing field far from level (Ishida, 1993, 2001).

Research in Japan developed out of my work in marginalised communities in the United States and the UK, where, in the former, 'race' dominates discourse and, in the latter, 'class'. Having lived and worked in Japan prior to beginning my official research, I knew that Japan was not homogeneous even though the common refrain from most people is that they are just middle class (Lie, 2003). In an attempt to explore and expose the complexity of this truth, I began conducting a survey with the assistance of four Japanese women regarding attitudes towards diversity. The process was not easy as one of the assistants was threatened with ostracisation when questioning her neighbour about attitudes towards the *Burakumin*, Japan's traditionally outcast group (De Vos and Wagatsuma, 1966; Inoue, 1969). Other informants gave superficial and politically correct responses. The survey technique is used extensively in Japan and people know what is deemed an acceptable se. In a country where *tatamae* (what is said publicly) and *honne* (what one shares from the heart) are daily realities, I am constantly amazed at how frequently surveys are still used, though I am aware that they serve a distancing function that enables detachment of oneself from the response. Against advice from Japanese researchers who had attempted work on critical social questions in the past, I decided to revert to my own methodology, which has served me well over the years in equally contested terrains: critical ethnography (Carspecken, 1996; Gordon, 2000a). Learning from this first attempt, I shifted my research to a less controversial topic: the changing image of teachers in Japan (Gordon, 2005b). Through my network of colleagues and friends I was able to access a variety of schools and interview teachers who trusted me with their knowledge of the contradictions facing contemporary Japan, in particular the education of immigrants, called Newcomers, and of the *Burakumin*.

I have written extensively about my work with both of these 'groups' (Gordon, 2008b, 2009) but what I have not discussed before, and will address in this chapter, are the ways in which teachers for both Newcomers and the *Burakumin* are differentially selected, viewed and rewarded for their efforts in educating children who, for a variety of reasons, do not fit within, or have not been accepted into, normative Japanese society. In all cases, work with marginalised youth required a re-negotiation of their expectations of themselves as teachers and professionals. The context of their teaching and the constraints placed on them through political and community agendas defined their pedagogy, practices and identities as they worked with children perceived to be 'unlike themselves', often with little preparation but with preconceived views about 'the other' that often translated into fear and uncertainty. However, it needs to be made clear that the situation of teaching children of *Burakumin* backgrounds who are Japanese nationals is radically different from the teaching of Newcomer youth, even though many Newcomers are also ethnically Japanese (Hirasawa, 1991). Most Newcomer youth in this study came from three general regions: South America (Brazil, Peru, Colombia), China (mostly descendants of orphans left behind after the Sino-Japanese War in the 1930s) and South-East Asians (children of refugees from Laos, Cambodia and Vietnam) (Shimizu et al., 1999). Most immigrants from South America, the *Nikkei*, have Japanese ancestry as do the Chinese *zanryukoji* (Reis, 2002; Tsuda, 2003).

The research for this chapter is based on 6 years of work in and outside of two of the main urban centres of Japan: Osaka and Yokohama, locations which have the largest percentages of either *Burakumin* or Newcomers. Over 200 interviews, both formal and informal, took place, with approximately 100 in each of the two settings. Approximately 60 of the formal interviews pertaining to Newcomers were transcribed from tapes by two Japanese translators. Others were transcribed by hand either by me or by an assistant. About half of the time either a Japanese colleague or a cultural ntermediary served as a facilitator and/or an additional source of information. For the *Burakumin* research, only about 30 of the formal interviews were taped, as this was far more sensitive work and required a much greater degree of protection for the individuals involved (Gordon, 2006b). Most interviews were conducted with someone who was either hosting me from the community or a trusted *Dowa* educator (see further) who served as my sponsor for this work. For both the research on Newcomers and the *Burakumin*, most of the conversations were conducted by the author in Japanese with the remainder in English, Chinese or Spanish. My findings and notes were later confirmed by colleagues or community activists as my knowledge of the overall situation increased. In addition to interviews with teachers, administrators, cultural intermediaries, community members, social workers and students in various school settings, numerous hours were spent in informal settings discussing the shifting political landscape of education as well as collecting governmental documents. Most of the interviews with teachers and principals took place at their local school site during a visit that included observing classes and participating in informal conversations. On average each formal interview lasted about one and a half hours. No such boundaries, however, limited the informal conversations which flowed into restaurants, coffee houses, community events and festivals, and even into homes. Tours of the community were frequent as were long conversations while commuting on trains and buses (Bestor et al., 2003). The research later took me to Brazil, which has the largest Japanese immigrant community outside of Japan. I will not go into details of that fieldwork at this time (Gordon, 2010).

Given the timing of the research, 2004–2010, when Japan was in the midst of an economic crisis (Tachibanaki, 2005), I could not help but document the cultural texture within which teachers were attempting to promote the academic and occupational success of their students as policy changes flowed from political circles (Gordon, 2005a). By the year 2000, increased unemployment, particularly among Japanese youth aged 16–35, had led to a new phenomenon called NEETS (no education, employment or training) (Yasuda, 2003). With competition for entry-level jobs at an all-time high, those whose social status left them at the bottom held few illusions about the value of education (Tsukada, 2010). It is within this political and economic context that the present research was nested. For clarity I will first discuss the situation for teachers and community workers staffing the *Dowa* schools who serve *Burakumin* youth in and around the Osaka area (Hawkins, 1989; Kiyonori, 2002). In the latter half the focus is on those who teach and direct the classes and extra-curricular programmes for immigrant youth in Yokohama where special services in language instruction, interpreting and/or cultural enrichment are offered (Ota, 2002). It is important to note that in Japan teachers do not select the schools in which they teach; rather, they are assigned by their prefectural Board of Education. Moreover, teachers are rotated on a regular basis, usually every 6–7 years. The situation is more extreme for principals who serve for only 3 years at a school. It is argued that the rotation policy allows educators an opportunity to work in a variety of settings and grow professionally. In reality, the process limits access to and, hence, the trust in and of the communities in which they work.

## The *Burakumin*

*Dowa* education (*Dowa Kyoiku* or anti-discrimination education) had been heavily funded for four decades by the national government at the demand of community activists in support of the *Burakumin* but was curtailed significantly after 2003 (Neary, 1989, 1997, 2003). Teachers who work in schools with strong *Dowa* programmes were caught in the centre of an ever-fluctuating political and cultural maze. On the one hand, they are held accountable for responding to the special needs of low-income youth from the *buraku* (an ancient term meaning village, now seen as enclaves of low-cost housing), but on the other hand, recent government policies have prohibited the identification of children's backgrounds (Akashi, 1995). Part of the reason for this shift in policy relates to concerns expressed that other groups, including *Zainichi* (Koreans born in Japan but not Japanese nationals, most with ancestors brought over as labourers in the 1930s), have not received the same degree of governmental support but remain the recipients of discrimination by Japanese society at large (Hicks, 1997). *Dowa* education, as a result, has broadened its scope to include other minorities, women and the disabled. In the process, a new name emerged, *Jinken Kyoiku*, which means human rights education (Nabeshima, 1995; Nabeshima et al., 2000).

But teachers who work in these communities know that little has changed in terms of how society views *Burakumin*, even as they examine their own attitudes (Nabeshima, 2000). Many teachers attribute the low academic achievement among *Burakumin* to child-rearing patterns in the community as well as lowered parental expectations (Ikeda, 2001). Pedagogically, in teaching for understanding and tolerance of differences, teachers are aware that they might inadvertently reinforce stereotypes and prejudices while raising questions that *Burakumin* parents might prefer to be left unasked. In other schools, *Dowa* education is seen as a source of strength and a point of departure for what Americans might call 'culturally relevant pedagogy'. But what is seen as part of one's cultural heritage is not always what one wants to claim for themselves today. In several interviews, I found that teachers, in their desire to 'relate' to *buraku* young people, actually imposed onto youth identities that the students clearly did not wish to embrace.

Changes in recent policy have also left many teachers confused about their own identities (Gordon, 2008b). *Dowa* education has been a major part of the pedagogy and practice of Japanese teachers in the Osaka area for over 50 years (Fukuchi and Nakamaru, 1969; Reber, 1999). Many teachers currently working in these schools became teachers in the 1970s and 1980s and have shaped their professional identities around their somewhat esoteric knowledge of *buraku* communities. Their expertise has enabled them to be spokespersons on social justice to the larger society as well as to fill positions within the educational and political system that requires an awareness of the nuances within *Dowa* education (Gordon, 2006b). However, for many, the changes in government policies, which have been designed to eradicate or rather deny the notion of lingering discrimination against the *Burakumin*, have forced some of these educator activists out of their former positions into schools where their past expertise and radical views will be diluted, hence neutralising their power within the community (Gordon, 2008b). The fact that these changes have been supported, if not encouraged, by the Buraku Liberation League (BLL) leaves many educators who have committed their lives to social justice with a sense of betrayal. The traditional triangle that has provided the crux for critical pedagogy to be implemented in the Osaka area – the Board of Education (BOE), teachers' labour union and BLL – has collapsed to an alliance between BOE and BLL, with the teacher unions standing to the left of the radical BLL, but with no official support. Teachers, lacking a strong identity or organised association, watch as the number of *Dowa* teachers is significantly reduced, while the number of *buraku* students remains the same (Gordon, 2008b).

Interviews with teachers and administrators who currently work in these schools reflect the complexity of issues involving pedagogy, practice and prejudice that can affect who ultimately participates in the education of youth in the *buraku*. It should be noted that in all of my time in these schools, I was only aware of one teacher who was 'out' as being *Burakumin*. Until around 2000 it was rare for a *Burakumin* youth to go on to college and far rarer for them to become teachers (Ikeda, 2001). Finding teachers to work in *Dowa* schools is not easy; few are so inclined. First of all, community and parental pressure on teachers who are not overtly supportive of *Dowa* education can be devastating and lead to ostracisation. While teacher rotation, as mentioned above, is systematically organised, teachers feign illness or incompatibility in order to be transferred out of *Dowa* schools. Second, teachers feel insecure and shut out. As explained by one principal, 'It is not unusual for teachers to see *buraku* culture as impenetrable, and having a closed atmosphere, even though it is understood that it is discrimination that has created the tight community.' Third, the schools carry a stigma, which can either enhance political capital or undermine self-confidence, depending on your position within 'the struggle'. The stigma is caused not only by association with an outcast community but also by low academic status and high rates of school refusal. Fourth, young teachers, who are entering the profession at a slow but gradual rate, have not been, and often do not want to be, socialised into the same social consciousness of the 1960s and 1970s. Their world view is far more materialistic and individualistic, causing many long-time teacher activists to wonder how the next generation will be educated if new teachers remain ignorant of *Burakumin* issues and unwilling to engage the community.

### Newcomers to Japan

While the vast majority of teachers might wish the best for all children, few teachers in Japan are educated or trained to work with Newcomers (Gordon, 2006a; Ninomiya, 2002; Okano and Tsuchiya, 1999). Japanese teachers also tend to have had little exposure or experience with foreigners of any kind and therefore often hold stereotypes that are difficult to break through (Tsuneyoshi, 2011). As a result, when international children come into their classes, teachers tend to be somewhat paralysed by the process of accepting full responsibility for the children within their care. Most of the administrators with whom I spoke agreed that teachers need to have special preparation for working in these schools. As one principal stated, 'It is so far from the reality of what most teachers have experienced themselves, especially the young teachers entering during these past 10 years.' And yet the reality in contemporary Japan is that more and more children are not fitting into the desired traditional mould of the conforming student. One teacher reminded me, 'The needs of these children [Newcomers] are not the exception. They are just working class.' To hear this uttered from a Japanese teacher is profound. Yet fears of working with foreign youth and stereotypes of their engagement in criminal activity abound, and alleged statements by government officials claiming that people who commit crimes in Japan are foreigners make it difficult to fault the average Japanese person's perception.

As the result of this perception, few teachers are interested in working with Newcomer youth, and those that do tend to come in three different categories. One is teachers who were trained by *Dowa* educators, often in the Osaka area, and see work with immigrant youth as another expression of their commitment to social justice and the fight against discrimination. These tend to be dynamic, thoughtful people who are asked to take on major leadership positions, such as opening up alternative high schools so that Newcomer youth can have an opportunity to continue their education even when they are rejected from regular schools due to their low exam scores. The second category tends to be teachers who have lived abroad and their children have attended school overseas for a short period of time. Knowing the difference between the way that Newcomers in Japan are treated versus the way their children were received and catered to in another country moved them to reconsider the type of teacher they would be upon their return to Japan. The last category is teachers who were pushed out of other schools due to their iconoclastic views or belligerent ways. For all three types of teachers, working with Newcomer youth in Japan was still a challenge as few had visited the countries of their origin or spoke their home languages. The fact that in most cases these children lived in low-income housing further stigmatised those who associated with them.

### Cultural intermediaries

One of the main obstacles to providing quality teaching to Newcomer youth and to appropriate selection and training of teachers is that only Japanese nationals (with few exceptions) are allowed to become public servants, including teachers. This means that individuals who have lived for several generations in Japan but are not of Japanese heritage, as well as immigrants of Japanese descent who were not born in Japan cannot become educators in public schools (with a few exceptions). As a result, teachers are often left clueless as to how to access the communities of the children in their care. Given this reality, special funding is granted to schools who enrol more than 10 per cent Newcomer students. This has provided for greater flexibility in the curriculum as well as a range of resources, including *cultural intermediaries*, who attempt to mediate and guide the difficult negotiations of life in Japan for these young people. This group consists of language interpreters, social workers and government and NGO workers. These intermediaries face their own set of marginalising factors. Since most are foreign born, and therefore unable to become Japanese nationals, they are ineligible for regular teaching positions and are employed as contractors at lower rates of pay, without benefits or a voice in the decision-making within the schools. Often these people work at two or three schools as well as other agencies and hospitals to assist immigrant families. Travel to and from schools is not paid for by the schools, a cost that can be exorbitant in Japan. Invited into the homes of many of the cultural intermediaries and seeing the conditions in which they have to exist, I could not help but wonder who else knew of the travesty.

Further conflicts and contradictions arose around the status of the cultural intermediaries. A few of these people were native-born Japanese nationals, often married to a non-Japanese Newcomer, and worked for prefectural agencies as social workers. These individuals enjoy higher status and rate of pay but still lack full access to school policy and practices and they are not considered teachers. They are also resented by the foreign-born intermediaries, who perceive that they, the foreign born, have greater knowledge of the Newcomer families and are able to penetrate and relate to the community but are not rewarded for such. The hierarchy of national versus non-national is outdistanced only by the pecking order among immigrants themselves, not only among countries but within. Of particular interest was the status differential between those who spoke Spanish versus those who spoke Portuguese (Takenaka, 2003). For both immigrants and cultural intermediaries, education and social status 'back home' play a role in not only how they perceive themselves but also how they are perceived by others, both inside their communities and within the larger society. Their education, where it took place and experience with other cultures beyond their own ethnic enclave, whether it be in São Paulo or Yokohama, positioned them differently as well as their pre-migration assumptions and prejudices about Japan and what it had to offer them.

## The UK

The search for teachers who are willing and able to work with marginalised youth takes on class overtones in the UK (Osborn et al., 1997). Regionalism, often demarcated by linguistic variation, can easily position someone in the class pecking order (Bernstein, 1973; Cannadine, 1999). Perhaps the finding of most surprise to non-British audiences is that, in the UK, it is the low-income White council estate residents, rather than the immigrant community, that causes the greatest concern for teachers (Corrigan, 1979). In the North of England, where most of my research takes place, teachers in urban schools who serve children living on government housing estates are seldom embraced by the local community; rather, they are viewed as outsiders who know little about their students and their families and have little interest in engaging them (Gordon, 2003). This perception is heightened by the fact that most teachers tend to live in what are called 'the leafy suburbs', miles from the estates which are clearly demarcated from one another with their own names and identities, often admitting only those for whom this is called home.

Few children from the estates ever aspire to become a teacher for fear that they will be viewed as betrayers of their own people, as someone who tried to become someone that they have always been told they could never be due to their 'station' in life. One result of this distancing is misinformation about 'the other' regardless on which side of this equation one lies. Low-income parents and students resist the efforts of middle-class teachers while simultaneously these very teachers create images of those youth based on their reactions to class differences, a difference often reinforced not only by the variance in quality of schooling received but also by the quality of life offered in these areas (Troman, 2000; Woods, 1994). Resentment flows both ways. Teachers perceive that parents do not support the ongoing education of their children, while residents question the effort required for success when unemployment is high and social benefits easy to come by. Within the tight community of council estates, the norm for success has little to do with education. Such a disconnect between school and community results in a disenfranchisement of teachers, who see themselves as professionals caught in a generations-old narrative of class resistance that they had little to do with creating, any more than did the children whom they serve.

In my research, teachers were uniformly unsettled, if not revolted, by the language and behaviour of low-income White students and their parents. In contrast to this, students from non-White families, mostly Pakistani, Bangladeshi and Indian, were seen as valuing education and respectful not only to teachers but also to their parents (Bhatti, 1999). Inadvertently, these non-White British youth were said to have a 'calming effect' on their low-income White peers. This assumption threw the three schools where I did most of my research into an intriguing light since one was an all-White school on an estate, another a school reflecting many different nationalities in a South Asian ethnic enclave and the third a multi-ethnic school in a predominantly White community adjacent to a council estate. In the two multi-racial schools, the troublemakers were almost always identified as White. The exceptional outrageous act by a child of colour was seen as an aberration and attributed to the negative influence of the White children. While such White students were considered unlikely by parents and teachers to succeed in any academically challenging field, most of the immigrant students, in contrast, were guided by their families towards careers with higher perceived status and income than teaching.

With the goal of mediating the problems of White youth, several reforms were made to bring in teachers who might be more understanding and reflective of the lives of the students. One such attempt began with a headteacher's (principal's) engagement with the mothers of the community, inviting them to assist in the pre-kindergarten programme. Over many years, with extensive encouragement, financial support as well as twisting of the rules, he was able to offer training and employment for the women who ultimately came into classrooms as aides and, in a few cases, moved into clerical and teaching positions. While this proved beneficial in some aspects, in other ways this was not a positive outcome, as some of these women were viewed as 'selling out' with repercussions as dangerous as having their homes attacked or being personally assaulted. Those who finally became teachers refused offers of employment on council estate schools and asked to be moved into areas where their past identity would not be revealed. In reality, it is hard to hide one's past, particularly in a country where class standing can easily be read and heard in the first encounter (Gordon, 2008a).

## The United States

The American educational system, with its complicated history of slavery, guilt about usurpation of land from both Mexico and Native Americans and confusion about immigration by whom and when, walks a tightrope, constantly questioning both the purpose of education for members of these two groups and how to hear their disparate voices. Teachers thrown into this cacophony are often undermined regardless of their ethnicity, their linguistic ability, their ancestral homeland or their skin colour (Gordon, 2000a). While access is open to all, historical memories, reinvigorated by community beliefs, no matter how outdated and reinforced by contemporary situations, prevent many African American, Native American and Latino youth from considering the profession for fear of 'selling out' (Ogbu and Simons, 1998). While this is changing gradually for Latinos, who see the need to improve educational conditions for success in their community, the stigma remains that education is what 'White' people do (Fordham and Ogbu, 1986). In contrast to this, Asian Americans from East and South Asia, whose primary motivation for immigration is access to education, often shun teaching, in part because of the social welfare demands it places on teachers as well as the perception of a desire for employment which will bring higher status and monetary gain (Gordon, 2000b). 'White' people, whether from South America, Africa, Central or South Asia, Russia or other parts of Europe, are grouped together as having a single voice of 'the oppressor', limiting what might be a multicultural chorus to a single chord.

While my work in urban education spans several decades, I continue to be amazed at how often I am told by teachers of colour that if a student from their own ethnic group is qualified enough to go on to college, they should shoot for something much higher than teaching (Gordon, 2000a). Comments such as 'S/he could be a doctor or a lawyer or CEO' were not uncommon in my research across the United States, which included interviews with approximately 200 teachers of colour. These assumptions parallel images held by some African American male teachers who claimed that due to the preponderance of White middle-class teachers, often those who went into the profession were viewed as 'goody-two-shoes' or 'tall children' (Gordon, 2001). Related to this was yet another factor that stigmatised teachers and served as a disincentive for some students to consider teaching: the assumption that they would teach students from the same ethnic group as they are identified with. While this varied amongst the groups interviewed, the concern was most pronounced amongst second-generation Latino males, who felt that simply because they spoke Spanish they would be expected to teach kids in ESL (English as a Second Language) classes at a level they felt was beneath them. They wanted to use their subject matter expertise and work with more challenging material and students.

Some of the African American teachers similarly objected to the expectation that they would be better equipped to work with African American youth than non-Black teachers and that they would want to work in predominantly Black communities. As they noted, this assumed that their background in terms of education, socio-economic class and regionalism and expectations were somehow in line with those of other children who shared the same skin tone. Since all of the teachers I interviewed were currently living in urban areas, many made a clear distinction between the way that they had been raised, often in the South, and the lives of their students, as noted in these comments: 'I came to Detroit and it frightened me. I have never lived in a ghetto; in the South we were just poor' and 'I wasn't trained for the inner city. I never experienced some of the things that these kids live.' These teachers wanted 'the freedom like all other credential teachers' to work in whatever school they chose based on their qualifications. A few of these teachers, finding themselves in difficult urban situations for which they were either not prepared or unable to respond to the demand, moved to more suburban areas and in at least one case to a private, all-White girls' Roman Catholic school. For some teachers the disciplinary issues they were asked to handle were more than they had bargained for, as often the most troubled children were sent to them. In some ways their work in less diverse schools alleviated their marginalisation and provided them with more freedom.

In 1996, I selected San Jose, California, as the US site for a continuation of the study of teacher perceptions of educational and career options for students from low-income and ethnic minority communities. I also wanted to explore how those perceptions shape teacher-student interactions which could influence students' choice of teaching as a career. While the complexity of the issues needed to be addressed in these schools is not unique to San Jose, the irony of the location is. The district under study is adjacent to the wealthy and technologically oriented Silicon Valley while struggling to serve a student body largely of first-generation Americans from South-East Asia, Mexico and Central America. More than 50 languages are spoken in homes from which approximately 85 per cent of students qualify for free or discounted lunch. Interviews were completed with several teachers in each of 14 schools and all major administrators of the district. My involvement in the district began first in the form of a resource to the most difficult schools in providing them with tutors from my undergraduate students. In the process of setting up these interactions, discussions with administrators and teachers led to more formal interviews, inquiring into the ways teachers work with students from backgrounds different from their own. As an outgrowth of this research, I was invited by an adjoining district to conduct a year-long collaborative study with 14 high school science teachers who had been identified by their district as having difficulty working with low-income students. Having many points of entry has provided access for me to situations and conversations perhaps less available to other researchers. The findings confirmed results from my previous research and those of many other scholars: most teachers, regardless of ethnic background, are ill prepared to work with the range of diversity exemplified in urban, multicultural, low-income, public classrooms. In addition, the results showed that many teachers across ethnic groups hold negative views of the teaching profession and freely share these opinions with their students. In this study, the vast majority of teachers at all grade levels discouraged their students from considering teaching as a career choice.

# China

China faces huge challenges as it moves towards mass schooling in a country where inequality of access and success for rural and urban population increases with each passing day. Being a teacher in today's China is not an easy task as parents demand more and more from schools with the expectation that education will position their child for future gain and status. Given that this is the first generation in which the hopes of four grandparents and both parents are directed on one child, the pressure to perform is exceedingly high. With the combination of the one-child policy and the increase in affluence, few middle-class parents want their children to become teachers, and even fewer young people hold that aspiration. Ironically, at a time in which the government is setting policies for not only increased educational access but also degrees required for basic employment, few individuals are interested in assuming responsibility for teaching the next generation and leading them into a world as of yet undefined (Li et al., 2011).

Yet it needs to be kept in mind that there is great variation within China. Approximately 70 per cent of the population live in rural areas and nearly 40 per cent live below the poverty line. This is a vast country where the divide between the haves and have-nots is growing daily as land is taken away from the poor to make way for development, and corruption becomes a necessity for success. The image that most non-Chinese have of China, largely created through knowledge of its eastern seaboard with skyscrapers towering within the dazzling centres of Beijing and Shanghai, is also one that the rural peoples of China hold – as a destination for their children. The desire to escape the village is great as millions attempt to move into more urban contexts (Murphy, 2004). The differences between these two parts of China, the rural and the urban, are vast, as is the range of backgrounds of these children and the teachers who serve them.

Little is written about rural China or the ways in which the government has attempted to infiltrate or assist, depending on one's point of view, the schools in providing a common education for all children. This has meant sending thousands of Han Chinese (the dominant ethnic group) teachers from the more urban areas into provinces where the Han population is still viewed with relative distrust, in particular in the west of China, home to more than 50 minority groups. These teachers attempt to disseminate a common culture through the use of Mandarin as the official national language, often at the loss of local dialects. To make this process more efficient and consolidate resources, rudimentary boarding schools have been set up in the far-flung parts of north-west China. This has also alleviated the need for children to walk long distances to school, often two to three hours, and allowed parents the freedom to leave for work in the towns and cities.

This phenomenal migration, which has fuelled the success and productivity of present-time China, has as one of its core motivating forces the desire on the part of parents to provide a better future for its youth (Kipnis, 2011). Education is the wheel on which families make decisions to leave their child behind with relatives, place them in boarding schools or bring them along into strange towns and cities. Parents who decide to take the last option face further challenges, of which the most daunting is the *hukou* system of registration. This bureaucratic structure is centuries old and was an attempt to maintain a semblance of order in the country by preventing people from moving freely, fearing that the countryside would be left barren. Moving out of your registered area often jeopardises your chance to obtain work permits, housing and schooling for your child. However, given the vast economic divide between rural and urban, along with the demand for labour in special economic zones and in preparation for the 2008 Olympics, it was hard to resist the temptation to move east. Parents make this decision knowing that they might be forfeiting their child's education but, as revealed to me in research conducted in 2007, many took the risk hoping that their child would miraculously have access to an education far superior to that in the village. It is upon this faith that 'illegal schools' have been set up and 'teachers' garnered from the ranks along with some assistance from NGOs and volunteers from universities. These 'schools', often no more than a room down an alleyway with a tap of water running outside for villagers to use, serve as the space in which a semblance of ongoing education is attempted. Given the fluidity of the situation, the degree of a child's acquisition of material usually rests solely with the degree of surveillance a parent can exert on the child in the home (often a wooden small shack connected to many others) to ensure that reading and writing is pursued.

However, for the urban middle class registered in their home city, educational conditions are radically different. Students from these families compete for seats in the best schools, which will then position them to move into top academic high schools and from there into leading universities in China or abroad (Kipnis, 2011). In China, like in many other countries, with a major exception being India, public schools are far more prestigious than private schools. These public schools are government funded and well resourced. Those at the top, including 'key schools', are truly remarkable in what they provide for and expect from their students. Being a teacher in either a rural or urban school no longer holds the esteemed status it once had. For the rural teachers, classes can be as large as 80 children demanding as much social care as education. For the urban elite, parents, who often have more education than teachers, work not as collaborative partners but as directors and dictators in their child's schooling.

## Bhutan

Set among the Himalayas and wedged between China and India lies Bhutan, a country shrouded in mystery and mysticism. What little is known about the country tends to include their public proclamation to uphold the value of gross national happiness (GNH) over gross national product (GNP) and their standing as being one of the most Buddhist countries in the world (Crossette, 1996). While both of these are true, there is yet another side to Bhutan seldom seen by outsiders and seldom acknowledged openly by those within this kingdom. This is the contested role of education and the marginalisation of the teachers who attempt to move this society into the 21st century. The crux of the problem lies in both its historical context and its location. Bhutan has for centuries existed under the powerful influence of Buddhism and its monasteries which served as the mainstay of the education of males (Denman and Namgyel, 2008). To send one's child to a monastery for education, rather than to a public school, is still an option which is attractive to many parents. Most formal secular education took place outside of the country, usually at Indian boarding schools in hill stations run by families of English or Scottish ancestry (Wangmo and Choden, 2011). Few were able to afford this education but it was not rare among current middle-class families. Several of the men I interviewed aged between 45 and 65, now living in Bhutan as teachers, managers or hotel keepers, had such an upbringing. The proximity to India not only influenced where the country would provide expanded education in the early years of its modernisation but it also dictated what kind of education would be adopted to guide Bhutan's effort in mass education. The curriculum was geared towards passing the civil service examination as set up by the Indian government, and similar in content to what was followed in Britain as well as China. Textbooks, curricular examples and end-of-year exams were not based in a Bhutanese reality but rather referred back to India. As a result, most of the teachers in Bhutan until recently were Indian.

Not until the 1980s did a shift begin to occur, when Indian teachers were asked to give up their privileged positions as teachers to native Bhutanese. While this might seem like a positive step, most Bhutanese were not prepared academically or psychologically to take on this responsibility. With the introduction of mass education came the demand for new schools and qualified teachers, neither of which was readily available. By this time, the elite of Bhutan had begun to send its children overseas to the UK and the United States for higher education, not only for exposure to a different world view but also to reinforce Bhutan's autonomy from either China or India. This process was facilitated by the recognition of two official languages, English and Dzongkha of monastic heritage.

Returning from impressive institutions of higher education and armed with new ideas as to how to benefit their country, some of these people decided to invest in assisting the government in its process of modernisation and mass education. However, few of them wanted to go into teaching, because to do so would require their movement out of the comforts of the capital, which is the only main town in the country, into the very rugged and isolated areas where the majority of people live. Drawing up plans for a school system in the abstract in an office in Thimphu, the capital city, is a far cry from convincing rural peoples that they should send their children, often an important means of labour, away to a school often one to two hours away by foot and to be taught things that have nothing to do with their current lives or their futures.

In 2011, I had the honour of conducting research in Bhutan at the invitation of the Royal Education Council. The goal was for me to assess how educational reforms that attempted to be more sensitive to local contexts were being received by teachers in the field. With the assistance of a driver, I visited 15 schools and interviewed 30 teachers and principals. Out of the educators with whom I spoke, less than a handful had chosen teaching as their career. Rather, they were placed, if not thrown into it. As they confessed, they and other teachers are the biggest critics of the profession. None of the teachers had a child who was going into teaching nor did they recommend the profession to anyone they knew. On a less than positive note, they attempted to ameliorate the distress that this pronouncement caused me by claiming that perhaps in the future more young people would enter the profession as, because of the significant increase in unemployment, they would have no other options in life.

At the beginning of my research I thought it odd that in a country that has more illiterate than literate individuals there would not be more children aspiring to become teachers and more parents encouraging their children to become these educated pillars of society within the village and town. However, as I probed more deeply, the reasons for this disconnect became clear, and, as bizarre as it might seem, the concerns of teachers in this small 'Third World' country corresponded in many ways to those of teachers in 'First World' countries. These included low morale among teachers, low pay, lack of significant compensation for work in difficult schools/areas, teacher isolation and, as stated repeatedly, lack of respect and status.

The main reasons for this lack of commitment to a profession had a great deal to do with the perceptions by the teachers of their marginalised status. These were reinforced by government policies that placed teachers in difficult schools for an undermined amount of time with no recourse for appeal. These schools were often in isolated places without modern conveniences as basic as indoor plumbing. Given that most teachers were educated in the capital or overseas, they were not accustomed to these conditions and resented being tossed into communities where they were not necessarily welcomed. They often had to leave their families behind, particularly if they had their own children, as most of the communities in which they taught only had primary schools and of rudimentary quality. The fracturing of families in the name of educating someone else's children was a common theme. In some cases a teacher agreed to the post for a year or two but ended up spending 10–18 years in such locations, often without colleagues or support. When asked for another posting, their letters to the Ministry of Education (MOE) went unanswered. In one case, the individual I interviewed was the only person in the school; he was the sole teacher, administrator and janitor. For 8 years he had no colleagues but had to manage 65 students of varying ages and educational levels.

An additional factor in marginalisation among teachers is misplacement of teachers according to training. Some teachers I met had been trained in a specified subject for secondary school but were placed in primary schools. Others were teaching subjects they had never studied themselves. In one school, someone who had been sent to do community work with adults had seen the conditions of the school and volunteered to teach students a full course load. In another case, a young man, who was supposedly sent for observation purposes, was teaching not only a full load but having four different subjects to prepare for every day. I dare say, these people were not happy and openly expressed their frustration (Dorji, 2009; Gordon, 2013).

## Conclusion

In this chapter, I have discussed how policies and practices can hinder the retention and selection of teachers willing to work with marginalised youth, and how teachers who share a common heritage with marginalised youth sometimes attempt to distance themselves from their origins. There is no simple or single solution for the problems I have discussed, especially as the exact nature of these problems varies considerably across contexts and groups of teachers. One beginning to a possible solution is expressed in the revised version of a Nelson Mandela quote from Hargreaves and Fullan (2012, p. 186): 'There can be no keener revelation of a society's soul than the way in which it treats its children *and their teachers*' (emphasis in original). That same volume with its vision of professional capital for the teaching profession is a solid contribution to understanding not only why teachers are marginalised but also how we can counter the forces that constrain them. Empowering teachers is not as simple as a professional workshop in a tidy conference room. The attitudes which shape who enter the field and the type of children they are willing and able to teach are determined by society at large. The demand for quality comprehensive education must be accompanied with respect for the profession and the individuals who commit their lives to educating someone else's children.

## References

Akashi, I. (1995) 'Zendokyo and others: Teachers' commitment to *Dowa* education', in Y. Hirasawa, Y. Nabeshima and M. Mori (eds.) *Dowa education: Educational challenge toward a discrimination-free Japan* (Osaka: Buraku Liberation Research Institute).

Befu, H. (2001) *Hegemony of homogeneity: An anthropological analysis of Nihonjinron* (Melbourne, VIC: Trans Pacific Press).

Bernstein, B. (1973) *Class, codes, and control* (St. Albans: Paladin).

Bestor, T. C., Steinhoff, P. G. and Bestor, V. L. (2003) 'Introduction: Doing fieldwork in Japan', in T. C. Bestor, P. G. Steinhoff and V. L. Bestor (eds.) *Doing fieldwork in Japan* (Honolulu: University of Hawai'i Press).

Bhatti, G. (1999) *Asian children at home and at school: An ethnographic study* (London: Routledge).

Cannadine, D. (1999) *The rise and fall of class in Britain* (New York: Columbia University Press).

Carspecken, P. F. (1996) *Critical ethnography in educational research* (New York and London: Routledge).

Corrigan, P. (1979) *Schooling the smash street kids* (London: Macmillan).

Crossette, B. (1996) *So close to heaven: The vanishing Buddhist kingdoms of the Himalayas* (New York: Random House).

Denman, B. and Namgyel, S. (2008) 'Convergence of monastic and modern education in Bhutan', *International Review of Education*, 54(3), 475–91.

De Vos, G. A. and Wagatsuma, H. (1966) *Japan's invisible race: Caste in culture and personality* (Berkeley, CA: University of California Press).

Dorji, K. (2009) 'Teachers' motivation . . . What causes teachers to leave?', in *Quality of education in Bhutan: Research papers from Proceedings of National Seminar*, Rinpung, December 7–10, 2008, 140–61.

Fordham, S. and Ogbu, J. U. U. (1986) 'Black students' success: Coping with the burden of "acting white" ', *Urban Review*, 18, 176–206.

Fukuchi, K. and Nakamaru, K. (eds.) (1969) *Practice of emancipation education*, Vols. I–IV (Tokyo: Meiji Tosho).

Gordon, J. A. (2000a) *The colour of teaching* (London and New York: RoutledgeFalmer).

Gordon, J. A. (2000b) 'Asian American resistance to selecting teaching as a career: The power of community and tradition', *Teachers College Record*, 102(1), 173–96.

Gordon, J. A. (2001) 'African Americans and the choice to teach', in R. Nata (ed.) *Progress in Education*, Vol. 4. (Huntington, NY: Nova Science Publishers).

Gordon, J. A. (2003) 'A shoelace left untied: Teachers confront class and ethnicity in a city of northern England', *Urban Review*, 35(3), 191–215.

Gordon, J. A. (2005a) 'Inequities in Japanese urban schools', *Urban Review*, 371, 49–62.

Gordon, J. A. (2005b) 'The crumbling pedestal: Changing images of Japanese teachers', *Journal of Teacher Education*, 56(5), 459–70.

Gordon, J. A. (2006a) 'Assigned to the margins: Teachers for immigrant communities in Japan', *Teaching and Teacher Education: International Journal of Research and Studies*, 22(7), 766–76.

Gordon, J. A. (2006b) 'From liberation to human rights: Challenges for teachers of the *Burakumin* in Japan', *Race, Ethnicity and Education*, 9(2), 183–202.

Gordon, J. A. (2008a) 'Community responsive schools, mixed housing, and community regeneration', *Journal of Education Policy*, 23(2), 181–92.

Gordon, J. A. (2008b) *Japan's outcaste youth: Education for liberation* (Colorado Springs, CO: Paradigm Publishers).

Gordon, J. A. (2009) 'Children of the Danchi: A Japanese primary school for newcomers', *Ethnography and Education*, 4(2), 165–79.

Gordon, J. A. (2010) 'Transnational migration and identity: Brazil and Japan share a workforce', in J. Dosch and O. Jacob (eds.) *Asia and Latin America: The encounter of two continents: Political, economic and multilateral relations* (London and New York: Routledge).

Gordon, J. A. (2013) 'Bhutan: Educational challenges in the land of the Thunder Dragon', *Ethnography and Education*, 8(3), 1–15.

Hargreaves, A. and Fullan, M. (2012) *Professional capital: Transforming teaching in every school* (New York and London: Teachers College Press).

Hawkins, J. N. (1989) 'Educational demands and institutional response: *Dowa* education in Japan', in J. J. Shields, Jr. (ed.) *Japanese schooling: Patterns of socialization, equality, and political control* (University Park, PA, and London: Pennsylvania State University Press).

Hicks, G. (1997) *Japan's hidden apartheid: The Korean minority and the Japanese* (Aldershot, UK: Ashgate).

Hirasawa, Y. (1991) 'The education of minority group children in Japan', in B. Finkelstein, A. E. Imamura and J. J. Tobin (eds.) *Transcending stereotypes: Discovering Japanese culture and education* (Yarmouth, MN: Intercultural Press).

Ikeda, H. (2001) '*Buraku* students and cultural identity: The case of a Japanese minority', in N. K. Shimahara, I. Z. Holowinsky and S. Tomlinson-Clarke (eds.) *Ethnicity, race, and nationality in education: A global perspective* (Mahwah, NJ: Lawrence Erlbaum).

Inoue, K. (1969) *History of* Burakumin *and theory of emancipation* (Tokyo: Hatada Shoten).

Ishida, H. (1993) *Social mobility in contemporary Japan: Educational credentials, class and the labour market in a cross-national perspective* (Stanford, CA: Stanford University Press).

Ishida, H. (2001) 'Industrialization, class structure, and social mobility in post-war Japan', *British Journal of Sociology*, 52(4), 579–604.

Kipnis, A. B. (2011) *Governing educational desire: Culture, politics, and schooling in China* (Chicago: University of Chicago Press).

Kiyonori, K. (2002) *50 Years of* Dowa *education* (Osaka: Human Rights Organization).

Li, G., He, M. F., Tsou, W., Hong, W. P., Curdt-Christiansen, X. and Huong, P. L. (2011) 'Teachers and teaching in Sinic education', in H. Zhao (ed.) *Handbook of Asian education: A cultural perspective* (New York: Routledge).

Lie, J. (2003) 'The discourse of Japaneseness', in M. Douglass and G. S. Roberts (eds.) *Japan and global migration: Foreign workers and the advent of a multicultural society* (Honolulu: University of Hawai'i Press).

Murphy, R. (2004) 'Turning peasants into modern Chinese citizens: "Population quality" discourse, demographic transition and primary education', *China Quarterly*, 177, 1–20.

Nabeshima, Y. (1995) '*Dowa* education as human rights', in Y. Hirasawa and Y. Nabeshima (eds.) Dowa *education: Educational challenge toward a discrimination-free Japan* (Osaka: Buraku Liberation Research Institute).

Nabeshima, Y. (2000) *Jinken mondai ni kansuru kyoshokuin ishiki chosa* (Mie Prefecture Research on Teachers' Consciousness Concerning Question of Human Rights) (Osaka: Osaka City University Research Centre for Human Rights).

Nabeshima, Y., Akuzawa, M., Hayashi, S. and Park, K. (2000) 'Human rights education in Japanese school system', *Dowa Mondai Kenkyuu*, 22, 101–25.

Neary, I. (1989) *Political protest and social control in pre-war Japan: The origins of* buraku *liberation* (Atlantic Highlands, NJ: Humanities Press).

Neary, I. (1997) '*Burakumin* in contemporary Japan', in M. Weiner (ed.) *Japan's minorities: The illusion of homogeneity* (London: Routledge).

Neary, I. (2003) '*Burakumin* at the end of history – History of social class in Japan', *Social Research*, 70(1), 269–94.

Ninomiya, M. (2002) 'The *dekassegui* phenomenon and the education of Japanese Brazilian children in Japanese schools', in L. R. Hirabayashi, A. Kikumura-Yano and J. A. Hirabayashi (eds.) *New worlds, new lives: Globalization and people of Japanese descent in the Americas and from Latin America in Japan* (Stanford, CA: Stanford University Press).

Ogbu, J. U. U. and Simons, H. D. (1998) 'Voluntary and involuntary minorities: A cultural-ecological theory of school performance with some implications for education', *Anthropology and Education Quarterly*, 29(2), 155–88.

Okano, K. and Tsuchiya, M. (1999) *Education in contemporary Japan: Inequality and diversity* (Cambridge, UK: Cambridge University Press).

Osborn, M., Broadfoot, P., Planel, C. and Pollard, A. (1997) 'Social class, educational opportunity and equal entitlement: Dilemmas of schooling in England and France', *Comparative Education*, 33(3), 375–93.

Ota, H. (2002) *Newcomer children in Japanese public schools* (Tokyo: Kokusaisyoin).

Reber, S. E. A. (1999) '*Buraku Mondai* in Japan: Historical and modern perspectives and directions for the future', *Harvard Human Rights Journal*, 12, 297–359.

Reis, M. E. F. (2002) *Brazilians in Japan: The human tie in the bilateral relationship* (São Paulo: Kaleidus-Primus).

Shimizu, K., Sakai, A., Shimizu, M. and Dotera, I. (1999) 'Invisible foreigners: The Japanese school culture and the "Newcomer" children', *Tokyo University Graduate Faculty of Education Research Seminar*, 39, 339–64.

Tachibanaki, T. (2005) 'The rising tide of poverty in Japan', *Japan Echo*, 32(5), 47–50.

Takenaka, A. (2003) 'Paradoxes of ethnicity-based immigration: Peruvian and Japanese-Peruvian migrants in Japan', in R. Goodman, C. Peach, A. Takenaka and P. White (eds.) *Global Japan: The experience of Japan's new immigrant and overseas communities* (London and New York: RoutledgeCurzon).

Troman, G. (2000) 'Teacher stress in the low-trust society', *British Journal of the Sociology of Education*, 21(3), 331–53.

Tsuda, T. (2003) *Strangers in the ethnic homeland* (New York: Columbia University Press).

Tsukada, M. (2010) 'Educational stratification: Teacher perspectives on school culture and the college entrance examination', in J. A. Gordon, H. Fujita, T. Kariya and G. LeTendre (eds.) *Challenges to Japanese education: Economics, reform, and human rights* (New York: Teachers College Press).

Tsuneyoshi, R. (2011) 'The "internationalization" of Japanese education and the Newcomers: Uncovering the paradoxes', in D. B. Willis and J. Rappleye (eds.), *Reimagining Japanese education: Borders, transfers, circulations, and the comparative* (Oxford: Symposium Books).

Wangmo, T. and Choden, K. (2011) 'The education system in Bhutan from 747 AD to the first decade of the twenty-first century', in Y. Zhao (ed.) *Handbook of Asian education: A cultural perspective* (New York and London: Routledge).

Woods, P. (1994) 'Teachers under siege: Resistance and appropriation in English primary schools', *Anthropology and Education Quarterly*, 25(3), 250–65.

Yasuda, Y. (2003) 'High school graduates who cannot find work', *Japan Echo*, 30(2), 56–62.

# 3
# A Question of Role and Respect: The Status of Female Teachers in Societies in Change

*Jill Sperandio*

## Introduction

In established education systems worldwide, men typically move from teaching positions in secondary schools to the administrative levels of education, where power over the management of resources and student outcomes commands respect and bestows status. Studies in the United States show that men envisage careers in school leadership and administration from their point of entry into the profession as teachers (Hoff et al., 2006; Young and McLeod, 2001). Women have traditionally represented the majority of teachers in the primary levels of education, where 'caring' trumps the ability to ensure the academic preparation of young children, and they are expected to demonstrate the mothering role they have traditionally held in society. The socially prescribed role of women teachers (with role defined here as the characteristic and expected social behaviour of an individual) and the association of women teachers with nurturing and mothering (see also Chapter 6), rather than with pursuing a professional career in the teaching profession (Lumby and Azaola, 2013), coupled with their predominance in the sector, have been used to explain the low status of the profession in many countries. The low status of the profession is in turn seen as lowering the quality of both male and female applicants to it when a choice of occupations exists, thus lowering the quality of the educational provision. This perception is despite the fact that women now represent the majority of primary and secondary school teachers in most regions of the world except South and West Asia, and sub-Saharan Africa (UNESCO, 2010).

There are many societies where women have not traditionally been employed as teachers and school leaders (Rogers, 2005). This situation may be a result of social taboos that prohibit women's work outside the home or limit the opportunity for them to obtain the education and professional qualifications they need to enter the profession, or because of ingrained patriarchal attitudes that restrict the education of youth and the remuneration and status awarded for this occupation to men (UNESCO, 2000; Wylie, 2000). As many of these nations moved to meet Millennium gender goals for the education of girls (United Nations, 2007) and adopt affirmative action to ensure the representation of women in government salaried occupations, women have been actively sought to take on teaching positions and responsibilities previously denied to them. They can contemplate careers that include educational leadership positions which have traditionally commanded high respect and status for the men who have accessed them. Women may also find, by virtue of the opening up of secondary and tertiary educational opportunities to female students which allow them to acquire higher educational qualifications than in the past, that they have a choice of occupations, some of them of higher status than teaching.

Parallel to the changes in gender balance in the teaching profession, in a number of countries efforts have been made to reform education, resulting in a changed understanding of what constitutes effective teaching. These policies have led to a move away from teacher as nurturer or as subject content expert imparting knowledge, to that of a practitioner skilled in developing lifelong learners. A key element in this shift is the review and improvement of teacher training, and of the entry requirements to access such training. This trend also has the potential to change the gendered construction of teacher (male subject content expert versus female carer), and to change public perceptions of the status and respect accorded to teachers (OECD, 2004; Zeichner and Bekisizwe, 2008).

Clearly, the factors influencing the roles and status of teachers, and of women teachers within the teaching profession, are many and interact in complex ways. This chapter will examine changes in the status and roles of female teachers over time in a number of national contexts including the United States, Uganda and Bangladesh, in an attempt to tease out common patterns of response to societal change. In addition, an exploration of how systemic changes aiming to draw women into different levels of educational organisations can influence public perceptions of teacher status and women's status in society is included. Such understandings are needed to ensure both gender balance within the teaching profession worldwide and gender-neutral expectations with regard to role and status within the profession.

## Women's role and status in the teaching profession

The status of women teachers is a multi-levelled concept, incorporating perceptions of the status of teaching as an occupation, as viewed by both teachers themselves and society at large, together with the status of women teachers within the teaching profession, as viewed by the women themselves, their male colleagues and those outside the profession. The status of teaching typically refers to its relative standing as an occupation in a hierarchy of all available occupations in a given society. It is dependent on perceptions of prestige or respect, remuneration (salary, benefits, working conditions and personal satisfaction), the characteristics of the students they teach (see Chapter 2) and the power the occupation affords those engaged in it. The interlinking of these variables suggests that an occupation highly valued by society because of its outcomes will be well rewarded, with those employed in it commanding high levels of respect and authority. Teachers, both male and female, responsible for educating new generations to the benefit of society in general, might expect to be both well rewarded and respected (Hoyle, 2001). A further assumption is that the status of teachers will thus be an indicator of the significance attached to education within each culture, a view promoted by L. L. Graves in 1870 when he stated that 'by the elevation of the teacher, we elevate the value of education and accelerate the progress of civilization' (Copelman, 1996, p. 80).

A further ramification of this theory of high occupational status commanding high rewards is that the higher the status of the occupation, the greater the competition for entry, and the higher the qualifications of those gaining the position, something which in turn reinforces the prestige and respect of the occupation. From this perspective, teaching will follow classic economic labour market theory of supply and demand: individuals will become or remain teachers if teaching represents the most attractive activity to pursue among all of those available to them. When teaching is perceived as a desirable high-status occupation, with a limited number of positions available creating competition for these positions, the status of the occupation will be further enhanced by highly qualified entrants to it (Guarino et al., 2006).

Determining the status of teaching as an occupation has typically been undertaken by asking both those employed in the occupation and society at large to rank the desirability of a range of occupations. This type of research indicates how the status of teaching fluctuates as a result of increases or decreases in the numbers of positions available, the number of candidates qualified to fill the positions and changes in conditions and benefits associated with the work required. Hargreaves and colleagues (2007), in a longitudinal study of the status of teachers and the teaching profession in England, note the changes in public and teacher perceptions of the status of teaching since 1960, from a high in 1967 to a low point in 2003. Part of the changed status was ascribed to the perception of changes in a teacher's role and responsibility with regard to management of classes and the need to deal with difficult student behaviour. They also note the effects of the way the profession is constructed in the media, with negative 'teacher bashing' a feature of the early 1990s, giving way to images of teachers as 'dedicated and committed professionals struggling against a broad range of serious problems and pressures' (Hargreaves et al., 2007, p. 5). The same authors also note the differences in perceptions of teacher status from inside and outside the profession. In particular, teachers tend to underestimate the respect the public has for them and the public perceptions of the desirability of teaching as an occupation, with teachers rating the occupation lower than the public at large. However, women and primary teachers tend to hold more positive views about the rewards and respect associated with teaching, even though secondary school teachers rank primary school teachers as being of lower status (Hargreaves et al., 2007).

A study of the social status of teachers in Taiwan indicates how societal changes, including at an ideological level, affect the status of teachers and teaching (Fwu and Wang, 2002). Traditionally, Taiwanese teachers were perceived as having high status as a result of being 'morally and intellectually superior' (p. 214) – characteristics traditionally assigned to teachers throughout the Chinese and Japanese empires. However, with political change in Taiwan came a transformation of the teacher's role, and they were no longer regarded as authoritative figures inculcating the nationalist ideology, but rather as facilitators preparing citizens for a democratic society. Yet, despite these new expectations and the fact that teaching has become 'one occupation among many in the pluralist society, rather than a highly respected mission' (p. 212), the status of the profession remains high as a result of the high value given to academic achievement in this particular context. Women teachers in Taiwan are well represented at all levels of the system (they make up 68 per cent of primary teachers, 67 per cent of junior high teachers, 58 per cent of secondary teachers, 49 per cent of vocational teachers and 34 per cent of college and university teachers). They are not perceived as having lower status than male teachers, although primary teachers are perceived overall as having lower status than secondary teachers.

While the status of teachers in Taiwan remains high and the country has enjoyed a long tradition of recruiting highly talented people into the teaching profession despite the changing roles of teachers, evidence suggests the appeal of teaching is declining in other parts of the world. In a study of who chooses to go into teaching in Australia, Richardson and Watt (2006) note that Australia, the United States, the UK and a number of European countries are having difficulties in attracting and retaining teachers. This situation is of particular concern as these countries also anticipate high rates of retirement of their teaching workforce within the next decade. Despite government recognition of the importance of education, and the importance of teachers in enhancing student learning and outcomes, the appeal of teaching as a career is declining. This relates to the perception that teachers' role is changing and that they are being asked to do more work for less reward as salaries fall relative to other professions. The resulting lowering of teacher status is typically associated with a change in the background characteristics of beginning teacher education, with candidates at all levels of schooling being typically female, young and from less than affluent family backgrounds (Richardson and Watt, 2006). For these groups the financial rewards from an early teaching career are in line with other occupations, more so than for similarly qualified males, perhaps reflecting the persistent discontinuity between male and female salaries in the nation.

These findings from Australia replicate similar findings in the UK and the United States. In these countries, the lowering of status of the profession appears to be associated with an increase in the proportion of women entering the profession and with a lowering of the quality of entrants as measured by formal academic qualifications (Ramsey, 2000). However, Flyer and Rosen (1997) note that in 1960 nearly half of women graduating from college went into teaching, whereas fewer than 10 per cent went into teaching in 1990, a change the authors ascribe to the increase in female labour force participation and the opening of a wider variety of job opportunities to women. While this in itself does not reflect a lowering of quality of women applicants, Podgursky and colleagues (2004) note that, in the United States, graduates entering teaching had significantly lower scores than the non-teachers, and that while women at all test score levels were more likely than men to enter teaching, high-scoring women were relatively more reluctant to do so than high-scoring men.

## Feminisation of teaching

The relationship between the status of the profession and its 'feminisation' (Bolton and Muzio, 2005) is complex and has led to many debates. The term 'feminisation' refers to the process of women coming to numerically dominate an occupation (Bank, 2007; Wylie, 2000), and in so doing having a potential impact on the status of an occupation, its attractiveness to new entrants and the roles of those employed in it. While historically women have been excluded from the teaching profession in most countries of the world, and still have limited access to it in a number of African and Middle Eastern countries, they are now numerically dominant in the teaching workforce of the majority of countries across the globe (UNESCO, 2010). The historical process by which women have moved into teaching highlights the current concerns and debates around the feminisation of teaching, including the location of a much higher percentage of women in the lower levels of the professional hierarchy, the under-representation of women at decision-making levels of the profession and concerns about the gender imbalance reinforcing traditional stereotypes of undervalued 'women's work' and the gendering of the nature of teaching itself (Fischman, 2007; Griffiths, 2006).

The impact of societal change on the feminisation of teaching is well illustrated by the example of the United States during the period before and after 1840, as interpreted by Leaner (1967). She notes that, during the revolutionary period prior to 1840, the relative scarcity of women in teaching enhanced women's status and position in society, while the Puritan world view in which each individual was expected to contribute to the economic development of the community made women as independent wage earners acceptable. Both of these conditions of colonial life led to an undermining of traditionally held beliefs in the inferiority of women and their subordinate position to men. However, after 1840, a change in societal attitudes towards women, in part due to a desire to limit competition for places in higher-paid occupations, led to the genteel lady of fashion becoming the model for American femininity. Women's work outside the home no longer met with social approval and was condemned. Those women forced to work to support themselves and their families and who entered in large numbers low-paid and low-skilled industrial work fixed such work by definition as low-status 'women's work'. Women's political status, while legally unchanged, had deteriorated relative to the advances made by men as a result of changes in the economic environment and societal perceptions of women and men.

Leaner (1967) describes how, in the United States, the 'professionalisation' of certain occupations, a parallel movement to the development of low-skill factory work, led to the exclusion of women from the professions, as did subsequent unionisation of high-skill jobs in factories. However, teaching and nursing were the exception, because both were characterised by a severe shortage of labour. In the case of teaching, the promotion of a national education system and opening of common schools throughout the nation caused this shortage. Women were available in great numbers and they were willing to work. As recalled in Leaner,

> The result was another ideological adaption about women and work. In the very period when the gospel of the home as woman's only proper sphere was preached most loudly, it was discovered that women were the natural teachers of youth, could do the job better than men, and were to be preferred for such employment. This was always provided, of course, that they would work at the proper wage differential 30–50% of the wages paid male teachers was considered appropriate for women. The result was that in 1888 in the country as a whole 63% of all teachers were women, while the figure for the cities only was 90%.
>
> (1969, p. 10)

The history of the movement of women into teaching in the United States thus illustrates 'the interface between gender, labor and economics, and a dialogue between issues of masculinity and femininity within societies' (Kelleher, 2011, p. 8), and the cumulative historical and social process involving subtle patterns of socialisation (Drudy, 2008) replicated in the industrialising countries of Europe, and later in other countries ranging from Latin America to Australia developing public education systems in the late 19th century. A similar process appears to be in operation in some nations of the world today, for example China, where male preferences to avoid occupations where they will have equal status to women is due to gender prejudices which are deeply rooted in society and which override political attempts to promote gender equity (Fu, 2000).

## Women teachers' status

The link between the feminisation and the status of teaching does not seem to be an inevitable or universal pattern. Countries such as Finland,

Korea, Ireland and Cyprus have highly feminised teacher workforces and high social status of the teaching profession with strong competition for gaining such positions (Drudy, 2008; Mavrogeni, 2005). Of more concern is the status of women *within* the teaching profession. Gender stereotyping in subject areas in schools and universities, particularly in science and mathematics, and around leadership capabilities have resulted in a dearth of women aspiring to secondary school teaching in these areas or contemplating leadership positions from where they could influence the direction and outcomes of education systems (Page and Jha, 2009). In contrast, men have been more likely to enter primary schooling to teach at the higher grade levels and as a first step to a career in school administration. The result is a predominance of women in primary school teaching positions, with a comparatively recent movement of women into primary school leadership and secondary school teaching. In most countries of the world, secondary school teaching is perceived as having higher status, and secondary school teaching may be considered of higher status than primary school leadership. Thus women are typically occupying the lower-status positions within the profession, projecting to society at large the impression that they are lacking in skills to gain entrance to higher-status positions, rather than that past discriminatory practices have established patterns that are difficult to challenge and change, even despite changes in the societal attitudes that produced them (Griffiths, 2006; Skelton, 2002). For example, there is evidence which suggests that young people in the UK no longer see a difference in status between primary and secondary teachers (Everton et al., 2007), although the distinction between primary and secondary school leadership persists. Given that both primary and secondary teaching are now dominated by women, but men still dominate secondary school leadership, this finding may not represent the societal change in attitudes that it appears to be at first glance.

## Gendered expectations of teachers

The discussion of the concept of teachers' role is typically limited to the work teachers are expected to perform in the classroom or within the school as an organisation. Such work is laid out in job descriptions, and may include the prescription of teaching pedagogy, the delivery of content, student outcomes and classroom management, in addition to contributions to whole school activities or school organisational duties. As such, the formal role assigned to a teacher will be a reflection of societal understandings about education and student outcomes, be they, for example, the acquisition of knowledge by rote learning or by student inquiry. As such, the role of teacher will differ from one educational context to another.

Discussions about formal roles take a gender-neutral approach; however, studies of the informal roles of teachers reveal the gendered nature of expectations of teacher behaviours and responsibilities. For example, both male and female teachers have been and still are expected to model 'moral' behaviour, an expectation written into law in many countries, but there have in the past been clear distinctions between what constitutes moral behaviour for men and women. For example, unmarried female teachers in the 19th-century United States were restricted in terms of their living conditions and behaviours by the school districts that hired them. Morgade (2006) notes that young girls enrolled in teacher training institutions in Argentina in the 1930s were under severe scrutiny to demonstrate the right moral standards – a 'moral burden' attached to the role of female teacher. A report of a meeting for female teachers in Ghana in 2009 notes that the opening speaker urges the teachers to lead upright lives full of virtue, and demonstrate discipline in all their activities both at school and within the community to inspire female students (GNA, 2009).

The expectation that part of a female teacher's role is to be caregiver, maternal and nurturing is deeply rooted in many societies. This has led to a social construct of the primary teacher being synonymous with constructs of female and mother, 'natural' rather than learned skills, resulting in a deskilling of the primary teacher role and subsequent loss of status in the eyes of society (Smith, 2004). Acker (1996), reviewing the literature around caring as an informal expectation of a female teacher's role, notes that 'The place of caring in teachers' work remains deeply contradictory, simultaneously the moral high ground of the teaching task and a prime site of women's oppression' (p. 124). Paradoxically, in those societies where teaching has been a male activity, either male teachers have been perceived as able to provide the caring and nurturing needed by children in school, or this trait has not been perceived as an integral part of the teacher's role, supporting Acker's comments that the 'discourses on women's nature and women's role seem to go beyond imperatives of capitalism' (p. 124).

In those countries where access of girls to schooling is still of concern, women teachers have been assigned the role of acting as 'attractors' for girls to attend school. Studies in Africa and Nepal (Kirk, 2004; Teas, 1993) suggest that parents are more likely to send their daughters to school if there are female teachers. Nepalese mothers indicate they feel more comfortable talking about their children with a woman teacher. Women teachers in India are perceived to be 'more sincere' and less involved in local politics (Staki, 2002). This aspect of their role was referenced by the Director-General of UNESCO, Irina Bokova, discussing the teaching force in sub-Saharan Africa, still predominantly male, where gender equity in all levels of schooling still has to be met. She asked, '...a low proportion of female teachers will mean fewer girls at school and consequently even fewer women teachers in the future... If qualified female teachers avoid postings in disadvantaged and rural areas, how can we convince reluctant parents to send their children to school?' (www.guardian.co.uk/global-development).

A further addition to the informal roles that female teachers are expected to take up has been their promotion as role models for girls, specifically at the secondary school level. This has been a feature of both developed and developing education systems. It is illustrated by the current concern in the United States for more women teachers in mathematics and science to encourage girls to see these subjects as more desirable, and by calls by UNESCO for female teachers to encourage more girls to enter the teaching profession in many African countries. Women teachers are frequently thought to be more supportive of girls' academic and personal development (Kainja and Mkandawire, 1995). However, studies of the lived experiences of teachers and of the perceptions of girls who have overcome the barriers to their progress through school suggest that there may well be tensions and conflicts between women teachers and girl students, 'suggesting the need to consider carefully the assumptions often made regarding the presence of women teachers and educational empowerment for girls' (Kirk, 2004, p. 277). For example, studies in Uganda suggest adolescent girls may see female teachers as being of low status both in the school and in society and unsympathetic particularly given their 'role' as enforcers of moral behaviour (Sperandio, 1998, 2003). Additionally, female teachers themselves who may have 'chosen' to enter teaching due to a lack of alternatives may feel reluctant to encourage girls to do the same (Mirembe and Davis, 2001).

## Women teachers and societal change

The following two examples suggest that interventions that increase women's access to and status in the profession can also allow women to be change agents within society, challenging ingrained stereotypes about gendered roles and social divides, even though this positioning as 'change agents' is not unproblematic, as also discussed by Brown and Brown in Chapter 10.

## Teaching as empowering in Bangladesh

Until recently, traditional village societies in Bangladesh placed restrictions on almost all aspects of women's lives and behaviour through the institution of *purdah*, the social, economic and even physical segregation of women from public life. This situation not only limited the education available to girls, but also resulted in gender-segregated government schools, the majority of which were for boys and staffed predominantly by men. What little private schooling was available in rural areas was also undertaken by men. However, the mid-1990s saw the government launching a campaign to end illiteracy by expanding non-formal primary education with the help of non-government organisations. One of these organisations, the Bangladesh Rural Advancement Committee (BRAC), set up village schools for children unable to access government primary education. The organisation recruited and trained village women, who were previously unable to work outside the home, to lead the schools.

Interviews with 152 of these women teachers (Sperandio, 2011) indicated the important changes that had resulted from the BRAC policy of recruiting women into teaching and leadership of the new schools. The women describe how by being awarded the role of teacher in their village, a role always previously occupied by a man, combined with becoming a formal wage earner, a role previously denied to most married women in the village, raised their status and challenged traditional societal divisions. The women noted, however, that their village societies may have been accepting of this change because they were still seen as fulfilling the nurturing role of mother and household organisation in their work with children, and as occupied in work that benefited poor families. They also noted that their application for the teaching position required the approval of male family members, and male village dignitaries. However, the support of BRAC as a nationally and internationally recognised advocate for social justice gave protection from any shift in family and societal tolerance of the changed status of these women.

Beyond the changed perceptions in their communities of who could teach, and the respect that came to the women who occupied the role of teacher, they commented upon their own growth in self-confidence and upon their ability to learn new skills and assume new roles. A number of them noted how the experience of teaching and leading the schools had empowered them to consider other opportunities that might exist.

Confronted with the low status of teachers in the private sector in the broader occupational landscape of Bangladesh, they looked for opportunities for higher-status work such as developing their own businesses, or seeking entry into the government school system, where long-term benefits such as pensions were attractive. Thus changes in government policy with regard to education, combined with the purposeful recruitment of women into teaching and school leadership, appear to have initiated changes in the deeper fabric of society (Sperandio, 2011).

## Uganda: Affirmative action in educational leadership

School teaching has long been a devalued profession in Uganda, often taken up as a last option by graduates who fail to find positions in Uganda's limited and highly competitive job market (Kagoda, 2000). Uganda's economy is largely dependent on agricultural production and only 12 per cent of the labour force works in the formal sector, of which 26 per cent are employed in government service (UBS, 2006). Teaching is still a male-dominated profession in Uganda, with women comprising only 20 per cent of secondary school teachers. Few women made it through the many hurdles to become school leaders, but those who did were held in high regard by both male and female students.

Secondary school teachers are classified as government officers with the rank of educational officer. Teaching may not be a popular choice of profession, but once qualified to teach in government schools, teachers have job security, various benefits and a pension. In a country with few opportunities for paid employment, these aspects make teaching desirable and place women in competition for teaching posts with men. Disincentives to becoming a secondary teacher include inefficiencies in the government appointment system leading to delayed payment of salaries, and periodic government recruitment freezes, which leaves probationary teachers unable to obtain teacher status and the increased salary that this bestows. In recent years, the Ministry of Education has exercised its options to move teachers from one school to another in an attempt to improve teaching quality, so that teachers can no longer count on permanent employment in one school.

Ugandan children have only recently had access to free secondary education, and parents' preferences to use limited financial resources to educate boys traditionally resulted in few women gaining tertiary education and the qualifications needed to become a teacher. This situation has limited the numbers of female graduates with the qualifications to allow them to compete for teaching posts and head-of-school positions.

In response to the gender equity requirements of the Millennium goals, Uganda decided on a course of affirmative action within government departments, including education, to ensure 33 per cent representation of women. In addition, all private and public secondary schools were required to have a male and female administrator. This requirement provided government support to the attempt to change the negative stereotypes attached to women leaders, and gave women highly visible and respected positions in what is a competitive education market, in which children vie for positions in the best schools and school administrators are the gatekeepers to a successful school career. The government action also placed women in contention for positions at the ministry level and created a clear career path that could, for women, offset the disincentives attached to entering teaching and raises the status of women teachers as viewed from inside and outside the profession (Sperandio, 2008; Sperandio and Kagoda, 2010).

## Conclusions

The continual assignment of additional 'informal' roles to female teachers – to be caring, to role-model 'moral' behaviour, to demonstrate that women are able to understand mathematics and science, to show that women do have the capacity to lead, to mentor adolescent girls, to reassure parents by their presence to place their daughters in schools – does nothing to improve the status or the respect accorded to women entering the teaching profession. If we are to achieve a gender-neutral situation in which teachers, regardless of gender or the level of schooling in which they practice, are equally valued, then the role of all teachers must be defined in terms of their ability to teach all students effectively, and their status defined by their willingness to continually enhance their own professional qualifications. Professional expertise, the ability to enhance student learning and the result of mandated training, should rate as equal to, or more important than, academic knowledge and nurturing.

In those societies where women must still overcome discriminatory gender practices to enter teaching and to progress to administrative and leadership positions, placing women in these roles and supporting them to ensure their success can challenge deeply rooted stereotypes of what women can and cannot do. The examples from Bangladesh and Uganda speak to this. In Uganda, while competition for teaching and leadership posts remains fierce, the pool of formally qualified candidates large and patriarchal practices embedded in most aspects of life, government intervention to ensure the visibility of women teachers and women administrators is an important contribution to ongoing national efforts to develop a gender-equal society. In Bangladesh, a similar process of hiring women for roles traditionally reserved for men in village communities challenges entrenched gendered hierarchies.

In societies where change is represented by women in large numbers gaining the formal qualifications to give them a wider (yet constrained) choice of occupation, the challenge is to ensure that highly qualified women enter the profession, and they enter it at all levels. This may mean increasing incentives for women to enter secondary school teaching and school leadership, to avoid children being socialised into believing that certain occupations are gender specific. Thus the role, status and respect commanded by female teachers must be carefully monitored worldwide to ensure women's equal participation in the development and leadership of the schooling of children for more gender-equal societies of the future.

## References

Acker, S. (1996) 'Gender and teacher's work', *Review of Research in Education*, 21, 99–162.

Bank, B. J. (ed.) (2007) *Gender and education: An encyclopedia* (London: Praeger Westport).

Bolton, S. and Muzio, D. (2008) 'The paradoxical processes of feminization in the professions: The case of established, aspiring and semi-professions', *Work, Employment and Society*, 22(2), 281–99.

Copelman, D. (1996) *London's women teachers: Gender, class, and feminism, 1870–1930* (London: Routledge).

Drudy, S. (2008) 'Gender balance/gender bias: The teaching profession and the impact of feminization', *Gender and Education*, 20(4), 309–23

Everton, T., Turner, P., Hargreaves, L. and Pell, T. (2007) 'Public perceptions of the teaching profession', *Research Papers in Education*, 22(3), 247–65.

Fischman, G. E. (2007) 'Persistence and ruptures: The feminization of teaching and teacher education in Argentina', *Gender and Education*, 19(3), 353–68.

Flyer, F. and Rosen, S. (1997) 'The new economics of teachers and education', *Journal of Labor Economics*, 15(1), 104–39.

Fu, S. (2000) 'Initial exploration of the phenomenon of the feminization of teachers', *Chinese Education and Society*, 33(4), 40–6.

Fwu, B. and Wang, H. (2002) 'The social status of teachers in Taiwan', *Comparative Education*, 38(2), 211–24.

GNA (2009) 'Female teachers advised to be role models for school girls', *Modern Ghana News*, 22 May 2009, http://www.modernghana.com/news/217886/

1/feamale-teachers-adised-to-be-role-models-for   scho.html   (Accessed   1   July 2013).

Graves, J. J. (1870). 'Address of the president of the National Union of Elementary Teachers at the first annual conference', King's College London, 10 September 1870, *Educational Reporter* (1 December 1870), 6–9.

Griffiths, M. (2006) 'The feminization of teaching and the practice of teaching: Threat or opportunity?', *Educational Theory*, 56(4), 387–405.

Guarino, C. M., Santibanex, I. and Daley, G. A. (2006) 'Teacher recruitment and retention: A review of the recent empirical literature', *Review of Educational Research*, 76(2), 173–206.

Hargreaves, L., Cunningham, M., Hansen, A., McIntyre, D. and Oliver, C. (2007) *Status of teachers and the teaching profession in England: Views from inside and outside the profession*, University of Cambridge Faculty of Education research report no. 831A, Cambridge, UK.

Hoff, D. L., Menard, C. and Tuell, J. (2006) 'Where are the women in school administration? Issues of access, acculturation, advancement, and advocacy', *Journal of Women in Educational Leadership*, 4(1), 43–60.

Hoyle, E. (2001) 'Teaching, prestige, status and esteem', *Educational Management and Administration*, 29(2), 139–52.

Kagoda, A. M. (2000) 'Determinants of career professional development of female teachers in Uganda', Unpublished paper delivered to the Human Services Today conference, Makerere University, Kampala, Uganda.

Kainja, K. and Mkandawire, F. (1995) *National SCSE Study on the role of female teachers in the enrolment and persistence of girls in primary schools*, Comparative Overseas Collection (Institute of Education, University of London, London).

Kelleher, F. (2011) *Women and the teaching profession: Exploring the feminization debate* (Commonwealth Secretariat and UNESCO, London and Paris).

Kirk, J. (2004) 'Impossible fictions: The lived experiences of women teachers in Karachi', *Comparative Education Review*, 48(1), 374–95

Leaner, G. (1967) 'The lady and the mill girl: Changes in the status of women in the age of Jackson', *American Studies*, 10(1), https://journals.ku.edu/index.php/amerstud/article/view/2145/2104 (Accessed16 July 2013).

Lumby, J. and Azaola, M. C. (2013) 'Women principals in South Africa: Gender, mothering and leadership', *British Educational Research Journal*, doi:10.1002/berj.3028.

Mavrogeni, L. E. (2005) 'The feminisation of the teaching profession in Cyprus', Unpublished MS dissertation, Institute of Education, University of London.

Mirembe, R. and Davis, L. (2001) 'Is schooling a risk? Gender, power relations, and school culture in Uganda', *Gender and Education*, 13(4), 410–16.

Morgade, G. (2006) 'State, gender and class in the social construction of Argentine women teachings', in R. Cortina and S. San Román (eds.) *Woman and teaching: Global perspectives on the feminization of a profession* (New York: Palgrave Macmillan).

OECD (2004) *The quality of the teaching workforce. Brief*, http://www.oecd.org/edu/29478720.pdf (Accessed 16 July 2013).

Page, E. J. (2009) *Exploring the bias: Gender and stereotyping in secondary schools* (London: Commonwealth Secretariat).

Podgursky, M., Monroe, R. and Watson, D. (2004) 'The academic quality of public school teachers: An analysis of entry and exit behavior', *Economics of Education Review*, 23(5), 507–18.

Ramsey, G. (2000) *Quality matters. Revitalizing teaching: Critical times, critical choices.* Report of the review of teacher education (Sydney: NSW Department of Education and Training).

Richardson, P. W. and Watt, H. M. G. (2006) 'Who chooses teaching and why? Profiling characteristics and motivations across three Australian universities', *Asia-Pacific Journal of Teacher Education*, 34(1), 27–56.

Rogers, R. (2005) *From the salon to the schoolroom: Educating bourgeois girls in nineteenth-century France* (Pennsylvania: Penn State University Press).

Skelton, C. (2002) 'The feminization of schooling or the re-masculinising primary education?', *International Studies in Sociology of Education*, 12(1), 77–96.

Smith, J. B. (2004) 'Male primary teachers: Disadvantaged or advantaged?', Paper presented to the Australian Association for Research in Education Conference, Melbourne, December.

Sperandio, J. (1998) 'Girls' secondary education in Uganda. Unintended outcomes of well-intentioned policy', Unpublished doctoral dissertation, University of Chicago.

Sperandio, J. (2003) 'Leadership for adolescent girls: The role of secondary schools in Uganda', *Gender and Development*, 14(4), 391–410.

Sperandio, J. (2008) 'Advancing women into educational leadership in developing countries: The case of Uganda', *Advancing Women in Leadership*, Spring (24), 1–14.

Sperandio, J. (2011) 'Context and the gendered status of teachers: Women's empowerment through leadership of non-formal schools in rural Bangladesh', *Gender and Education*, 23(2), 121–35.

Sperandio, J. and Kagoda, A. M. (2010) 'Women teachers' aspirations to school leadership in Uganda', *International Journal of Educational Management*, 23(1), 22–33.

Staki, S. (2002) *Women teachers empowered in India: Teacher training through a gender lens.* UNICEF Programme Division Education document no. UNICEF/PD/ED/02-1.

Teas, M. M. (1993) *Increasing women's participation in the primary school teaching force and teacher training in Nepal.* Policy working paper no. WPS1161. World Bank.

UBS (2006) *Uganda Bureau of Statistics, Statistical Abstracts* (Kampala, Uganda: UBS).

UNESCO (2000) *Increasing the number of women teachers in rural schools; A synthesis of country case studies. South Asia* (Bangkok: UNESCO).

UNESCO (2010) *Country case studies in early childhood care and education in selected sub-Saharan countries 2007/8: Some key teacher issues and policy recommendations: A summary report* (Addis Ababa: UNESCO).

United Nations (2007) *The Millennium Development Goals Report 2007* (New York: United Actions), http://www.un.org/millenniumgoals/pdf/mdg2007.pdf (Accessed 16 July 2013).

Wylie, C. (2000) *Trends in feminization of the teaching profession in OECD countries 1980–1995.* Sectoral Activities Department working paper 151 (Geneva: International Labour Office).

Young, M. D. and McLeod, S. (2001) 'Flukes, opportunities, and planned interventions: Factors affecting women's decisions to become school administrators', *Educational Administration Quarterly,* 37(4), 462–502.

Zeichner, K. and Bekisizwe, N. (2008) 'Contradictions and tensions in the place of teachers in educational reform: Reflections on teacher preparation in the USA and Namibia', *Teachers and Teaching: Teaching and Practice,* 14(4), 331–43.

# Part II
# Teachers, Equality and Identities

# 4
# Who Counts as a 'Real' Teacher? Australian Teachers as Respectable, Conservative ... and White

*Ninetta Santoro*

## Introduction

Australian society is one of the most culturally diverse in the world. One in four Australians has a language background other than English (Australian Bureau of Statistics, 2012) and there is an Indigenous[1] population with rich cultures and traditions. Yet teachers are drawn mainly from the dominant White Anglo-Celtic majority, a national identity shaped by powerful historical and political discourses. It is estimated that approximately 87 per cent of teachers are of Anglo-Celtic heritage (Hartsuyker, 2007), with 1 per cent of all teaching staff in government schools and 0.3 per cent of all teaching staff in Catholic schools being Indigenous (Department of Education, Employment and Workplace Relations, 2008).

Attempts to diversify the profession and, in particular, to recruit increased numbers of Indigenous teachers have been largely unsuccessful. Despite several decades of support for universities and teacher education initiatives aimed at increasing Indigenous teacher numbers and ongoing calls since the 1970s for a growth in the number of Indigenous teachers (Collins, 2000; Commonwealth of Australia, 1993; Hughes and Willmot, 1982; VAEAI, 2001), including Hughes' optimistic call for 1000 Indigenous teachers by 1990, Indigenous people are still under-represented in the profession. There are a number of reasons for the poor representation of Indigenous people in the teaching profession, of why they are not attracted to the profession and why those who do enter the profession leave prematurely (Santoro et al., 2011; Santoro and Reid, 2006). One significant reason is that the vast majority of Australian teachers are White and of Anglo-Celtic heritage, the 'norm' from which all other positions are usually marked as different, or 'Other'. These constructions make it difficult for Indigenous people to be seen, 'naturally', as teachers and for an Indigenous child to see her teacher as someone like herself, or someone whom she is like. The image of teachers as respectable, conservative and female is one that has prevailed in popular media for many years and is embodied in 'respectable' and conservative appearance and behaviours (Townsend and Ryan, 2012; see also Chapter 6). In their work into how teachers are represented in children's books, Dockett et al. (2010) found that teachers were overwhelmingly represented as White and from the dominant Anglo-Celtic majority. In the same vein, Mendoza and Reese claim that 'The omission of specific groups of people from picture storybooks, particularly in the powerful role of teacher, generates messages about who belongs...' (in Dockett et al., 2010, p. 38).

Furthermore, while Australian students, Indigenous and non-Indigenous, are unlikely to have been taught by an Indigenous teacher, some may have had varying levels of contact with Aboriginal Teacher Aides, also called teaching assistants or Aboriginal education assistants. Aboriginal Teacher Aides are often employed to liaise with Indigenous families and perform para-professional tasks in schools where there are relatively high populations of Indigenous students. They do not have teacher status and are always in subordinate positions to the 'real' teachers – the majority of whom are from the dominant cultural majority.

Nearly 20 years ago, Hesch asserted that in order to be accepted as a teacher, an Indigenous person needs to 'produce the practices that excluded many of them and that will continue to exclude members of their original social category' (1996, p. 271). This would still seem to be the case. Being accepted as a teacher is a deeply troubling process for Indigenous people because it requires them to immerse themselves in a schooling system that is still shaped by colonialist and post-colonial discourses (Hickling-Hudson, 2003).

As a result of research in North America, Canada and the UK over many years, there is a significant body of literature about Black and Minority Ethnic teachers in those countries (for example, James, 2002; Osler, 1997; Wilkins and Lall, 2011; see also Chapter 10). However, there is little research that has focused specifically on Australian Indigenous teachers. In this chapter I draw on data from a 4-year study that investigated the experiences of 50 Indigenous teachers in Australian schools. I consider how historical and contemporary discourses shape and position Indigenous peoples as the deficit 'Other' – the antithesis of 'the teacher' as a respectable, conservative, responsible and White citizen. Underpinning this prevailing image is a national identity deeply embedded within a colonial and post-colonial history. I conclude the chapter by raising concerns about the success of strategies to increase the numbers of Indigenous teachers if Whiteness is seen as central to 'legitimate' teacher status.

Before examining some of the data from the study, I provide an overview of elements of Australian history in order to highlight some of the discourses that position those who are not from the cultural mainstream as 'Other', particularly Indigenous Australians. This provides a background against which the current under-representation of Indigenous teachers can be read.

## Australia as an imaginary White nation: A potted history

Apart from the Indigenous population of Australia which totals about 2.5 per cent of the 21 million strong population (Australian Bureau of Statistics, 2012) and can be traced back more than 40,000 years (Isaacs, 1987), Australia is a nation of immigrants – mainly White immigrants who first arrived about 225 years ago. The ethnicities of these early settlers constituted those of Britain and Ireland, that is the English, Scots, Welsh and Irish. Generally, however, these British ethnic groups united into the White Anglo-Celtic core of Australian national identity, an identity that has significant currency today (Colic-Peisker, 2005).

At the turn of the 20th century, the Australian government introduced the Immigration Restriction Act, commonly known as 'The White Australia Policy'. It operated from 1901 until 1958 (Hodge and O'Carroll, 2006, p. 102) to restrict the entry of non-Whites into Australia. It was finally abolished in 1973 (DIAC, 2009). This policy 'consolidated the various measures the colonies had already put in place into a system of restrictions based on a hierarchy of desirable (European, especially British) and undesirable (Asians, Indians, Pacific Islanders) immigrants' (Ellinghaus, 2003, p. 185). In effect, this means there was virtually no non-White immigration to Australia after the 1850s when the Chinese arrived to work the goldfields, until 1976 when the first of the refugees from the Vietnam War arrived. 'The White Australia policy made Anglocentric whiteness the definitive marker of citizenship; and a form of property born of social status to which others were denied access including Indigenous people' (Moreton-Robinson and Nicoll, 2006, p. 79).

From 1946 until the late 1970s, large numbers of British people were enticed to Australia by preferential treatment that took the form of assisted passage to Australia and resettlement incentives (DIAC, 2009). Up until the mid-1970s, they were also not required to forgo British citizenship in order to have the same rights as Australian-born citizens (Lucas, 1987) and were able to become Australian citizens after 1 year of residency. Australia was 'British to the bootstraps' (Christie and Sidhu, 2006, p. 454), with legal systems, language and a monarchy inherited from Britain and food and cultural practices originating from various places in the British Isles. After World War II, and in response to the need to increase Australia's small population for reasons of national security, large numbers of immigrants from Europe were also accepted. While they were not British, they were White.

There has always been, however, a major barrier to Australia's construction of itself as a White nation, and that is the Indigenous population. These original inhabitants who have lived in Australia for in excess of 40,000 years became known as the 'Aboriginal problem' (Ellinghaus, 2003). From the late 19th to mid-20th centuries, government policies facilitated what Ellinghaus calls the planned 'disappearance' of Aboriginal people:

> ... it was to be a two stage process: firstly, the 'doomed race' theory posited that people of full descent would soon 'die out'; and secondly, it was believed that Aboriginal physical characteristics, and it was hoped, Aboriginality itself, would disappear altogether through biological absorption.
>
> (2003, p. 186)

In most areas of Australia, Indigenous people were forced to live on tightly controlled missions and reserves where tribal languages and cultural practices were lost. This practice led to the systematic erosion of the rich cultures and social structures of hundreds of tribes. Up until approximately the end of the 1960s, most Indigenous children received formal education on church missions and were taught by White 'teachers' and clergy whose role was to instil White values into them. However, the standard of education was poor and not comparable to that received by non-Indigenous children. It prepared them for little more than farm work or domestic service.

Further attempts to 'assimilate', 'breed out' or 'absorb' Indigenous people occurred by forcibly removing children who had some White heritage and relocating them in institutions or with White families.

Between 1909 and 1969, approximately 100,000 children, since known as 'The Stolen Generations', were removed from their families (Reconciliation Network, 2012). It was not until 2008 that the Australian government apologised to members of the Stolen Generations for a policy aimed specifically at eradicating Indigenous people from the profile of modern Australia.

Citizenship was not an automatic right for Indigenous people and it was not until 1965 that all Indigenous people in all areas of Australia were given the right to vote. It was not until 1967 that a referendum was held and the constitution changed to allow Indigenous people to be counted in the Australian census. In 1993, the High Court of Australia rejected 'the previous legal foundation of "terra nullius" that was founded on the idea the Australian land had belonged to no one before European settlement in 1788'. Thus the native Title Act, recognising Indigenous people's claims to land, came to be (Reconciliation Australia, 2009).

As a result of these shameful racist practices, some of which are in the not-too-distant past, Indigenous people have become the most socially and economically disadvantaged group in Australia (Doyle and Hill, 2008; SCRGSC, 2005). Relative to the non-Indigenous population, Indigenous people are more likely to have poor health and die earlier, be unemployed and be poorly educated (Australian Productivity Commission, 2011). Furthermore, they have been portrayed by some right-wing politicians and social commentators as a drain on the welfare system – a construction readily accepted by some in the Australian community. In an interview, Sarra, an Aboriginal researcher and educator, claimed that Aboriginal people are often described by non-Indigenous people in negative ways, as 'welfare dependent', 'lazy' and 'well kept by the government' (Gorringe et al., 2011, p. 7). Popular and enduring myths suggest they receive subsidised cars and subsidised housing loans. Affirmative action in regard to the creation of employment opportunities for Indigenous people is often seen as 'politically correct' and unfair preferential treatment.

## Post-colonial theory

Post-colonial theory is concerned with identifying the effects and the legacies of colonising practices on the contemporary social institutions and practices of previously colonised societies (see Bhabha, 1994; Said, 1993; Spivak, 1988). The subjectivities of those who have been colonised and those who have been colonisers are shaped by discourses of power and dominance, with the legacies of these asymmetrical power relations having long-lasting effects. In Australian schooling and education, these legacies are played out through racist discourses that construct Indigenous people as *recipients* of education but not as contributors and not as agentic. They are hyper-visible at the same time as they are made invisible. This is not to say that all Indigenous people in Australia are powerless and without a voice in the education arena. There have been significant gains made possible by the determination of many Indigenous people, the advocacy and political action of Indigenous leaders and the work of non-Indigenous people committed to social justice and reconciliation. However, Australian education is still largely ineffective for Indigenous people, and becoming and being a teacher is fraught for Australian Indigenous people because they must battle the discriminatory practices of an education system that is, in many cases, a re-inscription of colonial practices.

What follows in this chapter is an overview of the study from which I draw data to support my argument, a presentation of data from interviews conducted with ten teachers and a concluding discussion.

## The study

The study on which this chapter draws brought together a team of Aboriginal and non-Aboriginal researchers to investigate the experiences and career pathways of Indigenous teachers in Australian schools.[2] It aimed to understand some of the reasons for their under-representation in the teaching profession. There were two main components to the project's research design: (a) qualitative case studies of 50 current and former Indigenous teachers and (b) longitudinal case studies of four newly graduated Indigenous teachers. In total there were 54 participants who were selected from networks of Indigenous teachers to which the project's Aboriginal co-researchers were connected. This decision led to a snowballing method of recruitment whereby the teachers recommended other potential participants. Because there are few Indigenous teachers in Australia and demographic information about them is not readily available, this method of recruitment was deemed to be the most viable. The 50 current and former teachers ranged in age from 25 to 61 and included 14 males. Of the 50 teachers, 12 had either left teaching to take on administrative roles in schools or the wider education system, become teacher educators or left the field of education entirely and taken up other occupations. The 38 current teachers had taught for periods of time ranging from 1 to 17 years and were located in primary and secondary school contexts across metropolitan, regional city, rural and remote areas of Australia. Data collection occurred between 2005 and 2008 and comprised semi-structured interviews conducted by all members of the research team. The interviews lasted between one and two hours and elicited information from the 50 teachers about their schooling, their family backgrounds, their pre-service teacher education, induction into teaching and their experiences as new graduates and professionals, including the nature of their pedagogies, their relationships with students, parents and colleagues and the professional challenges, successes and disappointments they had encountered. As an additional data source, a focus group consisting of eight volunteer participants was convened in order to follow up issues that emerged as significant across a number of the individual interviews, and to validate the emerging themes of the analysis through a collective member-checking process.

The 3-year-long longitudinal case studies of four newly graduated Indigenous teachers who commenced employment in 2004 and 2005 included teachers who ranged in age from 25 to 40. They had all begun their teaching careers in rural schools in the Australian state of New South Wales. Data were collected via intensive semi-structured three-hour-long interviews twice a year. The interviews elicited chronological, experiential and evaluative accounts of their schooling, their family backgrounds, their pre-service teacher education, their induction into teaching and their experiences as new graduates and professionals, including the nature of their pedagogies, their relationships with students, parents and colleagues and the professional challenges, successes and disappointments they had encountered. All interviews for the study were transcribed verbatim and returned to interviewees for verification.

In this chapter, I draw on interview data from both components of the study and specifically from ten teachers. Deb,[3] a Gureng[4] woman and a former teacher, is now working as a senior administrator in the health sector after having worked as a primary school teacher for 5 years; Raelene is a Wiradjuri woman who has been teaching in primary schools for 8 years; Alicia has been teaching for 10 years in primary schools and is a Gulidjan woman; Christie, a Dharug woman, has been a primary school teacher for 5 years; Tom, a Wiradjuri man and a former secondary school teacher for 8 years, is now working as an advisor for a state education department; Colleen is a Ngaralta woman who has been teaching in primary schools for 18 years; Luke, who was a participant in the longitudinal case study and a Wiradjuri man in his late twenties, was in his first year of teaching in a secondary school in a small rural town at the time of the first round of data collection; Shirley, a

Dharawal woman, was a primary teacher for 8 years before becoming a teacher educator and then an education consultant; Carol, a Dharug woman with 15 years' teaching experience, is currently a deputy principal in a primary school; Clare is a Kamillaroi woman in her first year of teaching in a primary school.

Drawing on naturalistic methods (Lincoln and Guba, 1985), a thematic approach to analysis was adopted. The transcripts were read and re-read, looking for broad recurring themes, similarities and commonalities across the two data sets in terms of the teachers' professional experiences. The following questions were asked of the data: What is the dominant story being told? What are the recurring themes? Where is the repetition? Where are the silences? The broad themes that emerged were 'reasons for becoming a teacher', 'experiences during teacher education', 'experiences during induction into the profession' and 'relationships' – with colleagues, students and parents. In this chapter, the data highlighting the binary opposites of visible/invisible are presented. They have been organised under the sub-themes of 'perceptions of qualifications', 'perceptions of teaching competence' and 'relationships with colleagues'.

I do not wish to generalise from the findings of the study. The data presented here are not intended to represent the perspectives of *all* Indigenous teachers. Nevertheless, they provide valuable insights into the discursive practices that shaped how the teachers were positioned, not as 'real' teachers but as 'Indigenous teachers'. I am also acutely aware of the ways in which 'naming' is a discursive practice that serves to *produce* the subject rather than simply reflect it. 'What does it mean for a word not only to name, but also in some sense to perform and, in particular, to perform what it names?' (Butler, 1997, p. 43). In an attempt to categorise and describe, researchers can *produce* the identities of those whose identities they seek to understand. For this reason, I cautiously use terms such as 'Indigenous teacher' and 'White teacher', because neither of these categories is homogeneous and the identities of those marked by these terms are not fixed and immutable.

## Looking, speaking and acting like a teacher

Despite the shortage of Indigenous teachers, the majority of our participants reported difficulties in obtaining jobs after graduating from teaching degrees. This was sometimes because they were unable to move from their home communities to take up a position elsewhere. However, when there was a generalist teaching position available, as distinct from one targeting Indigenous applicants for positions as teachers of Indigenous Studies,[5] our participants were usually not successful. Some of the teachers applied for numerous positions after graduation. When they finally obtained a position it was usually in a school considered hard to staff, that is, a school with a large number of Indigenous students, students of low socio-economic status, culturally diverse students for whom English is a second language and students with special learning needs.

The participants also talked about the surprised reactions of other teachers, parents and students when they realised Indigenous people were teachers. Christie says: 'I feel good when I say that I'm a teacher. I'm proud. But a lot of people are so shocked.' Colleen recounts her interaction with a parent during her first parent-teacher interviews:

> This parent came up and says, 'Are you a real teacher? Are you a qualified teacher? Are you a real teacher?' 'Yes, of course, I am.' But you know what, I think that says a lot. There's the stigma of the ... If you're Aboriginal, you can't be a teacher.

These attitudes that position Indigenous teachers as less-than-legitimate professionals are also manifested in the scrutiny the teachers are forced to endure in relation to their qualifications and teaching competence. Alicia expresses the following about her colleagues, the students and their parents: 'They have this opinion that because I'm Black I'm not as well educated or trained as the White teachers.'

Indigenous people follow a diverse range of study pathways into the teaching profession including direct entry from school to university. However, most are of mature age and enter teacher education via special-entry enclave programmes. In some cases, additional economic, pastoral and academic support is made available to them through Indigenous support units in universities (Reid et al., 2009). The courses are of the same standard as those completed by non-Indigenous people, are equally rigorous and qualify them for the same national teacher registration. However, all of our participants reported that there were perceptions amongst their colleagues and the wider community that the courses were of lesser standard. Tom says:

> And one night a friend of mine was at a pub and talking to the parents of one of my kids [students] and it was like, 'Oh, the Black fella teacher? He probably got his qualifications out of a Weet-Bix packet ... they get qualifications handed to them'.

Tom also talks about how one of his colleagues would 'very regularly ask, "Which college did you go to?"' He goes on to say that while parents ask him about his teaching credentials, they never ask the other teachers the same question:

> You know, it's the same thing with every parent that you meet, 'What university did you go to?', or 'What "TAFE" did you go to?'

The parent's inquiry as to what college of TAFE (Technical and Further Education) Tom attended may reflect a genuine misunderstanding about the provision of initial teacher education being conducted exclusively within universities in Australia. However, that Tom chose to report this interaction suggests that he believes the query is intended to suggest he is less than a bona fide professional (colleges of TAFE generally specialise in less prestigious para-professional and vocational training). Clare says:

> People think that you've got this armour that things bounce off, but if you kept on getting told that 'You can't do that' and 'Why are you here?', 'Why would you want to teach, you're Aboriginal', you know basically you don't fit into this profession.

The teachers also report having to justify their practice to colleagues in ways that non-Indigenous teachers are not required to do. They feel they are watched constantly by their colleagues and by senior members of staff and that there is a basic lack of trust in their integrity as professionals and in their teaching competence. Most of our informants adopted an approach to teaching that is shaped by Indigenous ways of learning that focus on doing. Although taking specific examples of learning and suggesting they are applicable to all Indigenous peoples in all contexts is potentially problematic because it constructs Indigenous people as a homogeneous group, there is a significant body of literature that supports the notion that, in general, Indigenous people learn in practical ways involving observation and doing. For example, Barnhardt and Kawagley suggest that education for Indigenous Alaskans occurs through 'demonstration and observation accompanied by thoughtful stories in which the lessons were embedded' (2005, p. 10). Deb says:

> I got into a bit of strife about the way that I taught. I would do a lot of hands-on teaching, a lot of teaching by doing. On reflection, my style of teaching was probably teaching the way Aboriginal people teach. Not the way conventional teaching and learning

happens... We would do lots of hands on... and then the paper and pen stuff would come after concepts were well and truly understood. By not forcing them to pen and paper too early, it gave them that time to work it out for themselves. The Aboriginal kids were able to excel and it was just a great way to teach the others as well. But the Deputy Principal used to get annoyed because I'd have lots of equipment in the room. There was always plenty there for the other teachers, if they needed to borrow anything, it was always there, I didn't hog all the equipment. But it seemed to annoy her to some extent that I would use equipment.

Although it was not something expected of the other teachers, Deb was required to report to the deputy principal on a weekly basis so her teaching programme could be checked and scrutinised. Often, she was summoned to the deputy principal's office via a message delivered by a student:

Usually she had written about six pages in red writing about the things that she thought I should do and the things that needed to be addressed in the programme. So I did what she asked even though I knew what she asked for was trivial. You played the game, or you faced the consequences.

Not only is the deputy principal asserting her authority as a manager and a teaching expert, but she is also treating Deb like a student rather than a colleague by summoning her to her office and then handing her 'six pages in red writing' about her programme. Raelene reports similar levels of surveillance and requests for her to justify her practice: 'So it's sort of constant all the time, questioning you "Why are you doing it this way, why are you doing it that way." Cause you're constantly fighting all the time.'

Reflecting on her teaching experience as a student teacher, Colleen says: 'There was one supervising teacher who gave me a pass but she wrote on my prac [practice teaching] assessment report,... "I think she'll only ever teach Aboriginal kids." ' The supervising teacher's assessment of Colleen as *only* able to teach Aboriginal students implies that there are two categories of teachers: those who are able to teach non-Indigenous students and those who are able to only teach Indigenous students. This distinction further positions Indigenous teachers as less competent than their non-Indigenous peers because they are deemed to have limited teaching skills that are not suitable for teaching White children.

Some of our participants reported being constructed as Indigenous cultural experts (see Basit and Santoro, 2011; Santoro, 2012; Santoro and Reid, 2006). Usually they were the only Indigenous teacher in a school and were expected to take responsibility for all Indigenous matters, including liaising with Indigenous families and communities, being responsible for the pastoral care of Indigenous students, filling the gaps in the knowledge of White teachers about Indigenous education and taking responsibility for the implementation of Indigenous education policies and initiatives at school level. While all of the teachers were dedicated to improving education for Indigenous students and, in many cases, became teachers because they saw themselves as being able to do so, it is clear that many are resentful of the increased workload this entails, the lack of recognition they receive within educational communities and the ways they are constructed first and foremost as 'Indigenous teachers' rather than 'teachers'. In previous work, I have claimed that for many, if not for all, Indigenous teachers, 'this identity, once ascribed, becomes a means of identification, or a label, behind and beneath which individual difference and affiliation is (systematically) obscured' (Santoro and Reid, 2006, p. 298). According to Carol, 'The other teachers think, if that child is Black, a Black teacher can deal with it.' Shirley, reflecting on her experiences, says:

> I didn't want to be seen as the Aboriginal teacher. I think a lot of staff members in schools, when they see you coming as an Aboriginal teacher – you're Aboriginal. They don't see you as a teacher. And I tell the Aboriginal students who are going through university, 'First you're a teacher. You're not going through university because you're Aboriginal. You're not going to be qualified as an Aboriginal.'

Although Indigenous teachers are highly visible within schools because they are positioned as 'the Indigenous teacher' and are marked and signified as pseudo-professionals, at the same time, they are invisible. All of the participants spoke about being 'left off' the important school committees and rarely given opportunities to participate in or be heard in relation to the strategic planning and decision-making that occurred. With the exception of one of the teachers who was a deputy principal, none had school leadership responsibilities. Few engaged in the wide-ranging professional development opportunities afforded to other staff because they were seen by those in management as irrelevant to their work as 'the Indigenous teacher' or they were so busy that taking time away from the classroom was too difficult.

Most of the participants told stories during interviews about their experiences of negotiating what could almost seem like the impenetrability of teacher staffrooms and the feeling of social exclusion and invisibility that were engendered by staffroom relationships. Raelene says:

The staffroom makes me feel really uncomfortable because I don't talk the same sort of upper class talk like them [the other teachers], so it makes me feel uncomfortable. I stay in my room [classroom] at lunch time and eat my lunch there. I feel more comfortable because when I do sit in the staffroom I'm up this end of the table, the Kooris are up one end and all of the White people down the other end...which is you know really uncomfortable and then every now and then I'll talk to them a bit but a lot of times I sit on my own and I just feel like I'm looking at the walls...I feel like I am part of the furniture, they don't even notice me.

Here, Raelene alludes to issue of social class when she says 'I don't talk the same sort of upper class talk'. Having 'good manners' and being 'well spoken' are markers of the 'right' social class, all of which are also social constructs associated with Whiteness. Teachers are popularly thought of as role models who embody standards of respectability through their dress and behaviour. In other words, they have the right habitus to be a teacher. As argued by Bourdieu,

The habitus is a set of dispositions, reflexes and forms of behaviour people acquire through acting in society. It reflects the different positions people have in society, for example, whether they are brought up in a middle-class environment or in a working class suburb.

(2000, p. 19)

Raelene's habitus sets her apart from the other teachers and marks her as 'unteacherly'.

Christie recounts a situation whereby her Indigeneity appeared to be completely invisible to her colleagues:

One time something was brought up in the staffroom about Black people and I couldn't help myself, I'm not rude or anything but we were sitting at a table, I can't even remember what is was exactly, but anyway they were talking about something, something about Aboriginal people, Aboriginal kids in the school or something, I don't know. They kept going on and on and I was sitting and listening to it and when I'd sort of had enough, I said, 'Yeah, I hate Black people, my mum, my dad, hang on, I hate my whole family'. And this lady just looked at me, bright red, she just went bright red.

Of all the participants to the study, it was only Luke who gained the greatest status as a 'legitimate' teacher. However, he was only able to do so after he had transferred into a new position in a school where there were no Indigenous students and none of his colleagues or the students knew he was Indigenous. Although it is a commonly held view in Australia that all Indigenous people are dark-skinned and have particular physical features, Luke is relatively fair. In the absence of information about his background, his new colleagues assumed him to be White and therefore a 'real' teacher. He decided it would be easier for him to take the option not to reveal his background. Unlike his first two appointments where he was seen as 'the Indigenous teacher' and was expected to attend exclusively to the education of the Indigenous students and all Indigenous matters, at the new school he was able to teach his subjects of expertise, that is, maths and physical education. He was able to establish equal working relationships with other teachers, was given positions of responsibility and was able to plan a career path through professional development opportunities. He says: 'I was just like any other teacher' (see Santoro, 2012, for further details regarding this participant).

## Concluding remarks

Through classroom practices, curriculum, relationships with students and their engagement with education policy, teachers contribute to the preservation of existing values, practices and social hierarchies. Not only do they impart particular knowledge to young people and develop their minds and intellectual capacities, but they also teach them, either explicitly or implicitly, to behave in 'right', 'good' and 'morally' responsible ways – that is, to be the *particular* kind of citizens that fit into the existing social order. Therefore, those who are relatively powerful members of the social order and have a vested interest in its preservation are likely to take 'naturally' to the work of teaching and are likely to be seen as 'natural' teachers. In Australia, these people are White.

I do not want to suggest, however, that all White teachers unquestioningly preserve the values and practices of the existing social order through curriculum and teaching practices that are taken for granted as normal and natural. There are some teachers for whom the asymmetrical power relations between members of the social order and the differences between access to resources is deeply troubling. These teachers can have deep and nuanced understandings of how, as members of the dominant majority and members of the teaching profession, they are complicit in maintaining a social order characterised by inequality. Many are committed to working for social change. However, in general, it is difficult to clearly 'see' the discourses in which one's professional and personal life is embedded. It is also especially difficult to work towards changing the fundamental values and practices of a society, when one's job is to preserve them.

Therefore, in order to disrupt the values and practices that are rooted in the discourses of a colonial past and have become accepted as 'normal', it is important to change the profile of the Australian teaching profession to include greater numbers of Indigenous teachers. However, policies and strategies of affirmative action alone will not ensure Indigenous people being attracted to the profession or, indeed, remaining in the profession. Fifteen years ago, Jude claimed that Aboriginal teachers 'are still too few in number to effect major attitudinal change. They are still battling with the perception that their training and experience is inferior to their non-Aboriginal counterparts and they are faced with problems of such overwhelming magnitude that their unrealistic workloads often render them ineffective' (1998, p. 16). Almost 15 years on, little has changed.

What goes on 'naturally' and 'normally' in schools is closely connected with larger discursive constructions of racialised practices in Australian society. Therefore, it is absolutely imperative that education facilitates White Australians' understandings of the histories that have shaped their national belonging and nationhood and that they can critique why they, as a collective, are located where they are in the social order. The project of reconciliation between Indigenous and non-Indigenous Australians has meant that there has been a concerted effort in recent years across all aspects of social life to make visible to White people what has long been invisible to them, that is, the construction of Indigenous peoples throughout Australia's White history. This work has come a long way since the 1980s when school curriculum stopped teaching Australian young people that Captain Cook 'discovered' Terra Nullius in 1770, a land devoid of people. However, it is only within the last 10 years that *some* teacher education courses in *some* universities have made Indigenous Studies mandatory for teacher education students. Despite these initiatives, there is far more work to be done in order to counteract the effects of practices and policies from the not-too-distant past and post-colonial attitudes that position Indigenous people as deficient and needy. Until Australians stop imagining they live in a White nation, or stop longing for the imagined White nation of the past, it will be difficult for the image of a teacher to be anything other than conservative, respectable – and White.

## Acknowledgements

I gratefully acknowledge the contributions of the Indigenous teachers who were interviewed for this project and the support of the research team members, Laurie Crawford, Jo-Anne Reid and Lee Simpson.

## Notes

1. The term 'Indigenous' is the formal, institutional and policy term for First Nations peoples from mainland Australia (Aboriginal people) and First Nations peoples from the Torres Straits (Torres Straits Islanders), an island territory north of the mainland. In this chapter, I use the term 'Indigenous' when I do not differentiate between these two groups and 'Aboriginal' when I refer to only First Nations people from the mainland, while also acknowledging that there are Indigenous populations in countries other than Australia.
2. This research is funded by the Australian Research Council Discovery Program (Santoro, Reid and McConaghy) and includes Aboriginal researchers Laurie Crawford and Lee Simpson.
3. All names of individuals and places are pseudonyms.
4. There are about 300 Aboriginal Nations with different cultural practices and languages. It is common for Aboriginal people to introduce themselves by the name of the nation to which they belong, for example, Wiradjuri or Dharug. I foreground this important feature when referring to each of the participants for the first time.
5. Indigenous Studies are taught in schools and focus on the study of Indigenous cultures and histories.

## References

Australian Bureau of Statistics (2012) *2011 Census quick stats*, http://www.censusdata.abs.gov.au/census_services/getproduct/census/2011/quickstat/0 (Accessed 16 July 2013).

Australian Productivity Commission (2011) *Overcoming Indigenous disadvantage*, http://www.pc.gov.au/gsp/indigenous (Accessed 16 July 2013).

Barnhardt, R. and Kawagley, A. O. (2005) 'Indigenous knowledge systems and Alaska Native ways of knowing', *Anthropology and Education Quarterly*, 36(1), 8–23.

Basit, T. and Santoro, N. (2011) 'Playing the role of "cultural expert": Teachers of ethnic difference in Britain and Australia', *Oxford Review of Education*, 37(1), 37–52.

Bhabha, H. (1994) *The location of culture* (London: Routledge).

Bourdieu, P. (2000) 'The politics of protest. An interview by Kevin Ovenden', *Socialist Review*, 242, 18–20.

Butler, J. (1997) *Excitable speech: A politics of the performative* (New York: Routledge).

Christie, P. and Sidhu, R. (2006) 'Governmentality and "fearless speech": Framing the education of asylum seeker and refugee children in Australia', *Oxford Review of Education*, 32(4), 449–65.

Colic-Peisker, V. (2005) ' "At least you're the right colour": Identity and social inclusion of Bosnian refugees in Australia', *Journal of Ethnic and Migration Studies*, 31(4), 615–38.

Collins, J. (2000) *Report on the inquiry into the effect of education training programs for Indigenous Australians – Katu Kalpa* (Canberra: MCEETYA).

Commonwealth of Australia (1993) *National Aboriginal and Torres Strait Islander Education Policy 1993* (Canberra: Commonwealth of Australia).

Department of Education, Employment and Workplace Relations (2008) *National report to Parliament on Indigenous education and training 2007* (Canberra: Commonwealth of Australia).

DIAC (2009) *Fact sheet 8 – Abolition of the 'White Australia' policy*, http://www.immi.gov.au/media/fact-sheets/08abolition.htm (Accessed 16 July 2013).

Dockett, S., Perry, B. and Whitton, D. (2010) 'What will my teacher be like? Picture storybooks about starting school', *Australasian Journal of Early Childhood*, 35(3), 33–41.

Doyle, L. and Hill, R. (2008) *Our children, our future: Achieving improved primary and secondary education outcomes for Indigenous students*, Report published by the AMP foundation, http://socialventures.com.au/publications/#box_section_1 (Accessed 16 July 2013).

Ellinghaus, K. (2003) 'Absorbing the "Aboriginal problem": Controlling interracial marriage in Australia in the late 19th and 20th centuries', *Aboriginal History*, 27, 183–207.

Gorringe, S., Ross, J. and Fforde, C. (2011) *'Will the real Aborigine please stand up': Strategies for breaking the stereotypes and changing the conversation*, AITSIS discussion paper, http://www.aiatsis.gov.au/research/documents/AIATSISDiscussionPaper28.pdf (Accessed 16 July 2013).

Hartsuyker, L. (2007) *Top of the class: Report on the inquiry into teacher education.* House of Representatives Standing Committee on Education and Vocational Training, Parliament of Australia (Canberra: Commonwealth of Australia).

Hesch, R. (1996) 'Antiracist educators sui generis? The dialectics of aboriginal teacher education', *Canadian Review of Sociology and Anthropology*, 33(3), 269–80.

Hickling-Hudson, A. (2003) 'Multicultural education and the postcolonial turn', *Policy Practices in Education*, 1(2), 381–400.

Hodge, B. and O'Carroll, J. (2006) *Borderwork in multicultural Australia* (Crows Nest, NSW: Allen and Unwin).

Hughes, P. and Willmot, E. (1982) 'A thousand Aboriginal teachers by 1990', in E. Sherwood (ed.) *Aboriginal education: Issues and innovations* (Perth, WA: Creative Research).

Issacs, J. (ed.) (1987) *Australian dreaming: 40,000 years of Aboriginal history* (Sydney: Lansdowne Press).

James, C. (2002) 'Achieving desire: Narrative of a black male teacher', *Qualitative Studies in Education*, 15(2), 171–86.

Jude, S. (1998) 'Aboriginal education in urban secondary schools: Educating the educators', *Australian Journal of Indigenous Education*, 26(2), 13–17.

Lincoln, Y. and Guba, E. (1985) *Naturalistic inquiry* (New York: Sage).

Lucas, D. (1987) *The Welsh, Irish, Scots and English in Australia* (Canberra: Australian Institute for Multicultural Affairs).

Moreton-Robinson, A. and Nicoll, F. (2006) 'We shall fight them on the beaches: Protesting cultures of White possession', *Journal of Australian Studies*, 30(89), 149–60.

Osler, A. (1997) *The education and careers of Black teachers: Changing identities, changing lives* (Buckingham: Open University Press).

Reconciliation Australia (2009) *Aboriginal land rights Q&A*, http://www.reconciliation.org.au/home/resources/factsheets/q-a-factsheets/aboriginal-land-rights (Accessed 16 July 2013).

Reconciliation Network (2012) *Stolen Generations fact sheet*, http://reconciliaction.org.au/nsw/education-kit/stolen-generations/ (Accessed 16 July 2013).

Reid, J., Santoro, N., Crawford, L. and Simpson, L. (2009) 'Talking teacher education: Factors impacting on teacher education for Indigenous people', *Australian Journal of Indigenous Education*, 38, 42–54.

Said, E. (1993) *Culture and imperialism* (New York: Vintage Books).

Santoro, N. (2012) ' "I really want to make a difference for these kids but it's just too hard": One Aboriginal teacher's experiences of moving away, moving on and moving up', *International Journal of Qualitative Studies in Education*, doi: 10.1080/09518398.2012.724466.

Santoro, N. and Reid, J. (2006) 'All things to all people: Indigenous teachers in the Australian teaching profession', *European Journal of Teacher Education*, 29(3), 287–303.

Santoro, N., Reid, J., Crawford, L. and Simpson, L. (2011) 'Teaching Indigenous children: Listening to and learning from Indigenous teachers', *Australian Journal of Teacher Education*, 36(10), 65–76.

Spivak, G. (1988) 'Can the subaltern speak?', in C. Nelson and L. Grossberg (eds.) *Marxism and the interpretation of culture* (Chicago: University of Illinois Press).

Steering Committee for the Review of Government Service Commission (SCRGSC) (2005) *Overcoming Indigenous disadvantage: Key indicators 2005* (Productivity Commission: Allen and Unwin).

Townsend, J. and Ryan, P. (2012) 'Media narratives and possibilities for teachers' embodied concepts of self', *Journal of Media Literacy Education*, 4(2), 149–58.

VAEAI (2001) *Yalca. A partnership in education and training for the new millennium. Koorie education policy 2001* (Melbourne, VIC: Department of Education, Employment and Training).

Wilkins, C. and Lall, R. (2011) ' "You've got to be tough and I'm trying": Black and minority ethnic student teachers' experiences of initial teacher education', *Race Ethnicity and Education*, 14(3), 365–86.

# 5
# Grumpy Old Teachers? An Insight into the Life Experiences of Veteran Teachers

*Nicky Watts*

## Introduction

For societies where demographic trends produce an ageing population, questions regarding retirement and the management of older workers become increasingly political. This chapter explores how ageist stereotypes can affect the lives of female veteran primary teachers in England, although the implications of the study could have relevance in other countries too.

In the UK, to address the perceived problems caused by an ageing population, government policy is to defer retirement. It is thought that encouraging individuals to stay in employment, contribute to society and prolong economic independence will stop the drain on knowledge and expertise (Timmons et al., 2011). However, most large UK institutions are 'inclined towards the exclusion' (Taylor and Walker, 1998, p. 13) of older workers: whereas early retirement packages are common, proactive measures to retain an ageing workforce are rare.

In the teaching context, little effort has been made to retain older teachers. In the UK, where the 1988 Education Reform Act[1] linked the education system to government control, the primary curriculum has gone through constant changes driven by political ideologies (Cambridge Primary Review, 2011). Wyse and Torrance (2009) argue that the current top-down approach works directly against the global reform of education systems, which highlights the importance of creative teaching in raising the quality of education. This observation has implications for all teachers. However, this chapter gives some indication as to how present policy impacts on older professionals. Dominant discourses constructed around age and ageing workers in the educational context are examined together with evidence taken from my doctoral research project. The study suggests that attitudes towards teachers positioned as 'old' by school managers and expectations of their performance can be affected by social constructs influenced by institutional ageism (Taylor and Walker, 1998) and stereotypes. The chapter's title is intended to provide a focus on attitudes towards older generations,[2] and offer a prompt to question, expose and challenge popular assumptions about older teachers.

The areas that this chapter touches on include the role that age-related stereotyping plays in policy and performance, a perceived deskilling of the profession and lack of regard for older teachers' expertise and a worry that some institutions work to disempower older teachers and foster the development of a culture of fear. Older teachers do have a role to play in schools and some older teachers find new directions, specialise and take advantage of continual professional development (CPD) to offer valuable contributions to the education system.

## Methods

In my doctoral thesis (Watts, 2010), I studied the perspective of veteran female primary schoolteachers in Northern England, most of whom started their teaching career in the mid- to late 1970s. There is scant literature on older teachers' perspectives. Day et al. (2007) conducted a major research project which concentrated on teachers' perceived effectiveness. Klassen and Chiu (2010) also conducted a large-scale study on teachers, which explored job satisfaction in relation to years of experience. Although these authors have collected data on older teachers' perceived performance, not much has been done to allow for the voices of these teachers to be heard. As Klassen and colleagues admitted in their report, they have yet to factor in social and cultural elements. Building on the feminist premise that the personal is political (Oakley, 1974; Pateman, 1970; Sikes et al., 2003; Stanley and Wise, 1993), my research recognises the importance of the private as well as the professional exigencies of older teachers' lives, and strives not only to give older teachers a voice, but to provide a platform which offers space to expose vital insights that could affect management and employment policy.

The study aimed to set out a convincing portrayal of some older teachers' perspectives, using a range of methods, including in-depth interviews, focus groups, email correspondence, informal conversations and my own experience in teaching. I drew on Richardson's (1994) approach, which uses writing as a method of inquiry. As Sikes (2010) points out, research writing can be an extremely delicate area: it was essential that teachers' identities remained unknown as many of them were in precarious situations in their jobs. Consequently, I produced vignettes and monologues as I interacted with the data (see further). As a veteran teacher myself, my intention was to complicate existing stereotypes and prejudices and to offer a challenge to policy-makers.

Using a methodology uniquely structured to suit my research demands, I wrote and produced short dramas in the form of monologues which illustrate the experiences of some older teachers in their work environment. The stories were inspired by data collected from teachers in their mid- to late fifties and are grounded in my own knowledge and understanding gained from 25 years in the profession. All names are pseudonyms.

At every stage of the production, teachers were consulted through focus groups: from reading the script, meeting the actors and film-maker to viewing and analysing the finished product. The methodology was designed to encapsulate the fluid, sometimes indefinable, but deeply felt nature of emerging data. It drew on an auto-ethnographic approach favoured by Richardson (1994) and inspired by Denzin's (2003) creative analytical practice. This methodology recognises that the research process does not produce a static body of knowledge, but opens up platforms for alternative discourses. The stories that were produced did not reveal narratives of lives, but fictional constructions on screen that protected the identities of the participants. Their content raised issues that have been brought to the forefront by recent research on the well-being of the older teaching workforce.

The monologues were shown as a series of video clips which were shared with different audiences at conferences, focus group participants and a range of individuals. The audiences included retired and working teachers and headteachers, teacher educators and researchers. I also involved professionals and non-professional audiences who worked outside the teaching profession, such as artists, actors, film-makers and health workers. Reactions from these disparate audiences created an ongoing dialectic which informed the research process. This method borrowed elements from Boal's (1979) forum technique, creating not a static inquiry but an addition to a changing story, which gathers depth as it develops. The resource of short monologues provides a space for a unique and effective forum.[3] This approach proved useful in two ways: first, to invite discussion from older workers in a non-threatening environment, and second, to enable policy-makers to catch a glimpse of a range of perspectives that might otherwise be inaccessible to them.

## Ageist stereotypes and attitudes towards older teachers

This research found that stereotyping can have harmful and wide-reaching effects on policy and management of older teachers in schools. Foucault argues that grand theory and prevailing narratives present us with ways of thinking which dominate our perspectives of individuals and groups. He argued that by deconstructing the historic origins of these narratives, we can discover their genealogy and understand how they have evolved (Rabinow, 1984). By noting the influences which shape their construction, we can see how they are perpetuated and how other possible narratives have been overlooked. This applies to the depiction of older teachers in fiction,[4] the media and historic accounts. The narratives of older teacher stereotypes present an interesting genealogy which has historically prompted negative stereotypes, combining those of age, teachers and women. The most popular stereotype of older women teachers is either the near-angelic 'grandma' type or the old witch (Weber and Mitchell, 1995). In the case of women teachers, any attempt at gaining recognition of their professional prowess is seen to be martyrdom or idiocy (Britzman, 1991).

There are positive and negative stereotypes about people from older age groups. However, most people do not want to be associated with either. As Barry (2008) states, 'They are the old ones, they are the club that no one wants to join' (p. 185). It has been claimed by some psychologists that older people are more 'conscientious, modest, conventional, careful in interaction, sympathetic and helpful' (War et al., 2001, p. 177) than the young. The same research claims that older people have also proven to be less sociable and outgoing, less able to cope with abstract ideas and less career-motivated than their younger counterparts. However, Weber and Mitchell (1995, 1999) argue that the issues are far more complex, and that stereotyping profoundly affects how we view teachers. Redman and Snape suggest that attitudes in the workplace and 'negative stereotypes held by appraisers may override actual performance in determining appraisal outcomes' (2002, p. 5). They also argue that 'supervisors are often older than most of their subordinates, and it may be that they seek to distinguish themselves from the older group in an attempt to maintain a positive self image' (2002, p. 7). This view is supported by Maguire (2001), who discussed how discourses of ageism may be reproduced and performed by some middle-class professional older women managers who endeavour to distance themselves from uncomfortable stereotypes. An example of this is demonstrated by an experience related by a focus group member, Julie, aged 58. Julie's new head was only a few years younger than her, but had started teaching as a second career, and was ambitious. In Julie's words, she 'had less baggage' than Julie, and was keen to appear to be keeping up with the latest initiatives at the expense of upsetting some of the older members of staff.

Goodson et al. (2006) state that older teachers are often nostalgic for the 'golden days' (p. 52) and are resistant to 'changes that threaten patterns and purposes that teachers have cherished for decades' (p. 43). This perception reinforces the stereotypical view of older people's reluctance to change, a view which has far-reaching effects on the management of older teachers and the teachers themselves. The results of the NASUWT (National Association of Schoolmasters Union of Women Teachers UK) 2010 survey found that older teachers considered that their senior leaders did not think of them as being able to accept or adapt to change (NASUWT, 2010). I found that although some teachers alluded to the social and political nostalgia that Goodson and colleagues (2006) identified, they were not adhering to old and worn-out missions but harboured a reluctance to take on board iterative initiatives that had been introduced over their lifetimes. These initiatives, although presented as 'new', were what these teachers considered rehashes of old ideas and, to use the words of one focus group member, 'they didn't work the first time round'. Rather than harbouring backward-looking nostalgic perspectives, I found older teachers to adopt mostly a pragmatic attitude about past practice. They were reluctant to cast aside tried and trusted methods in order to accommodate ideas that they considered flimsy and recognisably untenable, and resented the fact that they were not listened to when they stated their concerns.

An example of this was expressed in a focus group where some older teachers expressed concern about the recent legislation Every Child Matters[5] that was designed to support children in England and Wales. When put into practice in conjunction with the National Curriculum,[6] this legislation seemed to work against a cooperative and supportive environment in the school. These teachers perceived this change to be bureaucratic and empty of values, increasing teachers' workloads. One teacher said, 'How can you have a curriculum where every child matters if there is no space in the timetable to even talk to the children in the mornings?' It has been well established by educational researchers that in order for change to be effective, practitioners need to be fully consulted (Goodson et al., 2006; Nias, 1989; Wilkins et al., 2004), yet these older teachers did not feel that their views were considered.

Some teachers who took part in my study were not committed to the transformations they could see taking place in the policy of education, and were weary of the constant changes being introduced to the primary curriculum. A number of them expressed a concern for younger teachers, realising that the stresses from the systems they are sure to face will have an effect on their health and well-being. Many demonstrated a deep concern and commitment to their own perception of how good education should be delivered, but had given up. While this attitude is not specific to older teachers, in the case of the older teachers who participated in my study, this often meant that they had succumbed to the pressure to retire and let younger teachers fill their places. Others carried on with an apparent cynical lack of commitment and an eye on the final retirement package. However, as one teacher stated, 'I've seen so many teachers keep their heads down, go into self preservation mode, and really not support or *know* [emphasis from interviewee] other members of staff!' She asked if this 'lack of commitment' was a result of the treatment they had received.

I also encountered older teachers who were 'surprisingly energetic, open, committed and optimistic' (Huberman, 1993, p. 246). A well-documented reason for teachers to stay on in their positions is an enjoyment of teaching and the interaction with children (de Beauvoir, 1988; Huberman, 1993; Nias, 1989; Peters et al., 2008). The National Union of Teachers (NUT, 2001) stressed the importance for all age groups to be represented in the teaching profession to enable children to benefit from a range of knowledge and experience. Wilkins et al. (2004) state that schools benefit from older teachers who have been given recognition for their expertise and given 'space' in schools. The NASUWT (2010) survey highlighted that many older teachers felt this was precisely what they were not being given.

## A perceived deskilling of the profession and lack of regard for older teachers' expertise

This research found that advantages of long service, such as familiarity with the community and the families, often seemed to be ignored. Although Sikes et al. (1985) found that some long-serving teachers felt that they were put in a 'difficult' position because of expectations placed upon them, I found older teachers who enjoyed the mutual respect they had established within the community. One focus group participant stated:

> When I looked forward to my last years in teaching, I expected to have a relaxed time, I have been there a long time, I know the area, the parents, I like the kids, they like me. You should be able, in the final couple of years, to reap the benefits of your experience, and enjoy your last few years.
>
> (Jean, aged 58)

However, it was felt by many participants that this knowledge and experience is often brushed aside. There was evidence that while older, more experienced teachers were encouraged to retire, 'experts' with no knowledge of the community, children or staff were brought in from successful local authorities and given *carte blanche* and a generous budget to lead the school to success. A research briefing from the Cambridge Primary Review[7] challenges the success of these restructured schools, questioning the long-term effectiveness of imported management driven by ' "fad theory" policy', and suspects that 'local contexts and personalities are more important than approved "styles" of leadership engagement' (Jones et al., 2008, pp. 1–4).

The Cambridge Primary Review also noted that teachers felt that the prescriptive curriculum was deskilling. This is supported in my study where some veteran teachers sensed that they were asked to become clones, delivering the same structure and content in lessons across the country. The statement from a focus group member illustrates this clearly:

> I thought there was a danger that I was only seeing it in a certain way ... because I had known something different. So I was contrasting it to how it was when I first trained and how much fun it was. The curriculum was actually very creative then. And it was very child centred then. Ok, it wasn't perfect; there were things that needed looking at. But I'm not so sure now, because what you've said about young teachers also feeling the pressure, then that surely it must be an indicator that it isn't just because we are looking back.
>
> (Sandra, aged 57)

Unlike their younger counterparts, older teachers were familiar with alternative approaches and although some, as Sandra, acknowledged that it 'wasn't perfect' before, they saw the heavy arm of government intervention as having a stifling effect on creativity in teaching.

## Disempowerment: Who is doing the disempowering?

Goodson et al. (2006) imply that older teachers have their heads in the clouds, dreaming of the 'good old days' and unable to accept the inevitable march of progress, and that this has contributed to their feelings of disempowerment:

> Our discussions with teachers suggest that rapid, imposed educational change, along with public disparagement of them as professionals, has engendered a deep sense of instability comparable to experiences of grief or bereavement... Experienced teachers in three of our schools provided moving narratives of nostalgia for working conditions that they remembered had empowered them and enhanced their sense of status, worth, and value.
>
> (p. 45)

My research suggests that it is not 'public disparagement' but disparagement from within the authority and in some cases the school itself that gives the fatal blows to older teachers' sense of status and self-respect: constant observations (by colleagues, senior managers or externals in the case of a school inspection) that have become part of teaching, insensitive appraisals, inconsiderate timetabling and even singling out for redundancies. All lead to feelings of worthlessness, and disempowerment. Ann, a teacher who watched the clips on her own, and filled in a response sheet, explained:

> I have had personal experience of having my life's work rubbished and my feelings of self-esteem/pride in achievements demolished. Even the praise and acknowledgement of many parents/ex-pupils can't compensate for that.
>
> (Anne, aged 55)

Discussion between focus group members also revealed the depth of this feeling of worthlessness:

> Most people are proud initially of what they are doing, but all that pride is lost because they are not appreciated.
>
> (Sara, aged 60)

Sense of pride seems to fizzles away somehow...

(Sandra, aged 57)

M [husband] said to me when I came home upset the other day, 'why are you worried?...you are going to leave anyway at the end of the year, so why bother?' Because it affects [me]...personally, and [I]...don't expect to feel like that at this stage of my career. I don't want to feel like they make you feel like.

(Julie, aged 58)

Wilkins et al. (2004) observed that some establishments make older teachers feel 'over-managed as if they are junior technical operatives who cannot be trusted' (p. 5), and claims from an NASUWT (2010) survey disclosed that many older teachers felt bullied and ignored or overlooked by their school management.

It is also well documented (see Hutchings et al., 2006; Peters et al., 2008) that, as they reach retirement age, some teachers look to downgrade from full to part-time work, or to give up some of their responsibilities: relinquishing management points (that is, financial rewards allocated to teachers undertaking management and leadership activities) in order to decrease their workload. For some, this is a reaction to the stress factors (Klassen and Chiu, 2010). For others, teaching has become too tiring and physically demanding (Hutchings et al., 2006; Peters et al., 2008). This does not necessarily signify that these teachers are less capable or knowledgeable, or even that they enjoy teaching less than their younger selves: although age affects physical abilities, personal identities can remain remarkably unchanged, and this deserves recognition (Athill, 2009; Oakley, 2007). This factor complicates the question of downgrading or a gradual progression into retirement and raises many complex issues regarding management of these teachers, in terms of the relative costs of employment, of the division of labour and of the status of the teacher. In some instances, teachers who had agreed to cut down their hours to work part-time felt their confidence and authority was being undermined because they were being demoted to teaching assistant timetables and duties: it was considered too difficult to manage these part-time teachers in conventional teaching roles. Conversely, some felt that they were being taken advantage of, and given extra responsibilities such as filling gaps in subject leadership roles and mentoring students, but not given the development time, status or resources to carry them out well. Teachers stated that this lack of support undermined their confidence, making them appear ineffectual or incompetent, which reinforces readily held negative stereotypes of older teachers.

It became evident in my research that it was difficult to assess and measure teacher effectiveness in isolation. Two focus group members and many older teachers from the audiences outlined how their teaching was assessed in unfair situations. They felt as if observations that were carried out on their teaching had hidden agendas: that they were identified as targets for redundancy or retirement. A few commented that observations were unfair, and picked up on practices that had been previously deemed acceptable or even good. Many issues needed to be considered. When I interviewed Diane Turner, assessor for Investors in People,[8] in 2009, she observed that a teacher who has performed appallingly in one situation can shine in another. This was borne out by one of the teachers who took part in this research. She wrote that she had always been considered an 'excellent' or 'good' teacher, but was told otherwise after being observed by a new headteacher. Soon after this, she received a merit for a different lesson with different people in a new setting. Observations of teachers' performances are powerful tools. Although they can be used to raise standards, when they are not considered within the cultural context of the setting, they can be used to disempower teachers and destroy careers.

## Is a culture of fear developing?

Some teachers who took part in my research felt strong pressure from their management to retire. Their situations in school were being made particularly difficult and they sensed that there was a general policy commitment within the authority towards 'getting rid of the old wood' (a common expression in British English). In some circumstances, the motive was to save money, as experienced teachers would have gained more increments and would therefore have higher salaries than beginner teachers. However, there is evidence that some veteran teachers felt that they were being used as scapegoats and that their dismissal was justified by assessments which used shifting criteria and hidden agendas. Evidence of 'hushing' was found: teachers who felt they were treated unfairly were told by management and, in one case, their union not to 'make a fuss', not to talk to the press. This teacher was given what was termed a gagging order. If she agreed not to mention the issues that were causing her concern, then she would be able to stop work at an agreed date, to receive her redundancy and retirement package and to work in school until that time. If she did not agree to the gagging order, she was to be put on paid leave until the date of her redundancy or enforced retirement, and not permitted on the school premises again. While she was considering what to do, a partial observation on a lesson was carried out, and she was deemed 'unsatisfactory' after 26 years of exemplary service in the school. This teacher was not the only one who had been treated badly: there was a general feeling of unease amongst many older teachers that their positions were not secure.[9]

There is also evidence that many teachers realised the extent of their maltreatment only when they left their teaching posts to go on to work in other establishments, where they found their skills were accepted and appreciated. These incidents build a bleak picture of the institutionalised victimisation which Taylor and Walker (1998) mention, which contributes to the elements of fear and mistrust in the perspectives of some older teachers. This is put into context by the statistics laid out by TAEN (The Age and Employment Network), which discovered that the number of age discrimination claims accepted by employment tribunals and that the number of people who believe themselves to have experienced age discrimination in the workplace are increasing (TAEN, 2010).

This research found many older teachers who felt compelled to declare that they were *not* 'grumpy'. Taylor and Walker (1998) state that where managers are proactive in creating a supportive organisational culture, making the equal opportunities policies a reality, older workers thrive and make positive contributions to the organisation. This is evident in my research, where teachers who had the support and respect of their establishment were specialising in their field of expertise, benefiting from CPD or changing direction to provide dedicated services.

## Way forward

This research aims to bring into focus the plight of older teachers, and to articulate some of their perspectives. My findings illustrate the precarious predicament of veteran teachers as the recession bites into the economy and prejudice against older workers deepens (Rothenberg and Gardner, 2011). Some veteran teachers are ready to leave and hand over to their younger colleagues, and some wish to stay, feel supported and have their skills appreciated. However, there is increasing evidence to show that a substantial number of teachers who wish to continue to make a contribution in education are being humiliated, or feel victimised because of their age, and live in a culture of fear or paranoia. As older teachers make up a large proportion of the teaching population, is it not in our best interests to utilise the experience and pedagogic skills these teachers have accumulated over the years?

In order to do this, policy-makers need to be persuaded to consider more fully the perspectives of older teachers. Taylor and Walker (1998) state that there is a need for organisations to take steps to identify and remove policies and practices which actively support prejudice against older workers. In order to do this, the experiences of older teachers need to become visible. Awareness needs to be raised about age-related discrimination, bullying and prejudice in schools. National and local government policy-makers need to become engaged to support schools and help develop strategies to tackle these issues.

## Notes

1. The 1988 Education Reform Act was presented as giving more autonomy and power to the schools through the so-called Local Management of Schools in England, Wales and Northern Ireland. In fact, it took power away from the local education authorities (LEAs) and the schools and transferred it to the secretary of state, to whom the schools have been made increasingly accountable.
2. The reference to 'grumpy old teachers' is a popular theme in the media in England at the moment. There are programmes on BBC TV about grumpy old men and women, and numerous books written about the phenomenon of age, and how this baby boomer generation of 'oldies' are making a lot of fuss, not taking ageing lying down as previous generations have done.
3. These can be seen on YouTube: http://bit.ly/ZZynaS (accessed 5 June 2013).
4. For an interesting glimpse at how teachers have been portrayed in literature from the 16th to the 19th century, see Egglestone (1892).
5. Every Child Matters (ECM) is a UK government initiative for England and Wales that was launched in 2003, partly in response to the death of Victoria Climbié.
6. National Curriculum was introduced into England, Wales and Northern Ireland as a nationwide curriculum for primary and secondary state schools following the Education Reform Act 1988.
7. The Cambridge Primary Review is a comprehensive independent inquiry into primary education in England.
8. Investors in People (1991–2010) was a nationally recognised business improvement framework administered by UK Commission for Employment and Skills.
9. My letter 'Stuck in a rut? I think not' to the *Times Educational Supplement*, published on 23 April 2010 (http://www.tes.co.uk/article.aspx?storycode=6041780), received heated comments.

## References

Athill, D. (2009) *Somewhere towards the end* (London: Grant).

Barry, S. (2008) *The secret scripture* (London: Faber and Faber).

Boal, A. (1979) *Theatre of the oppressed* (London: Pluto Press).

Britzman, D. (1991) *Practice makes practice: A critical study of learning to teach* (New York: SUNY Press).

Cambridge Primary Review. (2011). *National curriculum review–Curriculum in the balance: Entitlement or minimalism?* Accessed 20 January 2014, from http://www.primaryreview.org.uk/_UPDATES/news/newsarchive/homepagearticlesarchive/curricul um_in_the_balance.php

Day, C., Sammons, P., Stobart, G., Kington, A. and Gu, Q. (2007) *Teachers matter: Connecting lives, work and effectiveness* (Maidenhead: Open University Press).

de Beauvoir, S. (1988 [reprint]) *Old age* (London: Penguin Books).

Denzin, N. (2003) *Performance ethnography: Critical pedagogy and the politics of culture* (London: Sage).

Egglestone, E. (1892) *The schoolmaster in literature*, American Book Company, Library of the Ontario Institute for Studies in Education, http://archive.org/details/schoolmasterinli00skiniala (Accessed 16 July 2013).

Ellis, C. and Bochner, A. (2006) 'Analyzing analytic autoethnography: An autopsy', *Journal of Contemporary Ethnography*, 35, 429–50.

Goodson, I., Moor S. and Hargreaves, A. (2006) 'Teacher nostalgia and the sustainability of reform: The generation and degeneration of teachers' missions, memory, and meaning', *Educational Administration Quarterly*, 42(1), 42–61.

Huberman, M. (1993) *The lives of teachers* (New York: Teachers College Press).

Hutchings, M., James, K., Maylor, U., Menter, I. and Smart, S. (2006) *The recruitment, deployment and management of supply teachers in England*, RR738 (Nottingham: DfES).

Jones, L., Pickard, A. and Stronach, I. (2008) *Primary schools: The professional environment*, Primary Review Research Briefings 6(2), http://www.primaryreview.org.uk/downloads/Int_Reps/8.Settings-professionals/RS_6-2_briefing_Professional_environment_080418.pdf (Accessed 16 July 2013).

Klassen, R. M. and Chiu, M. M. (2010) 'Effects on teachers' self-efficacy and job satisfaction: Teacher gender, years of experience, and job stress', *Journal of Educational Psychology*, 102(3), 741–56.

Maguire, M. (2001) 'Beating Time?: The resistance, reproduction and representation of older women in teacher education (UK)', *International Journal of Inclusive Education*, 5(2/3), 225–36.

NASUWT (2010) *No experience necessary? A survey of the experience of age discrimination of older teachers in the UK* (Birmingham: NASUWT).

Nias, J. (1989) *Primary teachers talking: A study of teaching as work* (London: Routledge).

NUT (2001) *Who's leaving and why: Teachers' reasons for leaving the profession*, A report by the National Union of Teachers, http://www.teachers.org.uk/node/1095 (Accessed 16 July 2013).

Oakley, A. (1974) *The sociology of housework* (Cambridge, MA: Basil Blackwell).

Oakley, A. (2007) *Fracture: Adventures of a broken body* (Bristol: Policy Press).

Pateman, C. (1970) *Participation and democratic theory* (Cambridge, UK: Cambridge University Press).

Peters, M., Hutchings, M., Edwards, G., Minty S., Seeds, K. and Smart, S. (2008) *Behavioural impact of changes in the Teachers' Pension Scheme* (London: DCSF).

Rabinow, P. (ed.) (1984) *Foucault reader* (New York: Pantheon Books).

Redman, T. and Snape, E. (2002) 'Towards the over-50s ageism in teaching: Stereo-typical beliefs and discriminatory attitudes', *Work Employment Society*, 16(2), 355–71.

Richardson, L. (1994) 'Writing: A method of inquiry'. In N. Denzin & Y. Lincoln (Eds.), *Handbook of Qualitative Research* (London: Sage).

Rothenberg, J. Z. and Gardner, D. S. (2011) 'Protecting older workers: The failure of the Age Discrimination in Employment Act of 1967', *Journal of Sociology and Social Welfare*, 38(1) 9–30.

Sikes, P., Nixon, J. and Carr, W. (eds.) (2003) *The moral foundations of educational research* (Maidenhead: Open University Press).

Sikes, P. J. (2010) 'Teacher-student sexual relations: Key risks and ethical issues', *Ethnography and Education*, 5(2), 143.

Sikes, P. J., Measor, L. and Woods, P. (1985) *Teacher careers: Crises and continuities* (London: Falmer Press).

Stanley, L. and Wise, S. (1993) *Breaking out again* (London: Routledge).

TAEN (2010) 'Age discrimination claims rise by 37 per cent', *TAEN Newsletter*, Summer 2010, p. 12, http://taen.org.uk/uploads/resources/TAEN_Newsletter_Summer_2010.pdf (Accessed 4 March 2013).

Taylor, P. and Walker, A. (1998) 'Policies and practices towards older workers: A framework for comparative research', *Human Resource Management Journal*, 8(3), 61–76.

Timmons, J. C., Hall, A. C., Fesko, S. L. and Migliore, A. (2011) 'Retaining the older workforce: Social policy considerations for the universally designed workplace', *Journal of Aging and Social Policy*, 23(2), 119–40.

War, P., Miles, A. and Platts, C. (2001) 'Age and personality in the British popula-tion between the ages of 16 and 69', *Journal of Occupational and Organisational Psychology*, 74, 165–99.

Watts, N. (2010) 'Grumpy old teachers? A study of how perceptions of older teachers fit with older teachers' life experiences, and a quest for a transparent methodology', PhD thesis (Sheffield: University of Sheffield).

Weber, S. and Mitchell, C. (1995) *'That's funny, you don't look like a teacher!': Interrogating images and identity in popular culture* (London: Falmer Press).

Weber, S. and Mitchell, C. (1999) *Reinventing ourselves as teachers: Beyond nostalgia* (London: Falmer Press).

Wilkins, R., Head, M., Taylor, M. and Keaveny, B. (2004) *Supporting and utilising the experience and expertise of older teachers: Research report* (Canterbury: Canterbury Christ Church University College).

Wyse, D. and Torrance, H. (2009) 'The development and consequences of national curriculum assessment for primary education in England', *Educational Research*, 51(2), 213–28.

# 6
# Bodies and Binaries: An Examination of Women Teachers in the United States

*Christine Mallozzi*

## Introduction

The percentage of women in the teaching profession compared to men ranges greatly across nations (UNESCO, 2003). In the United States, where the author is located, women make up approximately 76 per cent of teachers and teacher education students overall (US Department of Education, 2012; Zumwalt and Craig, 2005) and 90 per cent of teachers at the elementary level (Ingersoll and Merrill, 2010). Being in the majority, however, does not equate to dominance, respect or professional status (see, for example, Chapter 3 or Chapter 9). People in many nations (see, for example, Department for Education, 2012; Van Riper, 2006) report respect for the profession, but that respect does not necessarily translate into support for individual teachers.

Women teachers' bodies are repeatedly used as evidence regarding women's suitability in the profession, in schools and in higher education (Freedman and Holmes, 2003). Teachers are often pressured to conform to and reflect established gendered norms in their bodily appearances and actions or risk being marginalised or pushed out of the profession. The common practice of objectifying women's bodies, the high percentage of women teachers and the likelihood of teachers being observed make these body-focused critiques particularly important for understanding the social pressures that women teachers experience.

## Theoretical framework

Organising principles such as binaries provide ways to make sense of one's surroundings. However, any organising ideology that separates the world into two categories is bound to be too simplistic for the complexities of life, as is the case for two sets of binaries, namely mind/body and public-professional/private-personal, examined here to provide a platform on which to understand the experiences of women teachers in the United States.

Descartes' ([1641] 1996) mind/body duality has been widely applied to human existence and positions the human mind as separate and superior to the human body. Women are usually associated with the body side of the binary (Kolmar and Bartowski, 2005). Foucault ([1975] 1976) offered a pointed challenge to this mind/body binary, arguing that institutions such as schools have practised disciplining and managing physical bodies, though outwardly claiming their practices are otherwise intended, such as shaping one's soul or mind. Foucault proposed that the architectural designs of schools mimic a Panopticon, a building and design philosophy that allows constant surveillance by authorities without revealing when and how that surveillance is occurring. By hiding the surveillance, people eventually self-regulate under the assumption that they are always being watched and thus subject to discipline. In this way, the Panopticon disciplines the body to encourage mindfulness, disrupting the mind/body binary. Although some of the realities of schools (such as existing architecture and immovable classroom furniture) may make them Panopticon-like (Gallagher, 2010), schools generally subscribe to producing docile bodies through surveillance paired with mindfulness. Therefore, the separation of mind and body is artificial.

Similar to the mind/body binary, the binaries of public/private and professional/personal have been used to organise human experiences in the world. What is considered public or private and who is welcomed into or kept from the public sphere and professional endeavours (what will be termed in this chapter as public-professional/private-personal) are consistent threads in US feminist movements, and the body is focal throughout. From Sojourner Truth's (1851) 'And ain't I a woman? Look at me!', Black women's suffrage plea to liberation, feminists' arguments against female biology (such as menstruation, reproduction and menopause) as barriers in (primarily White, middle-class) women's fight for the right to work, to the contested grounds of abortion, birth control, rape, pornography, sex trade/sex slave industries and breastfeeding, the role of women's bodies in the public-professional/private-personal binary has a long history (Kolmar and Bartowski, 2005).

## Women teachers' bodies as contested ground

Assuming a typical classroom in a ubiquitous school is impossible. For the purposes of this chapter women teachers are those who educate children (that is primary, elementary and secondary students) in academic classrooms (that is, in science, social studies, mathematics and language), where the overt school curriculum is focused on shaping minds. Teachers of children are considered moral leaders of vulnerable children (Grant and Murray, 1999), so teachers are often scrutinised, in both institutional and more informal ways, for their suitability to the profession. In the United States, high standards for women teachers have been set and teachers should embody 'all that is good, and wise, and lovely' (Beecher, 1846, p. 10). The optimal image is an earnest, well-mannered, conservative, stable person of high moral control (Waller, [1932] 1965), able to withstand being 'beyond reproach' (Lortie, [1975] 2002, p. 97) within communities where 'everyone is watching' (p. 97).

Foucault ([1971] 1972) described an institutionalised and authoritarian disciplining of bodies through surveillance. However, because the watchers (the teachers) are not hidden in schools as in other panoptic arrangements (Gallagher, 2010), those authorities are also being monitored. Students watch the teacher, waiting for instruction. Administrators (managers) observe faculty for effectiveness. Community members monitor teachers through interactions, public reports and students' stories. This watching has specific connotations for women in the feminised teaching profession whose sex has a history of objectification (see Bartky, 1990; Berger, 1972; de Lauretis, 1984; hooks, [1992] 2003; Mulvey, 1975). Examining the feminisation of the US teaching profession provides insight into the cultural and social pressures that women teachers are subject to or else lead to the risk of them being pushed out of the profession.

## A brief and recent history of feminised teaching in the United States

The late 1800s marked a change in the teaching population as one made primarily of men to a teaching population where women were the majority. In a historically and socially significant oral address, Beecher (1846) postured that women in the teaching profession should trade self-sacrifice in return for the power to shape society and save children from ignorance. By the 1930s, there were 5 times as many women as men teachers in the United States (Lortie, [1975] 2002). The cultural shift to teaching as a feminised profession was fraught with tension, and frequently women's bodies were critiqued for being ill fitting.

When men were in the majority, teachers served as disciplinarians, often using corporal punishment as a way to 'correct' and strengthen the mind. People questioned if female teachers, bred to have more genteel demeanours and frailer bodies, could do the same (Suggs, 1978). The first women teachers broke gender bounds by entering the public world of employment (Biklen, 1995; Hoffman, 2003; Lortie, [1975] 2002), but to be able to succeed as a teacher, a woman needed to prove her body was capable of handling the task. Femininity was replaced with a masculinised domineering presence, manifesting the female teacher into the pinched and strict schoolmarm (Donovan, 1974). Gaining employment opened women to critique as an independent and unfeminine woman. Moderate success in the public realm came with failure as a person. By the time women teachers were prevalent (1920s to 1930s), the role of the teacher shifted from disciplinarian to nurturer (Lortie, [1975] 2002). Despite rhetoric that women's presence in the classroom would be harmful to boys (Hall, 1904), the echo of which is heard in today's boy crisis discourse (Ringrose, 2007), teaching became acceptable women's work (Apple, 1985).

Feminisation of the profession and the accompanying 'schoolmarmitis' (Perrillo, 2004, p. 343), that is, seriousness, firmness, rigidity, brought a push for professionalisation through standards. The interwar and Progressive Era professionalisation movement aimed to produce compliant, feminine women. 'The anxieties over a female profession became expressed through anxieties over the female body, especially bodies that were seen as unproductive, inefficient, or self-indulgent', which is ironic considering schoolmarms were deemed too rigid. Policies were instituted to 'shape teachers' lives and bodies into an ideal American type: healthy, optimistic, and self-controlled' (p. 343). Gender-neutral laws and policies about undisciplined bodies (for example, being fat, being weak) were enforced almost solely against women teachers and often focused on what women did with their bodies during personal hours (such as drinking, smoking and sexual activity) to fire or restrict them. Although the official purpose of these rules was to develop healthier teachers, evidence points to the aim being a regulation of personal lives through surveillance of the body in the public forum (Perrillo, 2004).

The Progressive Era practice of watching women teachers' bodies under the guise of doing what is best for the teacher herself, the students and the school community remained. For example, in 1959 Louise

Singleton was officially fired for being too fat; although context indicates some racist motivations, the school superintendent stated they were hoping to help her (*Jet Magazine*, 1959). More recently, Ashley Payne, a teacher, was in effect forced to resign after a few (10 out of 700) pictures of her drinking alcohol on vacation and one instance of questionable language were posted on her personal Facebook page. An anonymous respondent claiming to be a parent stated she was 'disappointed and worried about my daughter's teacher' (Downey, 2009, n.p.) though the closest evidence of the respondent's concern for the teacher was a comment that Payne lacked discipline. The regulation of women teachers' bodies as weak in health, spirit or discipline is based on the assumption that flawed bodies means a flawed personal character and thus a bad teacher. The regulation of women teachers' bodies often falls into the categories of how a woman's body appears and how a woman's body acts.

## Problems with women teachers' bodies appearing

The discourse around women teachers' bodies appearing has been painted with a broad brush of professionalism, and often it includes discussion of dress. The *2009 Job Search Handbook for Educators* (American Association for Employment in Education [AAEE], 2008), a publication distributed to university career centres, advised new teachers to 'dress more conservatively and formally than you think is necessary', adding, 'It is far better to be noticed for being "over-dressed" than to have a reputation as the inappropriately dressed new teacher!' (Obrycki, 2008, p. 9). Teacher handbooks or dress codes from individual school districts indicate what is acceptable attire. More often and perhaps most effectively, teachers are acculturated into expectations for teacher appearance long before they enter the field.

Compulsory US education positions students to watch teachers in schools for 13 years or more. Through this 'apprenticeship of observation' (Lortie, [1975] 2002, p. 61), the people gain a clear expectation of how teachers should look; however, it is often only when a teacher breaches what is acceptable that her body becomes a focus of attention (MacLure, 2003). Still, both adults' and children's perceptions have been used to fuel the discourse on acceptable teacher images.

### Adult perceptions of women teachers' appearance

Women's bodies are regulated to serve institutional and external purposes (Sawicki, 1991). Perrillo (2004) maintained that during the 1920s and 1930s, when women became the majority of teachers in the United States, there was an effort to cultivate a muted beauty and glamour among women teachers as a way to shape the mind by moulding the body for the benefit of their students, men and the country. Achieving beauty was thought as an American woman's duty to the bachelors, husbands and bosses who fought in the war. This push towards beauty, health and hygiene, as an effort to combat 'schoolmarmitis' (p. 343), defined the new American modern woman, but teachers were seen as consistently lacking, described as maternal, not even trying to be stylish, and too cerebral (Perrillo, 2004).

Calling women teachers cerebral over body-conscious maintained the mind/body split and was an insult related to being unfeminine. In reaction, professional journals pitched the concepts of seeking the 'smart look' (Perrillo, 2004, p. 353) over looking like a schoolmarm, 'wearing clothes that were neither too revealing nor too heavy, hats that were stylish but not too large, and shoes that were "efficiently fit" and not too narrowly cut' (p. 353). Women teachers were encouraged to bridge mind and body by studying current fashions to embody 'design, forethought, and self-control' (Perrillo, 2004, p. 353). Their appearance was used as proof that they were committed to a better citizenry. Women who did not walk this fine line (that is, those seen as too schoolmarmish or too fashionable) were vilified, and the ripple effects can be traced in other periods in history and the present. For example, Munro (1998) shared the narrative of Bonnie, a secondary school teacher who recalled the regulatory practices a male high school principal initiated (see also Chapter 4 on the regimes of surveillance to which Indigenous teachers are subjected). This incident occurred in the 1970s when the rise of women's rights came with increased monitoring and critique. Bonnie wore open-toed sandals to accommodate swelling feet. The male principal, seeing her toe exposure as unprofessional, recommended Bonnie wear socks and asked a male teacher and male department administrator to 'counsel' (p. 102) her. When Bonnie was seemingly not self-regulating, the patriarchal system attempted to regulate her body for her.

Not all aspects of one's body are malleable, but because expectations for teacher appearance are so clear, teachers can even feel pressure to compensate for the unchangeable. In Alsup's (2006) study of teacher identity, when a prospective teacher could not control certain aspects of her teacher image, such as age and a petite body frame that made her look quite young, she recognised the need to mitigate with clothing what could be seen as flaws in her teacher image. Seeing oneself through the presumed eyes of others plagues women (Berger, 1972; Heldman, 2008; Levy, 2005), and for teachers, those 'others' are often their students.

## Children's perceptions of women teachers' appearance

Children play an integral role in organising teacher images. Waller ([1932] 1965) recognised that children sometimes superimpose pre-existing archetypal images onto teachers, images that hold different levels of prestige. More than 75 years later, inspired by the way they thought students saw them, pre-service teachers gave updated names to some of these archetypal images (Atkinson, 2008). They named them the *apple jumper teacher*, who hides her body with vests and jumpers with school symbols (that is with apples or rulers printed or knitted on it); the *teacher babe*, who wears trendy, form-fitting clothes; and the *bland uniformer teacher*, who wears non-feminine business casual clothes. The bland uniformer ranked as the preferred professional image.

Using students' and teachers' drawings, Weber and Mitchell (1995) found the typical teacher dress portrayed as dull and conservative, and students drew female teachers with their hair in a bun, wearing glasses and pearls, and usually a wide or sack-like skirt. The iconic classroom (a teacher at the front, students in front of her) is a readable and consistent symbol that controls the image, so much so that other images are 'alien or threatening' (MacLure, 2003, p. 14). Weber and Mitchell (1995) used the popular culture children's toy, the Mattel's Barbie doll, to interrogate an idealised image of the woman teacher. The Barbie doll as a student teacher in a Marvel comic was a shapely, smiling, manicured, young woman portrayed with a fun-loving nurturance and concern for her students. This image matches an ideal of a female teacher but is linked with the controversy of Barbie's critics, who are suspicious of the consumerism, glamour and overt sexuality. Barbie is a text of desire with real social effects, but incongruently as a toy, she cannot really be taken seriously. Even when Barbie succeeds in the stereotype, she is doomed. Barbie's contradictory meanings are reminders that iconic images can seem simple but are complex. For example, Chacon (2006) raises the point that women teachers' bodies in general are perceived according to multiple signifiers such as gender, race and sexuality, but also a specific teacher's body is understood within the context of other classroom dynamics such as what is being taught. hooks (1994), who as a Black woman in a predominantly White profession (US Department of Education, 2012; Zumwalt and Craig, 2005) stated being highly conscious of her body in the classroom, argued that erasing the teacher's body from the classroom is an attempt to override subjectivity in order to construct teachers as an objective source of knowledge. This approach may be more plausible with certain subject matters that bank on objectivity (such as the 'hard' sciences) than with others (like the humanities). Further, some embodied social identifiers (such as class and sexual orientation) may be easier to hide than others.

hooks (1994) stated that 'The person who is most powerful has the privilege of denying their body' (p. 137), and although there is danger in claiming a stagnant hierarchy of oppression (Lorde, 1983), the US history of racism, classism, sexism and heterosexism makes it likely that non-White, non-middle-class, non-male or non-heterosexual teachers will be less able to resist criticism of their bodies. Women teachers are in the majority, but as a population they are historically and presently subject to personal and systematic oppression. Therefore, they are less able to control how their bodily images are used for meaning-making and certainly not able to deny their bodies when society does so much to focus on them. The same is true of transsexual or intersex people. Non-White, lower- or working-class and non-heterosexual teachers further threaten the iconic image of the teacher (MacLure, 2003). Yet these teachers are deemed dangerous mostly for what they are capable of doing or inciting. It is this factor of bodies that act which extends the issue.

## Problems with woman teachers' bodies acting

Berger (1972) posited a binary for art history: 'men act and women appear' (p. 47). Although this structure may work for art history, it fails in reality where women both appear and act. Having explored the difficulties women teachers have in appearing, it should not be surprising that their actions are similarly scrutinised. Women teachers in the United States have been condemned for how they choose to use their bodies and for what purposes: in other words, what transgressions they engage in against expectations of them as women and teachers. For example, women teachers have been critiqued for using their bodies for professional resistance in conjunction with union movements (Perrillo, 2004) and disparaged as a woman's majority and thus barriers to male students' success (Galman and Mallozzi, 2012). Although many critiques exist, two are highlighted here. Women's extended presence in the teaching field and women teachers as sexual are closely aligned due to the intertwined public-professional/private-personal discourses of virginity, marriage, motherhood and sexuality.

**Women teachers' extended presence in the teaching field**

Bartky (1990) made the case that institutional structures objectifying women in general are more concerned with their sexualisation than with other qualities like motherhood. Looking at a history of US women teachers that accounts for marital status and reproduction evidences this. Blount (2000) delivered a historical analysis of educators transgressing gender expectations in US public schools. Transgressions are always situated, but Blount established that transgressions are consistently met with chiding, punishment or removal from the institution, until a point where a larger 'correction' of the system or culture occurs. One transgression, women entering the public sphere in the workforce, has already been outlined. This section presents a second gender transgression of women remaining single in the workforce, followed by a third transgression of married women remaining in the workforce. Keeping with Bartky's (1990) idea, the reactions to these transgressions are more about women teachers' bodies being sexual than being married with children.

In the early 1900s, women teachers were expected to work for a few years, then return to the private realm of the home, so that their attention was not divided between wife and mother duties and work tasks, for which teaching was presumed to prepare them. Though not necessarily dictated legally, this expectation was reinforced through sociocultural and systemic practices. Despite this, and because teaching was one of the only professions for women (Biklen, 1995; Hoffman, 2003), many women in the public realm remained single (Emerick, 1909). The term *schoolteacher* was no longer just a virtuous woman dedicated to her students, and it became associated with a type of difficult woman who evaded domesticity and eschewed deference to patriarchal sociocultural standards. Negative images of 'spinster', 'old maid', teachers in tight hair buns and pinched lips began to appear in popular-culture novels, comics and news stories (Weber and Mitchell, 1995) and were a sign that a transgression was afoot. Critics saw unmarried women not bearing children as resistant to serving men, as contributors to race suicide[1] (see Emerick, 1909), and contributing to the weakening of the White, middle class (Blount, 2000). Note the assumed equation of marriage with motherhood. Not only was an unmarried, childless woman in the workforce unwomanly, but she was acting un-American, due at least in part to refusing to fulfil her body's potential to bear children for the strength of her country that was reeling from World War I (Perrillo, 2004).

Acceptance of married women in the workforce presumably would have solved this dilemma, but common consensus was that a woman could not balance duties in both the public-professional and private-personal spheres (Biklen, 1995), a debate still ongoing. Married women in the workforce unsettled a neat household division of labour in which a man ventures outside the home to earn money and a woman stays at home caring for house and children, dependent on her husband's earnings. Eventually, several factors shifted the landscape towards the inclusion of married teachers into education. Peters (1934) and the National Educational Association (NEA, 1942) made cases for married teachers based on increased student achievement; marriage and motherhood were assumed to make women better teachers. Also, teacher shortage in the post-World War II era in the United States opened the doors for married teachers. Thus, the problem was solved at least in part because society needed the teachers – married or not. Now women could act in both marriage and career.

**Teachers as sexual**

As married women remained teachers, the older unmarried female teachers who were once common were now suspect. Why did they never marry if now they were allowed to have both marriage and a teaching career? One possibility that gained discursive favour marked another transgression, that these single, unmarried women were homosexual or at least 'not altogether heterosexual' (Blount, 2000, p. 90). A questionable interpretation of interwar, Progressive Era survey data presented approximately 26 per cent of the single women educators physically or sexually acting on intense same-sex feelings beyond 'ordinary endearments' (Davis, 1929, p. 247). Single women teachers, once useful to society by taking up teaching vacancies and for a cheaper price than men (Lortie, [1975] 2002), were now not as integral, less favoured than married teachers and more likely now to be seen as deviant. Eventually, spinster teachers were conflated with lesbianism, reinforcing married women and young women with the potential to marry as better choices for the teaching field compared to older single women. Thus, what was once transgressive (such as single and married women teachers) became acceptable when compared with questionable sexuality of a teacher in a heterosexist society.

Blount (2000) noted that in the 1940s and 1950s, at a time when Cold War US McCarthyism brought professional and personal activities under attack, any teacher's transgression was seen with suspicion. Teachers were dismissed or threatened with dismissal based on presumed homosexual activity, but how many is undetermined partially due to inexact records and teachers accepting termination on alternative grounds (Harbeck, 1997). To quell rumours of homosexuality, lesbians later reported marrying men and feminising their appearance, for example by wearing dresses, high heels and hosiery (Faderman, 1991). Social movements and organised resistance groups of the 1960s and 1970s increased the visibility of homosexual people leading to more protective rights; however, these actions towards security for homosexual teachers brought reactions like the Briggs Initiative of 1978 which proposed removing gay and lesbian teachers from classrooms (Harbeck, 1997). Throughout the 1980s until current times, homosexual teachers are at risk for discrimination in a heteronormative education system (Sumara and Davis, 1999) and have no federal protection under the US Equal Employment Opportunity Commission (US EEOC, 2004).

Tracing the histories of women teachers' marital status and motherhood as gendered expectations is wrapped in their sexualities (Bartky, 1990). The restrictive effect of these standards raises questions about women embodying their full heterosexual potential of marrying and bearing children or being condemned as faulty. If a woman is unwilling to marry, she may be suspected of being homosexual. If she is married but without children, her character as a nurturer is questionable or her body is found lacking as assumedly infertile. In the past, marriage, pregnancy and motherhood may have been used to solidify a female teacher's sexuality and sexual activity (Faderman, 1991), though with adoption and fertility treatments, it may now not have the same effect. However and moreover, it is questionable if a woman teacher's body is supposed to act sexually at all.

Maintaining that popular Hollywood movies represent a dominant cultural feature, Dalton (2004) examined teachers in the movies. In over 100 (mostly American) movies, cinematic representations of good teachers, bad teachers, women teachers and gay teachers reinforce current stagnant images of teacher. Dalton found that popular narrative cinema either ignored women teachers or reinforced the stereotypical woman teacher roles; both options maintain a narrow image of a woman teacher and, further, almost erase its image due to its ordinary presence. Tackling the issue of sexuality, Dalton (2004) stated, 'Hollywood continues its reluctance to give women teachers, whether lesbian or straight, stories in which they can act out their sexuality without being punished' (p. 20). Media are peppered with headlines, sound bites and images of women teachers' arguably egregious sexual indiscretions (Johnson, 2008), so it should be clarified that acceptance of a woman teacher as a sexual person is not an argument for her to act on that sexuality without wisdom or restriction. In fact, the all-or-nothing approach is a major factor in allowing people to be regulated, the assumption being that people are in need of regulation because they cannot regulate themselves from acting on their sexuality. In this way, it is the woman's bodily potential for action that is the focus, and this bodily potential points once again to binary thinking.

The virgin/whore or Madonna/whore duality, established in Judeo-Christian script (for example, the Virgin Mary/Mary Magdalene), cemented by psychoanalytics, and continued as a popular culture trope, positions women as either pure and good or sexual and bad. The ties of teacher as nurturer to mother as nurturer (Grumet, 1988; Lightfoot, 1978) place the proper teacher on the virginal Madonna side, leaving (potential, embodied or enacted) sex and sexuality linked to bad teachers. Becoming a mother (that is, through assumed 'natural' impregnation through sex) is incongruously subsumed under procreation as a pro-social action and fulfilment of a woman's bodily potential. Pregnant bodies effectively scream of (assumed) past sexual activity that is unspeakable in polite social interactions. The presence of a pregnant body in a public-professional classroom is evidence of the private-personal goings-on of the teacher. As long as the pregnancy occurred in a socially acceptable context, the pregnancy is usually greeted with favour (Biklen, 1995).

The norms around pregnancy and sex are socially, culturally and historically determined, with markers like race, class and religion being considerations. This point has been played out in current events with unmarried women teaching in Christian schools where premarital sex is condemned and legally supported grounds for dismissal (Hawkins, 1998). Regardless of the woman being engaged (Villalva, 2012), remaining pregnant based on religious beliefs (Tapper and Miller, 2006), even being pregnant through artificial insemination (see Walker, 2013), premarital pregnancy elicits backlash, though this is not necessarily the case for men (see Bindley, 2013; *US Catholic*, 2006). On the continuum of married sex for fruition of maternal destiny compared to single women's sex for pleasure, premarital sex resulting in pregnancy may evidence unfavourable bodily action.

As school structures seek to deny the presence of teachers' bodies in the classroom (Alsup, 2006; Johnson, 2008) and discipline teachers for being sexual, they incite discourse around teachers' sexuality (Bartky, 1990; Foucault, [1976] 1978). For example, Johnson (2004) interviewed female prospective teachers who reported being self-conscious under the gaze of high school students, especially the males. As a high school teacher, Johnson (2008), too, was the object of the gaze of a colleague who 'executed a flawless performance of "schoolmarm"' (p. 17) and questioned Johnson about the shortness of her skirt.

For decades, feminists have been struggling against being objectified for the pleasure of others (Berger, 1972; de Lauretis, 1984; hooks, [1992] 2003; Mulvey, 1975). Focusing the gaze on women teachers' body parts dismembers bodies as sites for meaning-making (Mallozzi, 2012). Walkerdine's (1990) oft-cited story of nursery school teacher Miss Baxter challenged the assumption that body objectification only happens in the perhaps hyper-sexualised environments of adolescence. After Miss Baxter redirected the misbehaviour of two 4-year-old boys, the boys told the teacher, 'show your knickers', 'show your bum off', 'take all your clothes off, your bra off' (p. 4). The gaze of students, colleagues and parents sends signals to a teacher about what is expected of her body. Other people regulate her body until she regulates herself, because she is pressured to function within the institutional expectations or risk being disciplined (Foucault, [1975] 1977).

## Conclusion

Boundaries of the public-professional and personal-private are blurred in teaching. Expecting teachers to maintain the mind/body split dooms them to failure in comparison to the uncomplicated iconic images of teacher, which ignore the teacher body, mask it or find it unproblematic. These binaries disservice teachers who cannot live up to their impossible standards of favouring the mind and disregarding the body or keeping the personal-private out of the public-professional (see also Chapter 9). When women teachers are unable to reconcile these dualities and unrealistic expectations, they are left to conform within established boundaries, resist the limits or leave the profession.

Of these three options, productive resistance provides optimism for change in the teaching profession. Women teachers are not simply victims of patriarchy and systemic oppression; they can act as agents for transformation when they do not conform to existing expectations (Munro, 1998). Incongruities abound, however. Using a woman's body for resistance requires accepting that she will indeed be an object of observation. One cannot use her body to create different teacher images and actions and then expect others not to watch her in that resistance. The purpose would be defeated. Resistance as an embodied practice raises the question posed by recent feminist work, which is that how women can ensure that bodily appearance and action are read by the observers in ways that subvert the system instead of reinforcing gendered expectations. In short, how can one cultivate the intended message of presenting a different kind of woman teacher body instead of reinforcing the new body as deviant? Further, how can teachers even envision a new kind of teacher body for themselves before being squeezed of the profession?

This kind of discursive change is slow. More complicated studies of past and present teachers' bodies are needed so that present and future teachers can see beyond monoliths. More importantly, perhaps, positive attention to teachers' bodies is needed so that the discourse shifts away from bodies that are 'alien and threatening' (MacLure, 2003, p. 14) to those that present possibility. Suppression of body-centred discourse or wholly negative attention to bodies can only serve to reinforce the mind/body binary, benefit those already in power and impair those currently at the margins.

## Note

1. A popular and (in hindsight) paranoid concept of the early 19th century, publicly touted by notables such as Theodore Roosevelt and Helen Keller, was that women seeking higher education was related to their remaining single and not bearing children, which would eventually lead to the dying out of White middle-class Americans.

## References

Alsup, J. (2006) *Teacher identity discourses: Negotiating personal and professional spaces* (Mahwah, NJ: Erlbaum).

American Association for Employment in Education (2008) *2009 job search handbook for educators* (Columbus, OH: American Association for Employment in Education).

Apple, M. W. (1985) 'Teaching and "women's work": A comparative historical and ideological analysis', *Teachers College Record*, 86, 445–73.

Atkinson, B. (2008) 'Apple jumper, teacher babe, and bland uniformer teachers: Fashioning feminine teacher bodies', *Educational Studies*, 44, 98–121.

Bartky, S. L. (1990) *Femininity and domination: Studies in the phenomenology of oppression* (New York: Routledge).

Beecher, C. E. (1846) *The evils suffered by American women and American children: The causes and the remedy* (New York: Harper and Brothers).

Berger, J. (1972) *Ways of seeing* (London: BBC and Penguin).

Biklen, S. K. (1995) *School work: Gender and the cultural construction of teaching* (New York: Teachers College Press).

Bindley, K. (2013) 'Teri James, pregnant woman allegedly fired for premarital sex, sues Christian school', *Huffington Post*, http://www.huffingtonpost.com/2013/03/01/teri-james-pregnant-woman-fired-premarital-sex-christian-school_n_2790085.html (Accessed 16 July 2013).

Blount, J. M. (2000) 'Spinsters, bachelors, and other gender transgressors in school employment, 1850–1990', *Review of Educational Research*, 70(1), 83–101.

Chacon, R. M. (2006) 'Making space for those unruly women of color', *Review of Education, Pedagogy and Cultural Studies*, 28, 381–93.

Dalton, M. M. (2004) *The Hollywood curriculum: Teachers in the movies* (New York: Peter Lang).

Davis, K. B. (1929) *Factors in the sex life of twenty-two hundred women* (New York: Harper and Brothers).

de Lauretis, T. (1984) *Alice doesn't: Feminism, semiotics, cinema* (Bloomington, IN: Indiana University Press).

Department for Education (2012) 'Teaching is now a top choice for high graduates', http://www.education.gov.uk/inthenews/inthenews/a00211810/teaching-is-now-a-top-choice-for-high-flying-graduates (Accessed 16 July 2013).

Descartes, R. ([1641] 1996) *Meditations on first philosophy* (Cambridge, UK: Cambridge University Press).

Donovan, F. R. (1974) *The schoolma'am* (New York: Arno Press).

Downey, M. (2009) 'Barrow teacher done in by anonymous "parent" e-mail about her Facebook page', *Atlanta Journal-Constitution*, http://blogs.ajc.com/get-schooled-blog/2009/11/13/barrow-teacher-done- in-by-anonymous-e-mail-with-perfect-punctuation/ (Accessed 16 July 2013).

Emerick, C. F. (1909) 'College women and race suicide', *Political Science Quarterly*, 24, 269–83.

Faderman, L. (1991) *Odd girls and twilight lovers: A history of lesbian life in twentieth-century America* (New York: Columbia University Press).

Foucault, M. ([1971] 1972) *The archaeology of knowledge: And the discourse on language* (New York: Pantheon Books).

Foucault, M. ([1975] 1977) *Discipline and punish: The birth of the prison* (New York: Vintage Books).

Foucault, M. ([1976] 1978) *The history of sexuality: An introduction*, Vol. 1 (New York: Vintage Books).

Freedman, D. and Holmes, M. (2003) *The teacher's body: Embodiment, authority, and identity in the academy* (New York: SUNY Press).

Gallagher, M. (2010) 'Are schools panoptic?', *Surveillance and Society*, 7(3/4), 262–72.

Galman, S. and Mallozzi, C. A. (2012) 'She's not there: Women and gender in U.S. research on the elementary school teacher, 1995–present', *Review of Educational Research*, 82, 243–95.

Grant, G. and Murray, C. E. (1999) *Teaching in America: The slow revolution* (Cambridge, MA: Harvard University Press).

Grumet, M. R. (1988) *Bitter milk: Women and teaching* (Amherst: The University of Massachusetts Press).

Hall, S. G. (1904) *Adolescence: Its psychology and its relations to physiology, anthropology, sociology, sex, crime, religion, and education* (New York: Appleton).

Harbeck, K. M. (1997) *Gay and lesbian educators: Personal freedoms, public constraints* (Malden, MA: Amethyst Press).

Hawkins, M. (1998) 'Liberties in conflict: The free exercise clause, Title VII, and morality based personnel decisions in religious schools', *Journal Law and Education*, 27, 335–42.

Heldman (2008) 'Out-of-body image'. *Ms.*, 18, 52–5.

Hoffman, N. (2003) *Woman's "true" profession: Voices from the history of teaching* (Cambridge, MA: Harvard Education Press).

hooks, b. (1994) *Teaching to transgress: Education as the practice of freedom* (New York: Routledge).

hooks, b. (2003) 'The oppositional gaze: Black female spectators', in R. Lewis and S. Mills (eds.) *Feminist postcolonial theory* (New York: Routledge) (Reprinted from hooks, b. [1992] *Black looks: Race and representation*, pp. 115–31, [London: Turnaround]).

Ingersoll, R. and Merrill, L. (2010) 'Who's teaching our children?', *Educational Leadership*, 67(8), 14–20.

Johnson, T. S. (2004) ' "It's pointless to deny that that dynamic is there": Sexual tensions in secondary classrooms', *English Education*, 37(1), 5–29.

Johnson, T. S. (2008) *From teacher to lover: Sex scandals in the classroom* (New York: Peter Lang).

*Jet Magazine* (1959) ' "Too fat" Louisiana teacher sues for lost job. Louis Singleton', 1 January, n.p.

Kolmar, W. K. and Bartowski, F. (2005) *Feminist theory: A reader* (Boston: McGraw-Hill).

Levy, A. (2005) *Female chauvinist pigs: Women and the rise of raunch culture* (New York: Free Press).

Lightfoot, S. L. (1978) *Worlds apart: Relationships between families and schools* (New York: Basic Books).

Lorde, A. (1983) 'There is no hierarchy of oppressions', *Bulletin: Homophobia and Education*, 14(3/4), 9.

Lortie, D. C. ([1975] 2002) *Schoolteacher: A sociological study* (Chicago: The University of Chicago).

MacLure, M. (2003) *Discourse in educational and social research* (Buckingham: Open University Press).

Mallozzi, C. A. (2012) 'Cultural models of bodily images of women teachers', *Societies*, 2, 252–69.

Mulvey, L. (1975) 'Visual pleasure and narrative cinema', *Screen*, 16(3), 6–18.

Munro, P. (1998) *Subject to fiction: Women teachers' life history narratives and the cultural politics of resistance* (Buckingham: Open University Press).

National Education Association (1942) 'Standards for eligibility', *NEA Research Bulletin*, 20(2), 56–63.

Obrycki L. (2008) *Professionalism: What it means for a new teacher. 2009 Job search handbook for educators* (Columbus, OH: American Association for Employment in Education).

Perrillo, J. (2004) 'Beyond "progressive" reform: Bodies, discipline, and the construction of the professional teacher in interwar America', *History of Education Society*, 44, 337–63.

Peters, D. W. (1934) *The status of the married woman teacher* (New York: Teachers College Press).

Ringrose, J. (2007) 'Successful girls? Complicating post-feminist, neoliberal discourses of educational achievement and gender equality', *Gender and Education*, 19, 471–89.

Sawicki, J. (1991) *Disciplining Foucault: Feminism, power, and the body* (New York: Routledge).

Suggs, R. S. (1978) *Mother-teacher: The feminization of American education* (Charlottesville, VA: University of Virginia Press).

Sumara, D. and Davis, B. (1999) 'Interrupting heteronormativity: Toward a queer curriculum theory', *Curriculum Inquiry*, 29, 191–208.

Tapper and Miller. (2006) 'Anti-abortion group backs fired pregnant teacher', ABC News, http://abcnews.go.com/WNT/story?id=1641467andpage= 1#.UV88M3CLFxE (Accessed 16 July 2013).

Truth, S. (1851) *Ain't I a woman?*, http://www.fordham.edu/halsall/mod/sojtruth-woman.asp (Accessed 16 July 2013).

UNESCO (2003) *Gender and education for all: The leap to equality* (Paris: United Nations Educational, Scientific and Cultural Organization [UNESCO]).

*US Catholic* (2006) 'Pregnant Catholic preschool teacher fired', *US Catholic*, 71(2), 9.

Van Riper, T. (2006) 'America's most admired professions', *Forbes*, 28 July, http://www.forbes.com/2006/07/28/leadership-careers-jobs-cx_tvr_0728admired. html (Accessed 16 July 2013).

US Department of Education, National Center for Education Statistics (2012). *Digest of Education Statistics, 2011* (NCES 2012-001), introduction and chapter 2; US Department of Education, National Center for Education Statistics, Schools and Staffing Survey, Teacher Data Files, 2007–2008.

Villalva, B. R. (2012) 'Cathy Samford fired by Christian school for unmarried pregnancy; teacher files lawsuit', *Christian Post Reporter*, 12 April, http://global.christianpost.com/news/cathysamford-fired-for-unmarried-pregnancy-by-christian-school-teacher-files-lawsuit-73103/#kAGZcc4rwYIuvhwS.99 (Accessed 16 July 2013).

Walker, K. (2013) 'Tussle over sex standards: Why are fired teachers still suing Christian schools?', *Christianity Today*, January–February issue, 16.

Walkerdine, V. (1990) *Schoolgirl fictions* (London: Verso).

Waller, W. ([1932] 1965) *The sociology of teaching* (New York: John Wiley and Sons).

Weber, S. and Mitchell, C. (1995) *That's funny, you don't look like a teacher! Interrogating images and identity in popular culture* (London: Falmer Press).

Zumwalt, K. and Craig, E. (2005) 'Teachers' characteristics: Research on the demographic profile', in M. Cochran-Smith and K. M. Zeichner (eds.) *Studying teacher education: The report of the AERA panel on research and teacher education* (111–56) (Mahwah, NJ: Erlbaum).

# 7
# Negotiating Sexualities, Constructing Possibilities: Teachers and Diversity

*Jukka Lehtonen, Tarja Palmu and Elina Lahelma*

## Introduction

Teachers are everyday agents in negotiating regimes of sexuality in school settings and other educational institutions. They tackle issues related to sexual diversity and harassment, and contribute to the definition of what constitutes 'proper' sexuality, in the context of a heteronormative school culture (see also Chapter 6 and Chapter 8). Their views and practices also influence the ways in which students think about sexuality. In this chapter, we use the concept 'heteronormativity' to refer to a way of thinking characterised by a restricted view in which heterosexual maleness and heterosexual femaleness represent the natural, legitimate, desirable and often the only possible alternatives of being a human and a member of a school or a work community. This type of understanding of heteronormativity is based largely on the thoughts of Judith Butler (1990, 1993), who uses the terms heterosexual matrix and heterosexual hegemony to describe the ideological power system which makes people understand sex, gender and sexuality in heteronormative ways. Heteronormative thinking is present in institutions, structures, interpersonal relations and practices. However, as a cultural and social construct, heteronormativity is open to challenge (Lehtonen, 2003). While all the time visible in informal processes that take place in schools (see, for example, Gordon et al., 2000; Kehily and Nayak, 1996), issues around sexuality are rarely raised in teacher education (Lehtonen, 2012).

In this article we explore the negotiation and construction of sexualities in educational institutions in Finland. We focus on teachers' views of sexual diversity. We also discuss the ways in which teachers' views and practices influence the way students think of sexuality. We draw on selective reading of several data sets, including a random survey of over 1000 teachers, which was conducted by the teachers' trade union magazine *Opettaja* ('Teacher' in English) and which explored teachers' views of sexual minorities (Lehtonen, 2012). We also discuss additional supporting qualitative evidence gathered from an ethnographic study of Finnish schools we conducted (see Gordon et al., 2000; Lahelma et al., 2000b; Palmu, 2003), from interviews with young people who defined themselves as non-heterosexual (see Lehtonen, 2003, 2010) as well as from letters and stories gathered from teachers who have been sexually harassed by students sent to Lahelma in response to an article published in *Opettaja* magazine (see Lahelma, 2002). This exploration of the negotiation and construction of sexualities in educational institutions in Finland focuses on teachers' non-heterosexuality and students' homophobic harassment of teachers. Through this analysis we intend to highlight the pedagogic importance of teachers' reflectivity in addressing sexualities in educational contexts – whatever their own sexual orientation is. The term non-heterosexual is used to describe a person with sexual feelings or practices directed at those from the same gender group and/or a person who identifies as lesbian, gay or bisexual (Lehtonen, 2003).

## Finnish teachers' attitudes to sexual minorities

Currently, in Finland, it is possible to register a relationship between people of the same sex, but there is no gender-neutral marriage law. Adoption of one's spouse's children is possible for those in registered partnerships; for instance, a non-biological mother can adopt her spouse's child if they have registered their relationship. However, they could not adopt a child from outside the relationship through, for example, international adoption, even if they had registered their partnership.

In schools, teaching about sexuality takes typically place in the context of Physical Education, Health Education, Home Economics and Biology. This teaching happens more often in lower and upper secondary schools than in primary schools, but primary school Biology lessons usually include some information on sexuality as well. Often, experts from health organisations come to school to contribute to the teaching. Yet it has been argued that information about sexual diversity is seldom properly dealt with in Finnish schools (Gordon et al., 2000; Lehtonen, 2003).

Based on the *Opettaja* survey, the attitudes of teachers towards sexual minorities and their legal rights appear, at first glance, to be positive. About 70 per cent of the respondents indicated that they approve of marriage for gay and lesbian couples and of these groups being granted adoption rights. If we approach these numbers from the opposite direction, however, the overall picture is not equally satisfactory. Equal rights, such as marriage or adoption for same-sex partners, would not be granted by almost a third. Moreover, 8 per cent of the teachers reported negative attitudes towards sexual equality. There seems to be a rather large group of teachers who find it difficult to accept evenhanded treatment and equal rights for non-heterosexual people. Thus, it seems relevant to consider how their negative attitudes are reflected in practices at schools. Are these teachers capable of treating their non-heterosexual colleagues or students fairly? Do their attitudes affect their teaching, and would they step in when the word 'homo' is used in a derogatory sense or when non-heterosexual students are bullied?

Teachers' awareness of sexual diversity seems to be very weak. Moreover, they do not necessarily regard this as a problem (see also Kontula, 1997). However, some distinct differences between non-heterosexual and heterosexual teachers were found in the *Opettaja* data (Lehtonen, 2012; see also de Graaf et al., 2003). The survey results suggest that 45 per cent of heterosexual respondents indicated that they had taught non-heterosexual students, 42 per cent mentioned that they had at least one non-heterosexual colleague and 23 per cent had encountered students with non-heterosexual parents in their work. The percentages for non-heterosexual respondents were, respectively, 73 per cent, 71 per cent and 38 per cent. Teacher respondents who belong to sexual minorities had thus been notably more sensitive to the range of sexualities that exists in educational institutions compared with their heterosexual colleagues. Non-heterosexuality is not equally easy to disclose to heterosexual teachers as it is to those who are assumed to be non-heterosexual themselves. Teachers belonging to sexual minorities could be seen as a resource in schools since they have a better chance of reaching non-heterosexual colleagues and students.

Of all respondents to the survey, 84 per cent indicated that they did not require more information about matters related to sexual orientation. Of non-heterosexual teachers, 64 per cent, in other words significantly fewer, responded thus. These figures are large, especially when considering the dominant view that schools represent an unsafe place for non-heterosexual youth to disclose their sexuality. The greater desire of non-heterosexual teachers for more information perhaps indicates that they would like information on practical methods they could apply to raise themes related to sexual minorities for discussion in their teaching and in the school community. Currently, there is almost no information or research on such methods or teacher training based on them.

Only 19 per cent of the teacher respondents answered that students do disclose their sexual orientation, while 76 per cent reported otherwise. Less than a third of respondents surmised that if a student disclosed their sexual orientation, the reaction would be one of acceptance, with the majority believing that the reaction to such a student would be rejection or bullying. It is, of course, self-evident that in some schools disclosure of non-heterosexuality by the student population can result in problems that the school community does not necessarily know how to deal with fairly (Lehtonen, 2003, 2004). The majority of teachers indicated in their responses that they do not consider schools to be a safe place for non-heterosexual youth if their sexuality became common knowledge.

## Hidden sexual diversity in schools

Our data suggest that teachers are usually aware of the constant presence of sexuality in schools. A lower secondary school teacher made the following comment on students' behaviour: 'everything that points to these themes makes them giggle'. However, sexuality is rarely openly discussed in the context of teacher education, teaching or learning, and relations and enactments of power that are involved are seldom questioned. Sex-based teasing and harassment are often regarded as natural in adolescence, part of normal relationships, an 'adolescent mating dance' (Kenway and Willis, 1998, p. 108; see also Haywood and Mac an Ghaill, 1995). One of the most hidden themes is non-heterosexuality. In schools, cultural and societal hierarchies and power dimensions surface in the concrete relationship between teachers and students. The role of the teacher can be considered as that of an embodied person teaching other embodied persons (Probyn, 2004). The primary question then is: what significance does embodiment get in current practices and classroom discussions? Non-heterosexual teachers, particularly, have pondered how much they are supposed to become 'visible' and 'out' about their sexuality (Epstein and Johnson, 1998; Khayatt, 1992).

It has been argued that schools are a major site of the production of hegemonic masculinity, constructed in opposition to the female and homosexual 'others' since it offers a condensed range of experiences in sustained and mandatory fashion (Gordon et al., 2000). As a lower secondary school teacher stated: sexuality is at the same time 'all over and visible' and 'the most sensitive sphere', which makes it of the utmost difficulty to discuss in school (Lahelma et al., 2000b). Some teachers have noted in interviews that schools are 'dragging behind' in relation to sexuality, particularly in relation to homosexuality. In relation to this point, one teacher observed that,

> In a way you have to be the point of contrasting reflection there all the time, though they [students] scrabble around and talk. You have to settle yourself as a model, to show how you are not supposed to speak about women and homosexuals.

The manifold ways of living and understanding sexuality are not easy to bring into classroom discussions, although homosexuality as a topic is visible in everyday school practices, mainly in the form of sexual name-calling as 'lesbian' or 'homo' (Gordon et al., 2000; Lehtonen, 2002). One teacher told in the interview how homosexuality came into the discussion when they were dealing with romance in a Finnish lesson:

> So, I thought that I would start by asking what romance means to them, what springs up to their mind first. So, there was, of course, talk about candles and good music and atmosphere and pink colour and some movies and ... One started 'man and woman', next said 'woman and man' and then somebody said 'man and man'. Then I only noted that, 'yes, of course, it could also be like this'. For example, being gay or lesbian it is, it is not visible in the schools' formal practices or curricula yet, but it comes from the students, and then you have to be ready to react in some way. But it is not an issue that belongs to things that are openly discussed in the school. Or I have not heard. Maybe in high school, but not with students of this age.

As the teacher in the quotation above notes, homosexuality is not a commonly discussed topic in schools. It is mostly invisible in the 'official school', but at the same time visible in the 'informal' and 'physical school' (see Gordon et al., 2000). Teachers have different perceptions of what is the most suitable age to discuss sexuality. One teacher stated that students at the age of 13 should see a movie that deals with homosexuality, whilst the teacher in the quotation above argued that discussions about sexuality should proceed not earlier than in the upper secondary schools (when students are over 15 years old). In the next quotation, a female teacher describes how she and her colleague pondered upon their own attitude and position towards non-heterosexuality, when they were collecting love poems for teaching material:

> I have not discussed this [homosexuality] with other Finnish language teachers, except for one,...but we tried to collect poems together. And there, when we were picking those love poems, this came up. We were discussing with each other what kind of position we should take.

Overall, sexuality and its diversity seem to confuse teachers and are seen as a potential source of emotional stress and shame. Thus, it seems preferable to avoid and silence these topics.

## Teachers' (non-)disclosure of their non-heterosexuality

Young people find it difficult to see their teachers as sexual beings, and, in some cases, a teacher's sexuality can lead to harassment or bullying (Lahelma, 2002; Lehtonen, 2004). Based on interviews conducted by Lehtonen (2003) with young people, it became clear that teachers appear to students for the most part as either heterosexual or nonsexual (see also Palmu, 1999). The young people interviewed as part of this study were interested in their teachers' familial and relationship status and were aware of the heterosexual marriages or other relationships and children of at least some teachers. They also indicated that teachers sometimes revealed their heterosexuality through stories or sexist jokes. In contrast, according to the students, teachers tended to remain circumspect about their non-heterosexuality. Discussion of their teachers' sexuality and sharing 'suspicions' of their non-heterosexuality sometimes occurred among students, but very few of the young people interviewed had experienced a teacher speaking openly about their non-heterosexuality. Some had met their non-heterosexual teachers outside school, for instance, at lesbian and gay meeting places, or after they had left the school, but typically these teachers, as well, had remained silent about their sexuality and thus appeared basically heterosexual in the school setting (Lehtonen, 2003). A boy called Petteri (a pseudonym like all the other names in this chapter) had met his Family Education teacher at a gay bar and commented:

> Petteri: She could never have imagined that I was gay, 'cause I was a board member of the students' union, and she used to be rather close to me then. I was the first student she ran into in a gay party.

JL: Did she tell you that?

Petteri: Yeah. We didn't talk much then. But in the next party we met again. Our Family Education teacher.

JL: She didn't bring up these issues in any way in her Family Education classes?

Petteri: No way, she was careful not to even mention gays.

JL: Did she say anything at all?

Petteri: I have talked a bit about it with her, 'cause she teaches Family Education. She teaches girls, and how would people react? And she said that she had told a couple of nice female teachers about it. Other teachers at her school don't know anything about it. But they don't ask either.

Several studies suggest that non-heterosexual teachers tend to hide their sexual orientation (see, for example, Epstein and Johnson, 1998; Harbeck, 1991; Khayatt, 1992). In the study by Lehtonen (2004), some teachers had revealed it to fellow teachers, but rarely to administrators or students. Some teachers who concealed their sexual orientation tended to avoid close relationships with their co-workers at school and avoided bringing up themes related to non-heterosexuality in their classes for fear of being disclosed (see Harbeck, 1991). Hence, the resources available to non-heterosexual teachers in teaching and addressing sexual diversity are not always put to use, particularly if they try to hide their sexuality and therefore often eliminate all signs of the existence of non-heterosexuality around them.

The assumption that teachers are heterosexual is either a spontaneous assumption or based on the teacher's stories or behaviour. Non-heterosexual Sara made an exception by asking her teacher directly whether she was straight:

Sara: At the beginning of upper secondary school I had a Finnish teacher whom I thought for a long time to be lesbian, but it turned out she's not. I asked her directly and she told me that she's not.

JL: How did you have the courage to ask?

Sara: She was quite young. I had just been in her class. I asked 'How about you, are you straight?', and she said 'I'm straight, but most of the people I studied with are gay'. Actually most of her closest friends were homosexual, she said. So she does have a rather personal touch with the whole issue.

A clear majority of the teachers who took part in the *Opettaja* magazine survey (70 per cent) felt that for a teacher, disclosing her or his sexual orientation was not a good idea (Lehtonen, 2012). The reasons for this, as indicated in the open responses, were that sexual orientation has no place at school, that it is a private matter whose discussion increases the risk of tension and bullying. Another interesting finding in the *Opettaja* survey was that the term 'sexual orientation' was used in the responses, but seemed to be viewed as referring to something other than heterosexuality. In other words, sexual orientation was seen as a synonym for belonging to a sexual minority. When sexual orientation is understood solely as belonging to a sexual minority, heterosexuality remains an unstated, self-evident norm. This norm is revealed when we turn this positioning on its head and ask if a teacher should be allowed to disclose his or her heterosexual orientation. If heterosexual teachers strove to conceal their heterosexuality, it would mean they would not tell their fellow teachers what they did with their different-gender partner and their children last weekend or over vacation. It would involve avoiding topics that might reveal them as heterosexual. It would mean not wearing engagement and wedding rings at school, not carrying photos of their children or spouse in their wallet, not inviting their opposite-sex partner to school events and not even picking them up from work. It would be reflected in their attire, make-up and gestures, what kind of voice they use and how they move as well as how they wear their hair. After all, traditional attire and a gender style in line with gender expectations often include clues that support the perception of a person's heterosexuality. Teachers might also be concerned about the impression that they make with their spouses outside of school – a colleague or student might see them and decide that they are heterosexual. This positioning might seem amusing, but many non-heterosexual teachers consider similar questions when thinking about how to construct a perception of themselves as something other than non-heterosexual – in other words, as something other than what they are (see also Lehtonen, 2003; Renold, 2000; Valkonen, 2002).

The coming out of teachers as lesbian or gay has been questioned in queer pedagogical texts (see Juvonen, under review). Teachers' identification as lesbian or gay can emphasise the idea of stable and clear sexual identities, which might not reflect students' experiences of their sexual pluralities. It might also give an impression that coming out is an easy process for students as well, which might not always be the case. How to express sexual orientation and sexuality in general can be a relevant question for heterosexual teachers as well (Holland et al., 2007; Palmu, 1999). They ponder upon how to deal with their own sexuality in relation to their school and teaching. They do not usually hide their sexual orientation, but negotiation of the boundaries of sexuality can be problematic: women teachers in particular are careful not to give signs that can be interpreted as erotic. Teachers may experience some tensions between the official demands of the school, and their gender and sexual identities. They try to perform the right kind of teacherhood and embodiment under the eyes of their students. Sometimes even the parents of the students can join in this discussion and get involved in controlling teachers' behaviour (Lehtonen, 2003; Palmu, 1999).

## Students' (non-)disclosure of their non-heterosexuality

Of the young people who sent in stories to Lehtonen, one had revealed her same-sex relationship to a teacher. The storyteller had mentioned the relationship immediately during the early stages of the study. The teacher had asked the reason for the student's move to a new town. She said that she had moved there because her same-sex partner had moved there.

> My teacher discreetly recommended that I do not mention the matter to my classmates, as it could cause unnecessary fuss, and I should spare myself from it. My teacher was diplomatically polite, even friendly, but her motivations remained a little unclear at that time.

The storyteller expresses some minor doubts as to the teacher's motivations to ask her to conceal her sexuality from the other students. Apparently, according to the teacher, telling about the relationship could have caused problems for the student, so it could have been a protective effort. On the other hand, the storyteller mentions causing unnecessary fuss 'that could result from telling'. This sounds more like the teacher's intent to protect the other students from having to deal with the matter, unless the intent was to protect the teacher from having to take a stand on the matter within the school community (see Epstein and Johnson, 1998). The storyteller, however, felt overall that she had received support from the instructor in question, even though her relationship was only touched on in their conversations. Receiving support as a non-heterosexual student is not an automatic given (see Lehtonen, 2003). The support offered by the teacher was important to the following storytelling student as well:

> Once, when we were enjoying a meal that we had prepared together as a class, my teacher asked me discreetly (we were sitting next to each other), that since I told I had got a part-time job, had my

spouse found work as well. I briefly explained my spouse's studies, and my teacher suggested that I should ask...about potential substitute positions...Several times during the first year I mentioned to my teacher something about my spouse and myself: our housing situation, studies, or job situation. My teacher seemed to be warm and approachable. I believe that my teacher was able to deal with the matter open-mindedly, and my openness with her had a positive influence.

## Sexual harassment of teachers by students

In my experience, sexual remarks directed at teachers are very rare...You might see writing on the wall, though: unpopular female teachers are naturally whores, and male teachers are homos.

This quote from a letter written by a female teacher is one of many letters, telephone communications and conversations expressly invited by two columns of Lahelma on sexual harassment in school, published in *Opettaja* (Lahelma, 2002; Lahelma et al., 2000b). Many of the letters contained strong reactions, anxiety and occasionally relief over the fact that the issue was finally being discussed. Most of the 37 teachers who felt strongly enough about the columns to contact Lahelma were women. Their accounts mainly involved the harassment of female teachers – the participant or a colleague – by male students. The female teachers had been subjected to distasteful remarks on their appearance, threats of rape, pornographic drawings and unwelcome physical contact. The quote above gives us an insight into how sexual name-calling or harassment of teachers by students in school operates and becomes normalised. First, the writer refers to the fact that openly sexual name-calling of teachers is not commonplace. Second, the name-callers tend to remain anonymous or hide in groups. Third, students may use sexual stigmatising as a means of expressing dislike for a particular teacher. Fourth, the use of the word 'naturally' implies that such language is perhaps considered a matter of course in school. Fifth, in sexual name-calling, women are usually labelled as 'whores', while men are called 'homos'.

There have been some lively debates on the increase of disorderly behaviour in schools, and the menace or even outright violence teachers are consequently subjected to. A survey by Janne Kivivuori (1997) indicates that 73 per cent of teachers have been subjected to insults, mainly in the form of sexual comments, by their students. However, teachers in

Kivivuori's study did not generally refer to students sexually harassing or commenting on their teachers' sexuality.

Dealing with problematic situations arising with students is part of teachers' professional skills. But when students use sexual name-calling against women teachers, the set-up is not one of teachers against students, but one of males against females in general. Such situations blur the power relations and thus make it difficult for the teacher to respond adequately.

## Male teachers' accounts of homophobic name-calling

The male teachers' accounts, or the female teachers' accounts of their male colleagues' experiences, usually involved homosexual stigmatisation. None of the letters indicated that the male teachers in question were non-heterosexual, and it was quite evident that the young male students' motivation for name-calling was not that they actually thought their teacher was homosexual. Homophobic name-calling is fundamentally about the construction of hierarchical masculinities, heterosexuality being at the top of the hierarchy. In some schools, homophobic name-calling is common among boys (Lehtonen, 2002). Those who have noticed its power to offend may use it to insult their teachers as well. However, this analysis is undoubtedly not the first to cross the mind of a male teacher suddenly being called homo by his students. The accounts in the letters suggest that dealing with these situations requires more than average professional skills.

One recurring topic of discussion involving schools is the shortage of male teachers (Lahelma et al., 2000a). In addition to the speech that polarises gender characteristics and is often hostile towards women, there is a pervasive assumption that male teachers are necessary male role models and compensate for the absence of the father, especially with regard to boys. This male role model is undoubtedly heterosexual – a thing so self-evident that it is never explicitly mentioned. Male teachers who do not conform to the image of a heterosexual male teacher may be attached the stigma 'homo'. A 30-year-old teacher with children had the following experience:

> I don't consider myself an average (male) teacher in terms of my appearance, or my views for that matter. People usually think I'm a rock musician, artist, etc. But with teaching I'm as strict as anyone, I am not the lax turn-a-blind-eye type. Once the initial curiosity waned, speculations, buzz and rumours of my homosexuality began

to circulate among students. In the end, the name-calling and even physical assaults became almost daily. I was sneered at in the hallways, the bus stop and the schoolyard. Writings like 'here comes a homo' appeared on my car, and finally I began to receive abusive phone calls in the night. There were a couple of those. I've found this whole affair very hurtful and offensive, since I myself uphold humanity and tolerance. I've tried to teach my students these values. This situation drove me so far as to even consciously change my style (hair, clothes) towards a more 'teacher-like', greyer look, because I couldn't handle the name-calling. Situations where my privacy was publicly offended made me flushed, embarrassed and so on, and I felt like smacking the brat, but of course that would have been out of order. I had no means of defending myself. Even if I'm not gay, I didn't argue or try to prove my sexuality to these bullies – I refuse to submit to that.

As we see it, the homosexual label is used because it is an effective means of offending and challenging the authority of a male teacher. It is also commonly used among boys themselves. Some adolescents interviewed trivialised the word and said it does not necessarily mean anything. The power of homosexual name-calling lies in the fact that whether or not it is used to imply a certain sexual orientation, the name-calling always negotiates hierarchies between males (see Nayak and Kehily, 1997). Masculinities are hierarchically organised in school and, in this hierarchy, heterosexual masculinity is at the top. Whatever the intended meaning of homophobic name-calling in school, it effectively manifests and maintains a social climate where non-heterosexuality is considered inferior. It is easy to see the deeply negative impact such a climate can have, especially on adolescents who have a non-heterosexual orientation or are confused about their own sexual orientation (Lehtonen, 2002, 2003). But being called a homo always presents a threat of sexual stigmatisation also for those young men whose developing masculine identity strongly relies on heterosexuality. Therefore, homophobic name-calling not only hurts those subjected to it but also influences the entire school's gender culture by reinforcing heteronormativity.

## Female teachers' accounts of homophobic name-calling

Female teachers are more likely to be called whores than lesbians, although the letters did include some experiences involving the latter label. The whore stigma is the more commonly used one against young girls as well (Aaltonen, 2002). Non-heterosexual women tend to be invisible – they are not considered a threat to gender and sexual hierarchies in the same way as homosexual men. One purpose of sexist name-calling is to reinforce heteronormativity. For example, in the case of a woman being called a whore, it implies her willingness to engage in sexual relations with a man.

The teachers' letters also contained astonishing stories where even isolated comments by students had caused anguish. These experiences were described as 'deeply aggrieving' or 'hurtful and embittering'. Some teachers had begun to fear certain places or experience problems in their own sexuality, while others had been compelled to change schools or seek therapy. Some letters showed the writers' bewilderment and embarrassment over such strong reactions to trivial comments by students, for a professional teacher should have been able to deal with such matters. The magnitude of such incidents is difficult to understand if one has not experienced it personally. The following is an excerpt from a letter written by a female teacher:

> [A boy] from primary school had called a colleague lesbian, which offended her deeply. That same year, we had work counselling, and in that context, discussed the matter. I remember wondering why Taina [teacher] took it so seriously – after all, the boy was only seven years old.

The writer herself later became the object of 'unfounded and outrageous talk', and that experience never escaped her memory. Of course, reactions vary from one teacher to another. Some letters contained stories that outwardly appeared similar to the above, aggrieved accounts, but the difference was that the writers expressed no distress over their experiences: 'These things should not be taken too much to heart.'

## Teacher and student power relationships

Teachers hold authority over students: they have the power to praise and to punish. This does not, however, mean that students are completely without power. Power is dynamic and contextual: according to the circumstances, students, girls or boys, can choose either to submit to the teacher's authority, to consciously and actively accommodate themselves to it or to challenge it. Students respond to teachers' authority in a variety of ways – and for a variety of reasons. In our society, power is intertwined with masculinity, and in particular with hegemonic masculinity (Connell, 1995) that is super-ordinate to other masculinities (such as homosexuality) and to femininities. By turning the student-teacher relationship into a gender-power relationship, boys can attempt to challenge and question the authority of teachers. By commenting on a female teacher's sexuality or anatomy, even young boys can – consciously or unconsciously – use masculine dominance over her by assigning her to a feminine position. The authority of male teachers can be questioned by attaching the homosexual stigma to them, leading to a renegotiation of school hierarchies.

Although it is impossible to give general guidelines for dealing with such a wide range of situations described in this chapter, we are all the same inclined to suggest that these matters be taken, if not to heart, at least seriously. Teachers who had managed to cope with their particular situation said they had laughed the comments off or simply ignored them, bearing in mind that the students are often trying to negotiate the teacher-student power relationships and undermine authority. But is this the right thing to do? A vocational upper secondary school teacher wrote: 'Should I as a teacher just accept it as normal practice that teachers are called pricks, or homos, which I was called as well?' Should such name-calling be condoned between students as well? If teachers ignore comments directed at them, do they at the same time signal that students should not react to name-calling either? And if the matter is laughed off, does this support a culture which permits offensive jokes related to gender and sexuality?

## Conclusion

Expressing heterosexuality is possible and actively supported in schools. Usually, heterosexual teachers do not consciously hide their sexual orientation, and disclosing a heterosexual relationship or heterosexual preferences is not seen as expressing sexual orientation. Heterosexuality, heterosexual couples and families are not seen as 'sexual orientation' or 'sexually oriented' in the same way as non-heterosexuality, which is regarded as 'a private matter' that should be silenced. For heterosexual teachers, sexual orientation is primarily a minority issue – and thus marginal. But this does not make it easy for heterosexual teachers either to tackle sexuality in the school context: they have to make decisions on how to face sexual diversity and harassment related to it, and how to keep up their own status as teachers in relation to sexuality.

In current teacher training, in Finland as in many other countries, the theme of sexual diversity remains for the most part disregarded as does heteronormativity, the problems it causes and the possible ways of dismantling it (see also Bedford, 2009; Koschoreck and Tooms, 2009; van Dijk and van Driel, 2007). Teachers' sexuality is not dealt with either. Yet things could be different. To begin with, teacher education institutions could allow and support teacher educators and teacher students in expressing their sexual orientation openly. This would reinforce the possibility for future teachers to be open about it, in the school communities where they work. Dealing with the topic of sexual diversity as part of teacher training could increase the capacity of teacher students to understand sexual diversity that exists in school communities and to deal with it in appropriate ways, for example, by calling into question heteronormative representations of the family which appear in the teaching material, by offering support to non-heterosexual students or by viewing the heterosexuality of a colleague as only one expression of the range of sexuality – not as an unstated, self-evident norm. Teachers should be encouraged to intervene when cases of sexual harassment occur, be it against another teacher or against a student. Since individual teachers are often completely taken by surprise when faced with harassment, there should be some discussion of the appropriate responses in teacher training and among the teaching community.

The relationship between teachers and students, as well as the question 'how is teaching "knowledge" linked to the personal experience?' are relevant here. The possibility for students to recognise themselves as part of the structure of knowledge is linked to experiential teaching. This is one of the main questions in the recent discussion about learning. What is the significance of affects in learning (Naskali, under review)? This question has been highlighted in feminist pedagogy related to higher education teaching, but it is equally relevant in the other levels of education, too. According to Britzman (1995), one task of teaching is studying boundaries: what kind of knowledge is thinkable, what is outside the thinkable and what is the knowledge we can deal with? The ethical questions about differences and choices are central. Also the curriculum should be based on knowledge that gives space for students to identify themselves. Those who are White, heterosexual and bourgeois settle easily in identity terms, without giving space to other subjectivities. For example, in teaching, performing homosexuality turns out to be a confession, while performing heterosexuality confirms normality (Naskali, under review).

If we understand teaching as an exercise of power that produces subjects, then the teacher embodies pedagogical power through their presentations of gender and sexuality (Juvonen, under review). Key issues for teachers and teacher educators remain: What are the pedagogical choices teachers make to reproduce 'normality' and stereotypes of gender and sexuality? How could teachers repeat these supposed continuums in a different way? A pedagogical task is to undermine the 'naturalness' of stereotypes, make visible their fragility and challenge the privileges granted because of them.

## References

Aaltonen, S. (2002) 'Told, denied and silenced. Young people's interpretations of conflicts and gender in school', in V. Sunnari, J. Kangasvuo and M. Heikkinen (eds.) *Gendered and sexualised violence in educational environments* (Oulu, Finland: Oulu University Press).

Bedford, T. (2009) *Promoting educational equity through teacher empowerment. Web-assisted transformative action research as a counter-heteronormative praxis* (Oulu, Finland: University of Oulu).

Britzman, D. (1995) 'Is there a queer pedagogy? Or, stop reading straight', *Education Theory*, 45(2), 151–65.

Butler, J. (1990) *Gender trouble: Feminism and the subversion of identity* (New York and London: Routledge).

Butler, J. (1993) *Bodies that matter: On the discursive limits of 'sex'* (New York and London: Routledge).

Connell, R.W. (1995) *Masculinities* (Cambridge: Polity Press).

De Graaf, H., van der Meerendonk, B., Vennix, P. and Vanwesenbeeck, I. (2003) *Healthy teacher, healthy school: Job perception and health of homosexual and bisexual teachers* (Amsterdam and Utrecht: Dutch Ministry of Social Affairs and Employment).

Epstein, D. and Johnson, R. (1998) *Schooling sexualities* (Buckingham and Philadelphia: Open University Press).

Gordon, T., Holland, J. and Lahelma, E. (2000) *Making spaces: Citizenship and difference in schools* (London and New York: Macmillan and St. Martin's Press).

Harbeck, K. (ed.) (1991) *Coming out of the classroom closet* (New York and London: Harrington Park Press).

Haywood, C. and Mac an Ghaill, M. (1995) 'The sexual politics of the curriculum: Contested values', *International Studies in Sociology of Education*, 5(2), 221–36.

Holland, J., Gordon, T. and Lahelma, E. (2007) 'Temporal and spatial relations in teachers' day at school', *Ethnography and Education*, 2(2), 221–38.

Juvonen, T. (under review) 'Kriittinen ja korjaava pervopedagogiikka luento-opetuksessa' (Critical and reconstructive queer pedagogy in lecture-based teaching), in J. Saarinen, H. Ojala and T. Palmu (eds.) *Feministinen pedagogiikka* (Feminist pedagogy).

Kehily, M. and Nayak, A. (1996) 'The Christmas kiss': Sexuality, storytelling and schooling', *Curriculum Studies*, 4(2), 211–27.

Kenway, J. and Willis, S. (1998) *Answering back: Girls, boys and feminism in schools* (London and New York: Routledge).

Khayatt, M. (1992) *Lesbian teachers* (Albany, NY: SUNY Press).

Kivivuori, J. (1997) *Opettajiin kohdistuva häirintä ja väkivalta* (Harassment and violence experienced by teachers) (Helsinki: Oikeuspoliittinen tutkimuslaitos).

Kontula, O. (1997) *Yläasteen sukupuolikasvatus lukuvuonna 1995–1996* (Sex education in lower secondary school in the year 1995–1996) (Helsinki: Sosiaali- ja terveysministeriö).

Koschoreck, J. and Tooms, A. (eds.) (2009) *Sexuality matters. Paradigms and policies for educational leaders* (Lanham, MD: Rowman and Littlefield).

Lahelma, E. (2002) 'Sexual name-calling of teachers – Challenging the power relations', in J. Lehtonen (ed.) *Sexual and gender minorities at work* (Helsinki: Stakes).

Lahelma, E., Hakala, K., Hynninen, P. and Lappalainen, S. (2000a) 'Too few men? Analysing the discussion on the need for more male teachers', *Nordic Studies of Education*, 20(3), 129–38.

Lahelma, E., Palmu, T. and Gordon, T. (2000b) 'Intersecting power relations in teachers' experiences of being sexualised or harassed by students', *Sexualities*, 3(4), 463–81.

Lehtonen, J. (2002) 'Heteronormativity and name-calling: Constructing boundaries for students' genders and sexualities', in V. Sunnari, J. Kangasvuo and M. Heikkinen (eds.) *Gendered and sexualised violence in educational environments* (Oulu, Finland: Oulu University Press).

Lehtonen, J. (2003) *Seksuaalisuus ja sukupuoli koulussa* (Sexuality and gender at school) (Helsinki: Yliopistopaino and Nuorisotutkimusverkosto).

Lehtonen, J. (2004) 'Lesbian, gay, and bisexual teachers: Invisible in the mind of the students?', in J. Lehtonen and K. Mustola (eds.) *Straight people don't tell, do they? Negotiating the boundaries of sexuality and gender at work* (Helsinki: Ministry of Labour).

Lehtonen, J. (2010) 'Gendered post-compulsory educational choices of non-heterosexual youth', *European Educational Research Journal*, 9(2), 177–91.

Lehtonen, J. (2012) 'Opettajien käsityksiä seksuaalisuuden kirjosta' (Teachers' perceptions on sexual diversity), *Finnish Journal of Youth Studies*, 30(2): 19–30.

Naskali, P. (under review) 'Turvallisuus vyöhykkeen tuolle puolen: yliopistopedagogiikka feministisen tietokäsityksen kehyksessä' (Higher education in the frame of feminist epistemology), in J. Saarinen, H. Ojala and T. Palmu (eds.) *Feministinen pedagogiikka* (Feminist pedagogy).

Nayak, A. and Kehily, M. (1997) 'Masculinities and schooling: Why are young men so homophobic?', in D. Steinberg, D. Epstein and R. Johnson (eds.) *Border patrols: Policing the boundaries of heterosexuality* (London: Cassell).

Palmu, T. (1999) 'Kosketuspintoja sukupuoleen. Opettajat, ruumiillisuus ja seksuaalisuus' (Touching on gender: Teachers, corporality, and sexuality), in T. Tolonen (ed.) *Suomalainen koulu ja kulttuuri* (Finnish school and culture) (Tampere, Finland: Vastapaino).

Palmu, T. (2003) *Sukupuolen rakentuminen koulun kulttuurisissa teksteissä. Etnografia yläasteen äidinkielen oppitunneilla* (Construction of gender in cultural texts in school: An ethnographic research on mother tongue lessons in secondary school) (Helsinki: University of Helsinki).

Probyn, E. (2004) 'Teaching bodies: Affects in the classroom', *Body and Society*, 10(21), 21–43.

Renold, E. (2000) ' "Coming out": Gender, (hetero)sexuality and the primary school', *Gender and Education*, 12(3), 309–25.

Valkonen, M. (2002) 'Gay, lesbian and bisexual teachers at work', in J. Lehtonen (ed.) *Sexual and gender minorities at work* (Helsinki: Stakes).

Van Dijk, L. and Van Driel, B. (eds.) (2007) *Challenging homophobia – Teaching about sexual diversity* (Stoke-on-Trent: Trentham Books).

# Part III

# Understanding Social Divides and Moving towards Social Change

# 8
# Lesbian and Gay Teachers: Negotiating Subjectivities in Sydney Schools

*Tania Ferfolja*

## Introduction

Sydney, in the state of New South Wales (NSW), Australia, is a cosmopolitan metropolis. In the past three decades, there has been a slowly developing, but increasingly liberal climate towards sexual diversity across the nation, particularly in cities. Changes to the NSW Anti-Discrimination Act in the 1980s made it illegal to discriminate on the grounds of sexual orientation in public institutions and more recent amendments to federal legislation in the areas of superannuation, taxation laws and so forth have enhanced access and equity to homosexuals not previously realised. Additionally, over the last decade, there has been greater visibility of sexual and gender diversity in popular culture and in the media – a virtual 'mainstreaming' of traditionally 'Othered' sexual subjects.

These kinds of changes have perpetuated a belief that discrimination based on sexual orientation is moribund or reduced to the point of irrelevancy, suggesting that lesbian and gay people should feel safe and accepted in the workplace. Yet homophobia still exists in Australian society and this form of inequality plays out frequently in schools; these remain common sites for discrimination and violence towards people who are, or are perceived to be, both sexually and gender diverse (Hillier et al., 2010). In the light of this knowledge, this chapter examines the workplace experiences of lesbian- and gay-identified teachers and the ways in which they negotiate their sexual subjectivities to accommodate the schooling cultures in which they work.

## Australian schooling cultures

Schools in the main are highly conservative, heterosexist organisations (Epstein and Johnson, 1998; Holmes, 2001). Policy, curriculum, pedagogical practice and schooling cultures produce understandings about sexuality and reinforce the normalisation and superiority of heterosexuality (Atkinson and DePalma, 2008; Ferfolja, 2013; Jackson, 2006). The international literature well documents how schools regulate the gendered and sexual subjectivities of both students and teachers (see Chapter 7). This process occurs through various means, including verbal and physical harassment, structural and interpersonal discrimination, cyber-bullying, ostracism, violence and coercion (Callaghan, 2007; Elia and Eliason, 2010; Hillier and Mitchell, 2008; Hohnke and O'Brien, 2008; Martino and Cumming-Potvin, 2011; McKenzie-Bassant, 2007; Meyer, 2009; Michaelson, 2008; Rudoe, 2010). The reification of heterosexuality in schools is intersected with a multitude of broader discourses that impact the working lives of lesbian and gay teachers. These include, but are not limited to, discourses that equate the 'professional body' with heterosexuality (Giuffre et al., 2008; Williams and Giuffre, 2011; Willis, 2011); that position teachers *in loco parentis* and as asexual (Khayatt, 1992); that socially construct childhood (and youth) as universally innocent, vulnerable and asexual, requiring protection from the corruptions of the 'adult' world (Robinson and Jones Diaz, 2006); that condemn non-heterosexual sexual practice for religious and moral reasons; and that position 'homosexuality' as abnormal, sick, hypersexual and predatory (Graydon, 2011).

These discourses are visible in, circulate throughout and are reinforced by broader social, cultural and political institutions (Weedon, 1987). For example, in Australia, homophobic discourse is used variously for political gain. At the time of writing, 'gay' and 'lesbian' teachers were being targeted by aspiring Australian political candidates from a conservative party. One candidate stated that she did not 'want gays [or] lesbians to be working in my kindergarten' (Willingham, 2013). Another candidate for the same political party tweeted, 'that he didn't want homosexuals teaching his children and he's not afraid to say it' (Willingham, 2013).

Such prejudice undermines how lesbian and gay teachers undertake their work. As a result, these teachers are often selective about revealing their same-sex relationships to colleagues and are careful to avoid revelation to students. Negative discourses that circulate about lesbian and gay subjectivities, combined with the potential for, and reality of, discrimination, compel many lesbian- and gay-identified teachers to shape the performances of their sexual subjectivities at work. This chapter, drawing on recent research with lesbian- and gay-identified teachers, explores some of the subjective locations strategically exploited by the participants to enhance their credibility, sense of safety and contextual power within largely heterosexist and heteronormative workplaces.

## Method

Fourteen teachers (six females and eight males) who worked in the Sydney metropolitan region of NSW, Australia, volunteered to participate in qualitative, in-depth interviews. Despite using a range of recruitment methods, the participants reflected the dominant teacher demographic in Australia, that is, White, middle class and English-speaking (Richardson and Watt, 2006; see also Chapter 4). Their teaching backgrounds were varied, however, and ranged from infants' school through to high school. These schools were managed by the state, were independent or were headed by the Catholic Education Office.[1] Eight teachers were in the early stages of their teaching career, two were considered mid-career and four had more than 25 years of experience. The school populations were demographically varied, but all were located within the Sydney region, where access to lesbian, gay, bisexual, transgender and queer (LGBTQ) support services and social groups is possible.

The interviews were undertaken in 2011–2012. They lasted up to two hours and were semi-structured in nature. This approach enabled the participants to convey their personal understandings of their experiences in relation to the questions in a relatively natural manner (Kvale, 1996). These interviews were professionally transcribed and then carefully read to identify codes which informed themes within and across the participants' narratives (Saldana, 2009). Feminist post-structuralist and Foucauldian perspectives were then applied to the analysis, interrogating how social, cultural and political discourses, used in the Foucauldian ([1978] 1998) sense, constitute subjective experience (Ezzy, 2002). Discourses produce power, meaning and knowledge; they may regulate behaviour, thoughts and interactions. They are simultaneously complex and contradictory and will constitute subjects as 'normal' or not (Foucault, [1978] 1998). According to post-structuralist feminist theory, subjectivity is constituted in discourse and refers to the 'conscious and unconscious thoughts and emotions of the individual, her sense of herself and her ways of understanding her relation to the world' (Weedon, 1987, p. 32). As a result, subjects are able to resist and challenge discourse and are also capable of selectively producing subjective positions that enhance their power in given contexts. These understandings inform this analysis and focus on how discursive and contextual factors shaped the construction of the participants' teacher and sexual subjectivities. It should be noted that to protect anonymity all names are pseudonyms and continuous narratives have been avoided within this chapter and across reports of the study (Ferfolja, 2009; Khayatt, 1992). Additionally, at times, the third-person pronoun is employed in this discussion to further protect participant confidentiality.

## Discussion

### Schools: Acceptance and discrimination

The cultural shift visible through greater social acceptance of sexual diversity was, to a degree, evident in this research. Many of the teachers spoke about how they were content in their workplaces and felt accepted by other staff. For example, one participant stated that colleagues were 'very accepting' which made his workplace experience 'a lot easier ... I mean at the staffroom table people talk about their husbands, their partners, their girlfriends, I talk about my boyfriend, and that's how it is, and everyone accepts that.' Another teacher stated, 'They just sort of caught on and they were fine with it actually.' Similarly one young male teacher indicated that, 'Once I realised that it was safe ... and I wasn't going to be ... disadvantaged by expressing who I was as a person genuinely, then no dramas.' Each teacher's experience was contextually determined and was largely dependent on a range of factors which have been reported elsewhere (see Ferfolja and Hopkins, 2013). Discriminatory practices, however, on an institutional and/or interpersonal level were apparent.

The discussion that follows provides insights into the kinds of discrimination and harassment reported by participants working in religious and then secular state schools. Although not comprehensive due to limitations of space and because this kind of discrimination, as alluded to earlier, is already well reported in the literature, it is critical to record for the following reasons. First, lesbian and gay teachers in the 21st-century Australia are still subject to unequal treatment at work, and homophobic harassment of lesbian and gay teachers is still a reality, despite the nation's generally more progressive stance in relation to sexual diversity. Second, experiences of discrimination (as well as the perceived potential for it to occur) regulate and police the ways in which lesbian and gay teachers perform and position their teacher and sexual subjectivities in relation to each other. How this is enacted is examined later in this chapter.

## Religious schools

Although contextually dependent on the school's administration and attitudes of management, participants who worked in schools with religious affiliations did not always feel comfortable with colleagues or management knowing about their sexuality. As Nathan who had worked in the Catholic system explained:

Largely you had to be silent around it [that is, one's sexuality]...You couldn't refer to it. You couldn't be open about it and you did all those things that closeted people do. You fabricate your social history. 'How was the weekend?' Well, you make it up. You gender-neutral it. Well, at first you just do the straight jump to, you know, change the pronouns to female ones. You do that.

This concealment reflected the fact that schools under the jurisdiction of religious organisations are exempt from NSW anti-discrimination legislation in relation to sexual orientation. Although it is illegal for government schools as public institutions to discriminate on these grounds, schools with religious affiliations are at liberty to do so. At the time of writing, proposed changes to federal anti-discrimination legislation were under debate. The Catholic Church claimed that discrimination on the grounds of sexual orientation is required to avoid 'injury to religious sensitivities' and that maintaining an exemption in anti-discrimination legislation 'would allow the school, in balancing those conflicting rights, to say to that teacher "wouldn't it be better if you found employment somewhere that is more consistent with what your beliefs are"' (ABC News, 2013). There is some irony in this position considering that one in four students who attend Catholic schools identify as non-Catholic, yet are officially enrolled in, and accepted by, this system (National Catholic Education Commission, 2011). Additionally, the continued exemption under the legislation is inexplicable considering that Catholic schools receive the majority of their funding from the government (Gonski, 2011). Hence, the public dollar that supports these institutions by extension indirectly condones the inequities imposed on lesbian and gay employees (and students). Another participant in this study highlighted how he perceived the position towards homosexual teachers in the ethos of the Catholic schools with which he had been affiliated and the apparent conflict and contradictions:

> The church has got this awkward theological stance on homo-sexuality that's nonsense really, where they will argue that being homosexual isn't sinful but homosexual behaviour is sinful. So you know, we support the homosexual but we condemn the behaviour. The behaviour is pretty much anything – anything – that normal human beings would say is expressive of their sexual identity . . . The gay thing sits, theoretically, in with the divorce issue and with other non-approved sexual practices that would be part and parcel of het-erosexual life, but we don't want to police that, we will only police the gay thing. So your gay teacher, we will make all sorts of assumptions about your sexual life that it is in contravention with Catholic teaching and therefore we will discriminate against you, but we won't take the same rubric and impose it on straight people because if you did, do you know what it would look like in an interview? It would look like something like: 'Do you orally pleasure your wife?', 'Do you allow your wife to orally pleasure you?', 'What kind of contracep-tion [do you use]?', 'Are you using artificial means to limit the size of your family?' . . . In terms of discrimination, you can tick the box that you've got a right to discriminate if you consistently apply these rubrics across your school population but you are not consistently applying these rubrics, you are choosing to apply them just on same-sex-attracted people. So if that's your choice then it's homophobia. It is not anything else.

As I have reported elsewhere (Ferfolja and Hopkins, 2013), for the les-bian and gay teachers in this study, experiences with religious-affiliated schools were variable; some participants stated that their sexuality was accepted by their colleagues and some participants claimed otherwise. However, virtually all participants who had worked in a Catholic school highlighted the need to be careful about their sexuality or not being too open about it. Experiences of perceived explicit and implicit dis-crimination were also described. One teacher related a story about a new gay teacher who was reportedly encouraged by his colleagues to invite his same-sex partner into a staff Christmas party, which the next day resulted in the teacher being formally reprimanded by the school principal, who advised him that his partner was not welcome at the school or to social events and that 'this is the only warning; one more warning and you are gone'. Another teacher described how he felt that his sexuality affected his opportunities for employment in a Catholic school in which he had been working on a temporary basis (Ferfolja and Hopkins, 2013):

> So I was there for two terms and I was hoping to extend, to stay over because there was an English position but both myself and my best friend who was also openly gay, they didn't hire any of us.

The exemption from anti-discrimination legislation for religion-affiliated institutions can have severe ramifications for lesbian and gay teachers in terms of acceptance, employment security, equitable practices and career opportunities as demonstrated by these examples. The teachers were aware of the importance of remaining silent about their private life at work, lest it affect their livelihood or career. This is a discriminatory imposition considering the liberties afforded to heterosexual teachers who can freely speak of their family relationships, partners, children, births and upcoming marriages. As Maggie pointed out:

> The things that grab kids often are the anecdotes you throw in, so you know, being very conscious of the gender-neutral language that I use... it is very draining I think and heterosexual teachers, I think, probably are very unaware and ignorant of how often they refer to their husbands and wives, you know, without giving it a moment's thought.

The normalisation of heterosexuality enables these relationships to be celebrated yet afforded private space with 'a right to more discretion' (Foucault, [1978] 1998, p. 38). Lesbian and gay individuals on the other hand, although silenced, remain as Foucault ([1978] 1998) highlights, marked, spoken about, regulated, under surveillance and marginalised (Chapter 7). Problematically, in religious schools in NSW, this discursive position as 'Other' and its attendant discrimination are reinforced by inequitable government legislation. This legislation permits the disciplining of subjects who transgress normative practices (Foucault, [1977] 1991), rewarding religious institutions and the discourses they perpetuate about sexuality difference, through state-condoned permission to discriminate.

## State schools

Despite the fact that NSW public schools are required to abide by the NSW Anti-Discrimination Act, which critically provides lesbian and gay teachers with security in their employment, the participants who worked in these institutions also spoke of experiencing various forms of homophobic discrimination from management, parents, other teachers and students, which occurred in explicit and implicit ways. Several teachers reported being targeted for derogatory comments by students 'in the playground' where 'kids [were] saying things behind me', and being 'called names in the class by students who I have had to remove'. Another participant communicated how students had identified a new teacher as gay when they located his Facebook page. The students' parents 'printed things out, brought it to school and said, "Look, this guy is this and he likes men with no shirts."...The parents tried to use it against him...Some parents requested their kids move [class].' Another reported how the threat of parental wrath was used by one student in an attempt to manipulate a male teacher into not reporting his misbehaviour to his father. It is interesting to note that even youth who have known an Australian society in the main legally protective and to an extent culturally 'accepting' of sexual difference are aware of the apparent 'abnormality' of lesbian and gay teachers and that this subjective position can be a site for violence, surveillance, regulation and coercion.

One young female participant, Casey, spoke of the ongoing harassment and ridicule that she experienced from students in a government high school:

> I had horrible times with my Year 10[2] kids. I actually had a lesson where I had to go and get my headteacher and leave the room because I just had a complete breakdown. I've never had that happen and that was because this girl told me that all gay people should be taken to the village square and hung. Then these other boys went on this big rant about how all fags and dykes should burn in hell. Oh my God, I lost it. It was like a pack. There was [sic] like five massive Year 10 boys all hovering over me and I just lost it.

This harassment by adolescents illustrated how homophobic discourse prevails in the lives of Australian school students who were aware of its power to intimidate and offend. It also demonstrated how homophobic language and sentiment can be used to undermine the institutional power inherent in the teacher subject, particularly when coupled with male physicality and mob mentality that threatens bodily violence. However, there is some irony in the students' selected modes of hypothetical punishment for 'fags and dykes' which, reflecting their outmoded attitudes, drew on archaic practices of civic shaming, public execution and religious discourses that condemn evil-doers to a fate of suffering in an eternal fire. Yet, despite the students' malevolence, when Casey reported to school executives another instance of homophobic abuse from students, the executive staff stated, 'We don't know where this is coming from because we don't have kids like that here.' Critically, even though she was pathologised as 'the problem' by their response (or lack thereof), Casey was aware of how homophobia is often normalised in schools to the extent that it is not seen. As she pointed out:

> But the problem is that people just don't believe you a lot of the time and they sort of just try and make it out like it is just your perception, the way that you are seeing things. I think – no, you're just so used to seeing it that you don't pick up on it.

This failure to 'see' is a result of the heteronormativity that operates in schools. Sexual minorities have been historically derided, and these discourses of derision are deeply ingrained in schooling cultures. Additionally, lesbian and gay teachers, as sexual subjects, have witnessed and experienced institutional and interpersonal discrimination, brutality and violence towards their communities; they have had their sexualities declared illegal or non-existent and they have been gaoled (Carbery, 1995). Heterosexuals, particularly those who are White and middle class, have experienced histories of power and privilege by comparison; as a result they may have little, if any, understanding of the symbolic scars that many lesbian and gay people carry and thus may be oblivious to the power of student harassment. After all, within the adult/child and teacher/student cultural binaries, teachers are discursively associated with power and authority. Students, on the other hand, are constructed as relatively powerless minors, in line with socially constructed understandings of childhood. Hence, homophobic student behaviours, if acknowledged by management, may be disregarded within discourses of the innocent child who is yet to 'grow up' and who is simultaneously perceived to be developmentally unaware of the impact of their language and behaviour on others.

Other participants also reported witnessing homophobia through silences and a lack of action by executive. James stated:

> I was in the staffroom and these fellows walked past and said the word 'faggot'!... I thought I've never heard that word for years! And I looked around at the headteacher and I said what are you going to do about that?... And he stopped. And he looked at me. And

he thought for about three seconds and then spun around and did nothing. And said nothing... That is what goes on in schools!

The intentions of silence are multiple (Cheung, 1993); however, as Foucault ([1978] 1998, p. 27) points out, silence 'is an element that functions alongside the things said, with them and in relation to them within over-all strategies'. Thus, by not responding, James' headteacher condoned the homophobic language being used by the student. Such language is constitutive of the discourses that circulate in society and in the micro-cultures of schooling and may problematically become the spaces in which subjects locate themselves and others.

### Negotiating complex workplaces

Despite experiencing homophobia, the teachers did not position themselves as 'victims' (Appleby, 1996); rather, they discursively positioned their teacher and sexual subjectivities in ways that aligned them with their colleagues, students, parents and/or institution. Although this reshaping at times involved technologies of the self (Foucault, [1977] 1991) through self-surveillance and self-management, these participants were productive in the construction of their subjectivities. They strategically and discursively positioned themselves in ways that responded to their professional context and enhanced possibilities of realising a safe, meaningful and fulfilling identity in the workplace.

This was achieved by drawing on dominant discourses of femininity and masculinity to forefront socially acceptable aspects of their subjectivity; positioning their subjectivity in (hetero)normalising ways, particularly regarding family and relationships; and positioning themselves in contextually powerful subjectivities within the workplace context such as being 'professional' and a 'teacher'.

### Gendered discourse

Experiences of homophobia and acceptance intersected and were, at times, simultaneous. Jake, who self-described as a queer activist, discussed his anxiety of being 'outed' because of the potential loss of credibility he thought he would suffer and the possible demise of the positive, professional relationships with the boys he taught. In the eyes of the majority of his male students, he was heterosexual, and Jake utilised this performance to maintain his relationships and authority as a teacher. He stated:

I'd definitely lose a lot of credibility with certain groups within the school... especially the boys... which is weird because like in my real life I don't care about... being accepted by boys, you know, I don't really... and I don't hang around straight men that are blokey or anything like that. But at school, it is like it is all these different sorts of standards of how things work. So I think a lot of the boys will feel like they can't joke around with me the same way or [participate in] the same banter with me in the classroom, if I was out.

Banter is used to engender camaraderie, particularly in relationships between males (Martino and Pallotta-Chiarolli, 2003). Although Jake does not engage in this kind of behaviour away from work, which he refers to as his 'real life', as he states, in the school context there are 'all these different sorts of standards of how things work'. The general presumption of heterosexuality provided him with a means to be accepted by the (male) students, enhancing his ability to bond with, and by extension engaging, these same students in the classroom. Jake's (assumed) heterosexuality fed the enactment of a stable and appropriately performed masculine gendered subjectivity (Butler, 1990). Destabilisation of his (assumed) heterosexuality would result in a questioning of his gender and a breakdown of his relationship and camaraderie with other males. With a different group of students at the same school, most of whom identified as queer and queer-friendly, and whom he had told he was gay, Jake was able to perform a different kind of masculinity and sexuality. As he stated:

One of [my students] asked me in the class, 'Why do you care about this [gay issues] so much?'... It was a girl with two mums. And I said, 'oh, because I am'. She said, 'Oh really, oh my God'. And they all started – 'Oh my God. It's amazing.' And then, um, see now obviously whenever I walk around the playground [the LGBTQ students] are all... coming up to me and telling me about their boyfriends and girlfriends... It has changed how they see me and what they can say to me.

Subjectivity is fluid, contextual and contradictory (Weedon, 1987), as demonstrated in Jake's narrative. On one level, Jake is anxious about how homophobia may mark him, and regulated his behaviour by agentically performing a heterosexualised masculinity in a particular context. In another context, with supportive students, he was the 'gay teacher'. This discursive shifting is a powerful position to hold and enabled Jake to operate in an unpredictable, changing and, at times, homophobic environment. This did come at a personal cost, however, as he pointed out:

> I almost see it like a performance basically. When I get on the train and I see my first student, there is a performance... I am not being myself, but I am modifying who I am.

Although it is true that if the student culture were different Jake may not have needed to perform his subjectivity in this way, this tension of 'modifying who I am' reflected his conscious decision to regulate his subjectivity in his workplace context to actively shift between discursive locations for maximum benefit. Another teacher, Barry, also highlighted the degree to which one regulates one's behaviour stating, 'It's an act, and you just sort of role-play that in the classroom.' He pointed out how these shifting performances and their repetition become ingrained in the teacher body, to the extent that they become part of who one is, where 'you sort of take it as part of your life'.

### (Hetero)normalisation

Several participants discussed how they consciously positioned their sexual subjectivities within normative frameworks. This was achieved by paralleling one's life to, and positioning one's relationships within, dominant heterosexual narratives. Clare, who worked in an executive role, explained how she made strategic decisions that gave credibility to her lesbian relationship through processes of normalisation:

> Everyone on my staff knows that I am a dyke. They all know that I am in a permanent relationship. Many people have met my part-ner... But I also think that I've structured some situations that might make it more comfortable, for instance, my staff have a thing of going away together with (their) families... And so I decided to join [them] and my partner and I decided we would take nieces and nephews and that would then present – it was quite strategic – that I could go and it would be normalising, but there I was with fam-ily... I think it was educative for people. It was like, 'Oh they're really normal; they're fun'.

In this way Clare enhanced her power within the school. She was not seen only as a 'sexualised being', which is the main lens through which many perceive and judge individuals who are lesbian or gay. As Kehily and Montgomery (2009, p. 85) state, 'In the modern era discourses of sexuality offer a complex means of policing the person, whereby individuals can be defined by their sexual activity rather than by any other aspect of their lives.' Although Clare's colleagues had met her partner, socialising with the two women and their extended family evidenced how their relationship transcended 'the bedroom'; they were re/positioned into the palatable, recognisable and safe discourse of family. This location enabled them to be read as 'fun' rather than weird, perverted or an abomination. The dominant discourse of family in Western society constructs it as a place of caring, nurturing and safety: as a stable, productive unit that forms a basis for society. Locating herself within and being positioned within the discourse of family was a measured strategy that enabled Clare to highlight to her colleagues her 'normality' by forefronting a commonly held positionality that is socially esteemed and celebrated. Locating herself within this heterosexual narrative illustrated her agency and power in her self-construction as a lesbian teacher. As Clare pointed out, this was 'educative' in its ability to diminish stereotypes and misconceptions about lesbian teachers and lesbians more generally.

Another teacher, Patrick, also related how he had made an active decision to share information on his relationship status with colleagues but only when it became socially acceptable, that is, normalised in terms of dominant traditional heterosexual discourses of commitment in relationships:

> [My sexuality] is just one aspect of who I am. And ... in the past I have had open relationships with people ... and I never felt this sense of I will be accepted like, because you know, the kids will ask, teachers will ask about relationships and stuff like that and I feel like people would see that sort of [open] relationship as less than what they have. So this year I am in a monogamous relationship and in some ways that also made me feel more comfortable to say, 'Yes, I have a partner, yes, I want to get married', stuff like that. Which is really in some ways silly but that is just the way it is, because I have conformed to this societal expectation of a relationship I have now got some sort of different confidence to say, 'Yeah', to come out and to try to be accepted or whatever. It is really weird.

Being in a committed relationship legitimated and made safe in Patrick's eyes the sharing of his personal life with his workplace colleagues.

Positioning his relationship in terms of the heterosexual narrative of finding a lifelong match that conforms to the social mores of monogamy, fidelity and marriage aligned his subjectivity as a gay man with his heterosexual counterparts. Like Clare, this process of heteronormalisation afforded him greater credibility and, by extension, confidence within the workplace context. Had he revealed his previous 'open relationships', he was aware that he risked being re-inscribed in discourses that position gay men as hypersexual, 'recruiters', emotionally unstable and unable to commit. However, he agentically connected with heteronormative discourses for a calculated benefit. He did not hide his sexuality; rather, he constructed his sexual subjectivity by selectively releasing information to his colleagues that positioned him in a more powerful position in the workplace context, where his gay relationship could be recognised and celebrated.

### Forefronting contextually powerful subjectivities

Another way that participants negotiated the intersections of their sexual and teacher subjectivities was by focusing on aspects of their professional role. This enabled them to comfortably silence their sexual subjectivity, particularly when dealing with students and their caregivers/families. As one participant explained:

> Yeah, and curiously, I am not uncomfortable with it; as I said I am out and not out. I don't publicise it, but I am not uncomfortable... Principals don't have sexuality. It's a position; you have responsibility, not sexuality.

The apparent asexuality of the teacher has been traditionally regulated and enshrined in discourses of morality and model citizenry. As individuals who are *in loco parentis* (Khayatt, 1992), they are deemed to have responsibility and rights over students in lieu of their parents' presence. Thus, as a principal this participant bore considerable responsibility for school organisational processes and student well-being, and this was the significant discourse in which they were positioned as a visible leader in a school. The principal was able to forefront this aspect of their subjectivity, which was a particularly powerful position within that professional context, rather than having their sexuality being the focus.

Participants who were classroom teachers commonly undertook a similar strategy around the intersection of their sexual and teacher subjectivities. When positioning themselves in the workplace context, they chiefly highlighted that aspect of their subjectivity that reflected their professional role as 'teacher' or subject specialist, with comments such as 'There is a place for every issue and you know you can't be political about it because *as a teacher* it is not my place'; '*As a teacher* I am quite happy with the attitudes of my colleagues, with being able to maintain a professional personal life balance or separation in the classroom'; and 'I am not saying [to students who ask], "no I am not gay," which I did say once at my last school ... And there is a point, this is my private life, *this is English, let's talk about English*' (emphases added). These positionings of the gay/lesbian teacher body as apolitical, separated from the political public sphere, and disconnected from the scholarly operations of the classroom enabled the participants to actively locate their subjectivities in ways recognised by, and acceptable to (heterosexual) colleagues and the (heteronormative) institution of schooling. Obviously, all sexual subjectivities are political, and sexualities pervade classrooms and playgrounds (Britzman, 1997). For teacher subjects, it is only those whose sexualities that are marked, that is, those who are not heterosexual, who are required to become disembodied. What is critical to this discussion is that the self-positioning within the professional discourse of 'teacher' reflected the participants' active and conscious negotiations of their sexual subjectivities in the workplace; as *teacher*, they were able to demonstrate considerable power within their own institution.

## Conclusion

This chapter has illustrated that lesbian and gay teachers 'work' and are 'working in' the margins; as such, they negotiate their sexualities in relation to their teacher subjectivity. Their stories and experiences revealed some of the ways that they accommodated and resisted the persistent heteronormative and heterosexist nature of schools, creating spaces in which they could comfortably operate in their employment. Regulation of speech and the construction of particular gendered/sexual performances enabled them to actively forefront aspects of their subjectivities that aligned them with their professional duties and/or with acceptable and normalising heterosexual narratives. Knowledge of the potential for both institutional and interpersonal discrimination compelled them to consciously work the margins in which they were discursively located as a result of their sexual subjectivities – work not required of heterosexual colleagues. It is time that schools not only as educational institutions but, critically, as workplaces create equitable employment conditions by proactively addressing the ongoing discrimination and inequities that many lesbian and gay teachers encounter in their profession.

## Acknowledgements

I would like to thank the University of Western Sydney for funding this study and Dr. Lucy Hopkins, who worked with me on this project. I am also grateful to the participants who gave freely of their time and their stories to make this research possible.

## Notes

1. School education in Australia is largely funded and regulated by the state or territory government in which it is located. Government (or public) schools, which enrol approximately two-thirds of the school-age population, offer free education. Catholic schools operated by the local parish, diocese or Catholic state department, as well as independent schools, generally charge students to attend (in addition to receiving government funding). All schools are expected to observe the same curriculum framework as articulated by their state or territory; however, flexibility within the documentation allows for various approaches and perspectives to be implemented.
2. In Australia, 'Year 10' is in principle the tenth (and final) year of compulsory education, with pupils aged 14–16.

## References

ABC News (2013). Catholic bishops defend right to discriminate, 24 January, http://www.abc.net.au/news/2013-01-24/catholic-bishops-defend-right-to dis-criminate/4482732 (Accessed 16 July 2013).

Appleby, Y. (1996) ' "Decidedly different": Lesbian women and education', *International Studies in Sociology of Education*, 6(1), 67–86.

Atkinson, R. and DePalma, R. (2008) 'Imagining the homonormative: Performative subversion in education for social justice', *British Journal of Sociology of Education*, 29(1), 25–35.

Britzman, D. P. (1997) 'What is this thing called love? New discourses for under-standing gay and lesbian youth', in S. de Castell and M. Bryson (eds.) *Radical interventions* (Albany, NY: SUNY Press).

Butler, J. (1990) *Gender trouble. Feminism and the subversion of identity* (New York: Routledge).

Callaghan, T. (2007) *That's so gay* (Saarbrücken, Germany: VDM Verlag).

Carbery, G. (1995) *A history of the Sydney gay and lesbian Mardi Gras* (Parkville, VIC: Australian Lesbian and Gay Archives).

Cheung, K. K. (1993) *Articulate silences: Hisaye Yamamoto, Maxine Hong Kingston, Joy Kogawa* (New York and London: Cornell University Press).

Elia, J. P. and Eliason, M. (2010) 'Discourses of exclusion: Sexuality education's silencing of sexual others', *Journal of LGBT Youth*, 7(1), 29–48.

Epstein, D. and Johnson, R. (1998) *Schooling sexualities* (Buckingham: Open University Press).

Ezzy, D. (2002) *Qualitative analysis. Practice and innovation* (Crows Nest, NSW: Allen and Unwin).

Ferfolja, T. (2009) 'Lesbian teachers, harassment and the workplace', *Teaching and Teacher Education*, 26(3), 408–14.

Ferfolja, T. (2013) 'Sexual diversity, discrimination and "homosexuality policy" in New South Wales' government schools', *Sex Education*, 13(2), 159–71.

Ferfolja, T. and Hopkins, L. (2013) 'The complexities of workplace experience for lesbian and gay teachers', *Critical Studies in Education*, doi:10.1080/17508487.2013.794743.

Foucault, M. ([1978] 1998) *The will to knowledge. The history of sexuality. Volume 1: An introduction* (New York: Vintage Books).

Foucault, M. ([1977]1991) *Discipline and punish: The birth of the prison* (London: Penguin Books).

Gonski, D. (2011). *Review of funding for schooling – Final report* (Canberra: Australian Government.

Graydon, M. (2011) ' "Kids not rights, is their craving": Sex education, gay rights and the threat of gay teachers', *Canadian Review of Sociology*, 48(3), 313–39.

Giuffre, P., Dellinger, K. and Williams, C. L. (2008) ' "No retribution for being gay?" Inequality in gay friendly workplaces', *Sociological Spectrum*, 28, 254–77.

Hillier, L., Jones, T., Monagle, M., Overton, N., Gahan, L., Blackman, J. and Mitchell, A. (2010) *Writing themselves in 3: The third national report on the sexuality, health and well-being of same sex attracted young people* (Melbourne, VIC: Australian Research Centre in Sex, Health and Society, La Trobe University).

Hillier, L. and Mitchell, A. (2008) ' "It was as useful as a chocolate kettle": Sex education in the lives of same-sex-attracted young people in Australia', *Sex Education*, 8(2), 211–24.

Hohnke, M. and O'Brien, P. (2008) 'Discrimination against same sex attracted youth: The role of the school counselor', *Australian Journal of Guidance and Counselling*, 18(1), 67–75.

Holmes, J. (2001) ' "If there was any hint": An analysis of the perceptions that lesbian and gay educators have of teacher sexuality and education', *Leading and Managing*, 7(1), 61–75.

Jackson, J. M. (2006) 'Removing the masks: Considerations by gay and lesbian teachers when negotiating the closet door', *Journal of Poverty*, 10(2), 27–52.

Kehily, M. J. and Montgomery, H. (2009) 'Innocence and experience', in M. J. Kehily (ed.) *An introduction to childhood studies* (Maidenhead, UK: Open University Press).

Khayatt, M. D. (1992) *Lesbian teachers. An invisible presence* (Albany, NY: SUNY Press).

Kvale, S. (1996) *Interviews: An introduction to qualitative research interviewing* (Thousand Oaks, CA: Sage).

Martino, W. and Cumming-Potvin, W. (2011) ' "They didn't have out there gay parents – They just looked like normal regular parents": Investigating teachers' approaches to addressing same-sex parenting and non-normative sexuality in the elementary school classroom', *Curriculum Inquiry*, 41(4), 481–501.

Martino, W. and Pallotta-Chiarolli, M. (2003) *So what's a boy? Addressing issues of masculinity and schooling* (Maidenhead, UK: Open University Press).

McKenzie-Bassant, C. (2007) 'Lesbian teachers walking the line between inclusion and exposure', *JADE*, 26(1), 54–62.

Meyer, E. J. (2009) *Gender, bullying and harassment. Strategies to end sexism and homophobia in schools* (New York: Teachers College Press).

Michaelson, M. T. (2008) 'Inclusion and social justice for gay, lesbian, bisexual, and transgender members of the learning community in Queensland state schools', *Australian Journal of Guidance and Counselling*, 18(1), 76–83.

National Catholic Education Commission (2011). *Australian Catholic Schools 2011*, http://www.ncec.catholic.edu.au/index.php?option=com_docman& task=cat_view&gid=41&Itemid=53 (Accessed 16 July 2013).

Richardson, P. W. and Watt, H. M. G. (2006) 'Who chooses teaching and why? Profiling characteristics and motivations across three Australian universities', *Asia-Pacific Journal of Teacher Education*, 34(1), 27–56.

Robinson, K. H. and Jones Diaz, C. (2006) *Diversity and difference in early childhood* (Maidenhead, UK: Open University Press).

Rudoe, N. (2010) 'Lesbian teachers' identity, power and the public/private boundary', *Sex Education*, 10(1), 23–36.

Saldana, J. (2009) *The coding manual for qualitative researchers* (Phoenix, AZ: Sage).

Weedon, C. (1987) *Feminist practice and poststructuralist theory* (Oxford: Blackwell).

Williams, C. and Giuffre P. (2011) 'From organizational sexuality to queer organizations: Research on homosexuality and the workplace', *Sociology Compass*, 5(7), 551–63.

Willingham, R. (2013) 'Katter party hopeful in gay furore', *Age*, http://www. theage.com.au/opinion/political-news/katter-party-hopeful-in-gay-furore-20130123-2d75p.html (Accessed 16 July 2013).

Willis, P. (2011) 'Laboring in silence: Young lesbian, gay, bisexual, and queer-identifying workers' negotiations of the workplace closet in Australian organizations', *Youth and Society*, 43(3), 957–81.

# 9
# Making Sense of Their Career Pathways: The Work Narratives of Women Primary School Principals in Hong Kong

*Anita K. W. Chan*

## Introduction

The under-representation of women school leaders has been an important concern in the field of educational management and leadership. The traditional focus (Hoyle, 1969; Lortie, 1969; Tropp, 1959) tends to blame women's deficiencies and orientation for this under-representation. Women are said to lack confidence, self-esteem, role models, aspiration and career planning as well as to be more family than career oriented and to prefer teaching and interacting with children to leading and managing (see also Chapter 3 and Chapter 6).

However, a critical examination of the practices of school organisations and of societal norms and values indicates that the barriers are not a problem inherent to women, but are structural, cultural and subtle (Bell and Chase, 1995; Boulton and Coldron, 1998; Kruger, 1996; Limerick and Lingard, 1995; Ozga, 1993; Shakeshaft, 1987). When gender norms in society prescribe different, and often 'inferior', roles to women, these shape not only their career orientations but also the ways schools are organised and the social perception of leadership. As women are usually seen as emotional, nurturing, collaborative, dependent and family based, they are more often assigned pastoral duties, which are often perceived as requiring low levels of commitment and competence, and risk receiving negative evaluations, resistance and even hostility when they aspire to leadership positions (Chan, 2011; Coleman, 2002; Cubillo and Brown, 2003; Fennell, 2008; McLay, 2008; Stufft and Coyne, 2009). Sexism tends to prevail when the school management or selection committee is dominated by men, who are more likely to hire and promote other men who look, think and act like them (Cushman, 2008; Shakeshaft, 2006; Smulyan, 2000a). Moreover, organisational norms and practices that appear to be gender-neutral actually privilege male experience and career trajectories. For instance, promotion practices that are based on seniority tend to favour men rather than women. As men are more likely to have linear and continuous career paths, whereas women are more likely to discontinue their teaching job, shift to part-time employment or take career breaks in order to accommodate family responsibilities, the latter are disadvantaged by the criterion of 'seniority' (Evetts, 1994; Sperandio, 2010). Furthermore, the images, qualities, expectations and characteristics associated with leadership seem to favour men and masculinity. As strong and competent school leaders are usually expected to be goal oriented, instrumental, competitive, assertive and totally committed to their work, these stereotypes devalue qualities associated with femininity and easily marginalise those who have family responsibilities (Blackmore, 1999; Chisholm, 2001; Deem, 2003; Grogan, 1999; Mahony et al., 2004; Smulyan, 2000a).

Studies of this kind have successfully revealed various institutional, organisational, cultural and discursive impediments that have enhanced our understanding of the difficulties women may experience when aspiring to a career in education. The usefulness of such studies notwithstanding, scholars also see the need to explore the rise of women leaders in given educational systems, an emerging phenomenon in the 1990s, and assess the extent to which gender equality has been achieved. Some studies have in fact identified different factors and expressed mixed views of the rise of women leaders. In countries such as England, Israel, Norway, Singapore, South Africa and Sweden, the rise has been attributed to the introduction of gender equity policies, the expansion of schools and positions of leadership, the practice of a centralised, meritocratic promotion system or a change of career strategies among women principals (see Chisholm, 2001; Davis and Johansson, 2005; Evetts, 1994; Moller; 2005; Morriss et al., 1999). In the case of Israel, the increase was somewhat linked to the exit of male principals, the steady erosion of the occupational prestige of all educational professions and the improved educational attainment levels of women (Goldring and Chen, 1994). In Singapore, Luke's study (1998) on the improved situation of women in the school workforce has usefully widened the focus from facilitators and barriers to women's work narratives. Her interviews with female administrators in higher education have illustrated how the codes of feminine propriety and filial responsibility, the 'politics of face' and an ethos of patronage have continued to constrain the life experiences of accomplished women.

Many other studies have expressed interest in the work narratives of accomplished women or women leaders, in particular whether and how they have downplayed or are unwilling to articulate gender problems in their narratives. For instance, studies in the UK and the United States note that women principals and administrators tend to regard hard work as the most important determinant of success and believe in using individual efforts to succeed (Coleman, 2002, 2007; Hoff and Mitchell, 2008). Studies in Australia, Canada and Norway also find that it is increasingly common for young educated women leaders to believe that gender equality has been achieved and subscribe to the 'professional success script' – a discourse that celebrates hard work, merit and professionalism (Blackmore, 2002; Moller, 2005; Reynolds, 2002). Local studies have also found that educated and professional women do not complain of a patriarchal structure or culture hindering their career progress (Lam, 2004; Luke, 2004). Where they did report gender discrimination, it was seen as something to work around rather than something that could be changed (Ford, 2007). Because of their acceptance of the ideologies of meritocratic equality and individualism, educated women believed they could succeed, even if it meant working harder than their male counterparts (Lee, 2003).

This chapter hopes to contribute to the current discussion by examining the career pathways of eight female principals in Hong Kong – a place where a steady rise of women leaders has been noted in primary schools in the past decade. The chapter will explore in particular the ways in which women make sense of their career development, the qualities and strategies they regard as important, whether and what costs they may have to bear when aspiring to become school leaders and the extent to which gender equality is achieved in Hong Kong. Before the discussions, further details on the contextual background and methodology will be provided.

## Gender equality in Hong Kong

Hong Kong used to be a patriarchal Confucian society which placed lower value on girls than on boys. While Chinese society had a high regard for education, daughters, especially elder daughters, were expected to sacrifice their own schooling to support their brothers' study or make financial contributions to their families (Salaff, 1995).

However, women's social status has changed significantly in recent decades. According to the 2011 population census, the percentages of women aged 50–54 and 20–24 who received no education or only primary education were 41 per cent and 2 per cent, respectively. Almost 40 per cent of women in the latter age group had received a tertiary education (Hong Kong Census and Statistics Department, 2011). Where primary school teaching is concerned, significant improvements were also observed. Primary school teaching was once a male-dominated occupation but, since 1950, has become dominated by women (Chan, 2012). The percentage of female teachers rose steadily over the years and stabilised at 78.6 per cent in 2011 (Education and Manpower Bureau, 2011–2012). More importantly, the male-dominated teaching hierarchy was transformed in the past decade too, as the number of female principals in primary schools rose. The percentage of female principals has risen from 29.4 per cent in 1991–1992 to 50.6 per cent in 2003–2004, and to 61.8 per cent in 2011–2012 (Education and Manpower Bureau, 1991–1992, 2003–2004, 2011–2012). However, the Hong Kong government, colonial and post-colonial, has not played an active role in promoting gender equity. Instead, it has tended to regard matters related to women as family concerns, relegated these to the private sphere and encouraged traditional Chinese familism to help meet the needs and welfare of family members (Lee, 2003; Pearson and Leung, 1995).

As already discussed elsewhere (see Chan et al., forthcoming), in the absence of gender equity policies, the expansion of career opportunities in Hong Kong's primary school teaching was more a product of historical contingencies and political uncertainties, and women's access to leadership positions was made possible by the strong cultural values placed on, and women's active pursuit of, education, and by encouragement and (partial) support received from senior colleagues, family members and waged household workers. In other words, where facilitators existed, they were incidental, informal, familial and personal, and women received little institutional support in their career development. That said, it remains to be seen how women make sense of their career progression, especially the strategies and gendered discourses that they have employed to develop or make sense of their careers, and whether and how gender relations are becoming more equal. It was against this background that I chose to explore the work narratives of women principals in Hong Kong.

## Methodology

This chapter is based on the experiences of eight women who are part of a wider research project that examines the life histories of primary school principals in Hong Kong.[1] We purposely looked for experienced and successful female primary principals with more than 5 years of headship experience and whose schools have been commended by the Education Bureau as excellent/high-quality primary schools or who have earned a good reputation in the primary sector.[2] The eight women principals interviewed are all ethnically Chinese and grew up in Hong Kong. When the first interviews were conducted in 2010, their ages ranged from 46 to 59. Six were married, one was divorced and one remained single. Seven were mothers; they had 14 children between them, the youngest of whom was 16. Their experience as a principal ranged from 9 to 24 years, while the youngest age at which they became school head was 34, the oldest was 46, and on average it took almost 16 years for them to become principal.

We adopted a life history approach by asking questions on their biography, career trajectory, leadership practices and work–life balance. The interviews were less to collect facts and evidence than to link their present to their past, their meaning-making processes to the social and cultural frameworks within which they live and work and their activities and lived experiences to the changing historical, institutional and social contexts (Fennell, 2008; Goodson and Sikes, 2001; Reynolds, 2002; Smulyan, 2000b). Each woman was interviewed at least twice. The interviews were conducted in their offices or meeting rooms and tape-recorded with their consent. The recordings were later transcribed and translated. We employed a qualitative data analysis software package (NVivo) for coding and analysis.

As our focus is on work narratives, we found particularly useful the ideas proposed by Catherine Risessman (1993, 2002) and Susan Chase (1995, 2005). Narratives, as they propose, are acts of storytelling which do not mirror a world out there and convey self-evident meanings. Instead, we are reminded that 'storytellers make use of available resources to construct recognizable selves; how they make sense of personal experience in relation to culturally and historically specific discourses; and how they draw on, resist and/or transform those discourses as they narrate their selves, experiences and realities' (Chase, 2005, p. 659). In other words, by examining narratives as the negotiation and construction of preferred (gendered) selves against the existence of culturally and historically specific discourses, we will gauge whether and how the culture in Hong Kong of primary teaching constrains and shapes women principals' self-understanding and how they struggle against and mediate those constraints. These will be the foci of the following analyses.

## Work narratives of women principals in Hong Kong

The work narratives of these eight principals[3] presented us with a common conundrum: while they admitted experiencing unequal treatment related to gender during childhood, they reported no discrimination at work. Growing up in the 1950s and 1960s, almost all our women principals stated that their families were patriarchal or sexist as their fathers enjoyed a greater say and higher status and sons had more resources and educational opportunities than daughters. Some even recalled how they had to cut short their schooling or turn to primary teaching to contribute financially to their families or to their brothers' education. Nevertheless, while one would assume women who entered primary school teaching and developed their careers in the 1980s and 1990s – when male domination was still the norm – would be equally aware of gender inequalities, only a few women from that generation mentioned 'gender practices' in the workplace, including the impression that 'principalship was a male territory' (Carina Lo, Hannah Ho and Alice Fung), that 'an old boy network existed' (Carina Lo and Hannah Ho), that there was a preference for men over women teachers (Carina Lo and Alice Fung) and that male physical education (PE) teachers enjoyed advantages in obtaining promotion (Carina Lo). However, these women were also quick to point out that gender inequalities were 'a thing of the past', as if gender was no longer an issue.

Furthermore, while our women principals have successfully crafted careers in primary teaching, they professed no interest in promotion or planning to reach their headship position, and thus denied devising any active or conscious career strategy. Though most agreed on the importance of hard work, they did not seem to use the discourses of meritocracy or individualism to construct their stories or selves. Nevertheless, as we are going to show, the women's narratives on their career progression, promotion and work–family balance are clearly gendered, and the discourses which are institutionally and culturally available for women principals in Hong Kong remain very limited and constraining.

### No planning, but dutiful, diligent and modest

It has been found that women usually stay away from school administration because they prefer teaching and find more satisfaction in interacting with children (Bell and Chase, 1995; Blackmore, 1999; Young and McLeod, 2001). Those who entered administration often saw their career progression as unplanned and 'unexpected' (Coleman, 2002), they felt that it 'just sort of evolved' (Young and McLeod, 2001), that they were 'pushed into' (Smulyan, 2000b), or 'tapped on the shoulders' (Young and McLeod, 2001). Such narratives could easily be treated as signs of a lack of confidence or aspiration, and therefore as signs of the personal barriers inherent to women teachers. However, feminists suggest that women's career progression narratives should be linked to the gender scripts which prevail in a specific societal context and to the way individual women perform gender. For instance, when women present themselves as lacking control or planning in their career progression, this presentation could be their way of maintaining traditional feminine norms – modesty and denial of ambition, the socially acceptable traits for women (Bloom and Munro, 1995; Hoff and Mitchell, 2008; Reynolds, 2002; Skrla, 1999; Young and McLeod, 2001). Indeed, desirable traits of Chinese femininity, such as obedience, diligence and teachability, can be detected when the narratives of our women principals are placed under closer scrutiny.

Several principals have described themselves as 'obedient and follow[ing] the rules of the church leaders' (Alice Fung), 'submissive and never argu[ing] with people' (Bonnie Chu) and 'obedient and non-confrontational' (Diana Yuen). However, the self-portrayal of Hannah Ho was slightly different. Her promotion was considered fast as she became Assistant Mistress (a senior administrative position, AM hereafter) 5 years after becoming a teacher. Part of the reason was because she entered a newly established school, where the chances of promotion were greater; she was also rewarded for her good performance. When evaluating her smooth career progression, Hannah made the following assertions:

> I think I am very teachable and very willing to learn. I was not bright, but very willing to work hard. I diligently did what I was assigned, so my former head kept supporting me...I was very lucky, very lucky indeed. He also saw my potential in recital and assigned me to lead students for the recital competition. We won some prizes, and because of these, I was promoted rather early...He was a principal with vision and I learned a lot from him. He is really my mentor...I still followed him closely after I became a principal. When a new policy came, I always consulted him first. If he said no to it, I would say no too. If he told me to do it, I would dutifully say yes.

It is undeniable that her former head provided important mentoring and greatly aided her career development. Nevertheless, what also clearly emerged in Hannah's narrative was her self-portrayal as a teachable teacher, willing to learn, work hard and, not least, diligently carry out the duties assigned by her mentor. Yet, her 'teachability' is not gender-neutral; it clearly comprises of feminine qualities such as diligence, obedience and modesty. Hannah did not just follow the guidance of her mentor when she was a teacher; she continued to do so when she became a principal. Her accounts of the mentor-mentee relationship are very similar to the discourse of 'the dutiful daughters' as narrated by women principals in post-war Canada (Reynolds, 2002): both reported diligently accepting the rule and guidance of strong but caring 'fathers' within the system. We are not suggesting that Hannah *consciously* performed the role of dutiful daughter in order to be mentored, but it seems possible that her diligent, agreeable and submissive character might have enabled her to get help at work and explains why she believed being a woman could be an advantage in Hong Kong:

> Honestly, I think being a woman can be advantageous. Women give people an impression that they need protection. Most of the time, the men I know would tell themselves, 'I need to protect women'. I don't know how true this is [elsewhere], but at least in Hong Kong, I think my observation is quite true.

Unlike Hannah, who repeatedly described herself as 'not smart but diligent', 'obedient and willing to learn', Fiona Lee appeared to be a confident principal in our interviews. Fiona had an exceptionally good memory and could recall the names of her students and colleagues and many other details. When asked about her career progression, she was initially very upbeat about her job performance and shared stories about how good she was at organising school activities and managing students of different backgrounds. However, as she continued, the emphasis of her narrative changed:

> About my promotion, yes, some colleagues actually thought my promotion came rather early, as it only took me 12 years to become AM. I actually felt that I deserved promotion, as I *did not disappoint anyone* in those years; I have never failed in my responsibility as a teacher. I was very good at disciplining students, no matter what their background was... At that time, my principal knew that I was very *hard-working*, so one day he told me to develop a school bulletin

and asked me to take charge of this. He knew that I would *never say no to him*, and every time he gave me an idea, I would help him develop it into an action plan. Even though I was just a junior AM, he trusted me.

(emphasis added)

Fiona did not just present herself as a competent teacher, but she also described herself diligent and *agreeable*, as she did not disappoint anyone and never said no to her boss. If Hannah diligently accepted the instructions of her mentor and won his guidance, Fiona appeared to be another type of dutiful daughter, who diligently submitted herself to satisfying the wish of her former head and won his trust and praise. The positioning of herself as a 'dutiful supporter' is made clearer when she evaluated her career pathway:

> Honestly, I think I am more suitable to be a deputy head. I believed I could win much praise and admiration from the head if I were a deputy head. In fact, this happened when I was a deputy head. I could easily meet his requests and help him succeed as I always stayed several steps ahead by preparing several options for him. Yes, if I could choose again, I'd rather be a deputy head.

The importance of diligence was also evident in the narrative of Evelyn Ma when she recalled her smooth career pathway. Evelyn was the high-flyer, as she was promoted to AM and then principal within 10 years. At the time of interview, because of her community involvement, she had earned herself several accolades and was a highly regarded principal. Unlike other women principals in our study, Evelyn was the only woman who admitted to making a conscious effort to improve her chances of promotion. Working in a big school, she knew very well that she needed to improve her performance and visibility if she was to improve her chances of promotion:

> When several colleagues of mine were promoted, I began to wonder what I could do better so that people would have confidence in me. I noticed that those who were promoted used to be panel heads, so I took the initiative and asked the principal if I could be the panel head for Chinese. That year it also happened that there was no teacher responsible for Girl Guides, so the principal asked me to head it and I accepted ... Did it help [promotion]? I probably scored some brownie points ... It turned out the Girl Guides gave me many

opportunities to network with external groups and people. The experience was very valuable. It might have helped my promotion too. When my senior wrote me a reference letter, she could mention my involvement in Girl Guides...

However, when we asked her to evaluate her career pathway, she appeared to change her position and redefined the meaning of her initiatives and past experiences:

In retrospect, the most important thing is *to do your duty well*. You must, of course, grasp the right opportunity, but... you *cannot be too instrumental, too intent* on getting it... Life is very profound. It might not be what I have done. Maybe because I was not so instrumental, people would look at my work closely. When they found my work was up to the standard, they gave me chances... When I was promoted to be a school principal, I overheard some gossip. Some people wondered why I was promoted so soon. Some questioned whether I was too young. I didn't get it [headship] by stepping on others' toes. It wasn't a premeditated scheme. I never thought about it. It just happened that my former head invited me to apply and *I didn't want to decline his offer.*

(emphasis added)

Although Evelyn volunteered to be a panel head and agreed to lead a service group to win people's confidence, in her recollection she played down any *intentional* and *instrumental* planning in developing her career. Instead, she attributed her success to her diligence – 'doing one's duty well' – claiming this was the most important factor that helped her win people's approval and chances. Apparently she changed her self-understanding from an active agent who crafted her career pathway to a diligent and dutiful teacher who quietly waited for people's recognition. There might be reasons for her inconsistency or 'revised identity' (Chase, 2005). It seems possible that the modest (re)presentation is an attempt to maintain her femininity as non-instrumental and non-aggressive, and thus fend off any gossip and criticism of her quick promotion as a young woman. It is also likely that in Hong Kong, even in primary teaching – a feminised occupation – women's career ambition was and is still not highly valued, and it is probably more acceptable for accomplished women to assert their modesty and denial of ambition when recounting their successes.

## Working hard and 'doing my duty well'

If working hard has been an important quality in the presentation of these 'dutiful daughters', it is featured even more prominently in the narratives of other women principals. As mentioned earlier, hard work is an important element of the 'professional success script', and its endorsers – the accomplished women – are likely to support the notions of meritocracy, individual efforts and personal achievement in their work narratives. Hard work, however, seems to carry different meanings and significance for women principals in Hong Kong.

Grace Yau came to primary teaching, having worked in the commercial field for more than 5 years, as she thought its bi-sessional[4] practice would allow her to perform her mothering role. As a firm, disciplined and dedicated teacher, Grace was promoted to AM and principal within 10 years, which was considered fast. In fact, her promotion could have been further escalated if she had accepted the offer of another school, but she declined:

> In the commercial field, promotion is based on tactics. As some people know the tricks, they get promoted very early. However, in education, it is based on merit. If you are really capable, even though you don't seek promotion, chances will still come and find you. I am a good example. I *never thought about promotion*... The principal talked me into accepting his offer. He knew my chances of promotion in the current school were not as good as his. I told him that I *couldn't care less about promotion. I was not interested in being AM*. All I wanted was to be a responsible teacher and fulfil my duties.
>
> (emphasis added)

At first glance, Grace's narrative seems to affirm her belief in meritocracy and the fairness of the education system in rewarding good and capable people. However, this belief is very soon overridden by her denial of ambition, disinterest in promotion and emphasis of fulfilling basic duties. Although she agreed that hard work did pay off, she was more eager to assert that her success was more to do with her fulfilling her duty, her loyalty and work commitment:

> Me: Looking back, how would you account for your career development?
> G: There is a Chinese saying, 'As a loyal servant, I will solve the worries of my master'. Anyone who hires me, gives me a chance or

nurtures me, I will repay their greatness. I won't let my boss worry. Whether in the past, when I worked in a commercial firm, or now in education, I am always *a responsible worker*. They only have to give me a target, and I will deliver the desired results...In the past, I was always assigned to teach students with the poorest English, but they always improved by the end of the term...Some colleagues wondered how I did it and secretly checked my assignments; they then learned that I really put serious effort into my teaching and worked hard for my students...*I am stoic and take my work seriously*. From a young age I knew I needed a job in order to survive. Now I probably don't need a job to survive but I know that if I have to retire, I don't owe anyone.

(emphasis added)

One may find some surprising similarities between the narratives of Grace cited above and those of Fiona mentioned in the previous section. Both presented themselves as good at satisfying and anticipating the needs and worries of their employers. However, what differentiates the two is the ways in which Grace positions herself as a loyal servant, or responsible worker, and relates her work commitment to her resilient personality, which developed out of the difficult environment into which she was born – a poor, broken, patriarchal family that expected its members, especially daughters, to survive on their own. In other words, in downplaying the importance of promotion, Grace is also refusing to present her hard work as a personal strategy for success, but rather as a sign of personal strength.

Carina Lo is another principal who tried to convey to us the idea that her hard work had no instrumental purpose. Carina became AM 9 years after her entry into primary teaching and became a principal after another 6 years. When asked about her career planning, especially her choice of a rural school as her first assignment and why she stayed there for her whole career, Carina provided us with some definitive answers:

I didn't think much about career development. I am actually a very lazy person; lazy in the sense that I don't like to move around, but prefer to stay in one place. *I am very loyal*. I stayed at the school because of the students. I never thought about job prospects. I never thought of moving to the town or a bigger school to maximise my chances of promotion. *I never thought of promotion*. No, I never thought...never thought of this kind of calculation. *I just focused on doing my job well*. In fact, I never thought of becoming AM...Since the first day I started work, I have been very committed. When I joined primary teaching, many people said it was a half-day job. I worked in the morning session, but always stayed until 5 pm.

(emphasis added)

Me: You were very hard-working.

C: I don't know if I was the most hard-working member of staff. I always designed worksheets for my students, and every day I would ask some of them to stay behind and give them extra tuition. I never thought that the school might give me [promotion] chances if I did this... My mum always told me that I should not think of being disadvantaged when I had to work harder than others. She told me that I should treat this kind of 'disadvantage' as a learning opportunity. My mum did not receive any schooling, but she knew a lot and had a great influence on my values.

Carina, a very soft-spoken principal, was in fact very strong and firm in her views about the issue of promotion and career development. She repeatedly told us, seven times, that she *never thought about* promotion and was not interested in calculating and maximising her own interests. Rather, she was more concerned with maintaining herself as a committed person who did her duty well. Working hard was definitely not a strategy, but a work ethic and even a moral value – again, something that she had developed from a young age – that drove her to do the best for her students.

The narrative of 'hard work' is worthy of closer scrutiny. When these hard-working women categorically deny their interest in promotion, they make it clear that they did not feel the need for promotion to affirm their ability and performance. Furthermore, by reaffirming the importance of hard work as a trait of self-determination and a work and moral value that sustained their career commitment, their narratives could be read as a refutation of the values of individualism and instrumentalism that have been encouraged by the discourse of meritocracy.

Nevertheless, moral or otherwise, the discourse of hard work available to women principals in Hong Kong encompasses selflessness and attentiveness to others' needs – qualities that appear to be conventionally associated with femininity. Such emphases also bear much similarity with the caring discourse popular in primary teaching (Duncan, 1996; Miller, 1996), except that this cultural possibility seems to be closely related to the historical and social context of Hong Kong. In a context where the colonial government involved itself minimally in the welfare and well-being of its population, diligence, as Grace and Carina maintained, is a stoic and resilient attitude developed to manage adverse social conditions. More importantly, a danger of this discourse is that those endorsing such views are likely to overwork and burn themselves out. In fact, six out of eight women indicated a wish to retire early and they all reported having worked more than 60 hours a week; Carina spent almost 100 hours a week on school and student affairs. Below are some of their retirement plans:

> I have been very busy. I don't even have time to exercise, or go shopping or go for a facial treatment. There was a period where I felt very upset and asked myself: 'Have I only lived for others and lost myself?' I have been thinking seriously about what my life could be after retirement. After retirement, I hope to have more time and space for myself. I hope to have more time for my daughter too.
>
> (Diana Yuen)

> If I could choose again, I would like to spend more time with my children, especially my daughter. She is really talented, but there was a period where she had relationship problems and was frustrated. I was not close enough to her... This is the area where I felt regretful. I have spent too much time on my students... Upon retirement I am thinking of raising my two grandchildren for my daughter to help relieve her burden.
>
> (Carina Lo)

### Work–family balance as women's duty and personal choice

It is not difficult to detect feelings of struggle and guilt in the retirement plans of these women principals, especially when they expressed the wish to spend more time with their children. In fact, women's work narratives are intricately linked to family responsibility, and work–family (im)balance is an oft-cited career impediment, hindering women from taking up leadership positions (Evetts, 1994; Grogan, 1999; Hoff and Mitchell, 2008; Oplatka, 2006). Where Hong Kong is concerned, family responsibility remains a challenge for working women (Ho, 2013). 'Women should be homemakers' is still a prevalent public attitude (Women's Commission, 2010), and, regardless of their employment status, wives still take up more family duties than their husbands (Young Women's Christian Association, 2008).

When we asked our women principals whether their careers have ever been affected by their family members or responsibilities, surprisingly, almost all provided us with positive replies. They stated that their husbands had been supportive of their jobs and that they were able to manage both work and family roles because of the support and help that they had obtained from family members and other waged household labour. In addition, they were mindful that they were engaged in family responsibilities at a time when primary schooling was still bi-sessional and the educational reforms had not yet been heavily implemented. Fiona, a proud mother of three bright children, recalled the help and social context that allowed her to juggle her teaching job and her childcare responsibilities:

> I was very lucky that the educational reforms had not started yet. I was already AM at that time, but when necessary I could still get home at around 2 pm to supervise [the children's] homework, as primary schooling was still bi-sessional. I am very grateful to my mother. We only hired a full-time foreign domestic worker in the 1990s, when my third child was born. Before that, I had a part-time helper to do the cooking and my mum lived with me to babysit my two sons. I supervised their homework myself.

Evelyn, who became a mother in the early 1990s, recounted how she managed the demands of her mothering role, a 4-year part-time degree course and her responsibilities after she became principal:

> Things were smooth because of the great support from my family. After my son was born, I sent him to live with my mum and my sister, and only took him home at the weekend. He came back to live with me when he was about to enter kindergarten, but my mum still came to my place every day to take care of him... Furthermore, the educational and curriculum reforms had not started yet, so the school's demands and tasks were simpler. It also happened that it was still bi-sessional, so I could still afford to attend courses in the evening.

However, although the women principals claimed they could accommodate the demands arising from different domains and had supportive husbands, a closer probing revealed that women still took primary responsibility for childcare and the help from their spouses was more theoretical than 'real'. Fiona is a vivid example:

> When the children were young, I gave them very close supervision. I believe this was essential and I now also lecture parents on this. I told them that they have to sacrifice 10 years. For myself, I had

no entertainment for almost 10 years; I didn't watch movies or meet friends... For a very long time, every day after work, I came home and worked full gear again. I checked [the children's] homework, supervised their piano practice and did revision. Every Sunday after church service, I started supervising homework at 3 pm and worked till 11 pm.

Me:   Did your husband share the responsibility?

F:   He is very supportive and very family oriented, but he is not as patient as me when it comes to homework supervision. He didn't actually do any supervision during those years, but he has played a mediating role between me and the children. Sometimes when I lost my temper over their homework and started yelling, he would walk away. When I turned my anger on him, he would hide himself in the bedroom and would not argue back. He has been very tolerant of my bad temper. Although he is also a teacher, he does not give as much attention to details as I do, so he would rather play with the kids and develop their non-academic interests in IT, hi-fi and photography. I think God has given us a very well matched partnership.

It is not difficult to see how hard Fiona tried to defend her 'supportive' husband. She might want to excuse his 'impatience' regarding homework supervision, but it appeared that she was the one who lost her temper whereas he had to stay calm and cool. It is equally easy to imagine the stress that she was under as she claimed to have expended all her free time and energy for almost 10 years on drilling her children for academic excellence. Furthermore, with her justification, self-'imprisonment' and lecture to parents, it is also crystal clear that Fiona still considers childcare, especially academic nurturing and homework supervision, as a woman's duty that good mothers/women, employed or otherwise, have to be ready to sacrifice themselves for.

The idea that mothers are the main care providers for children is also expressed in others' narratives, including that of Alice Fung – the only single woman principal in our study. Alice has been a committed teacher since she joined the teaching profession, giving up all her free time on weekdays to counsel students and attend to their needs. When she became a principal, she was very conscientious in providing a family-friendly environment. She would never ask colleagues to stay behind after school for meetings and introduced a 'curfew' requiring all staff to leave the school premises not later than 6 pm. However, when it came to the work–family balance of women and men teachers, her views were inconsistent:

> I always tell male teachers that they have to work harder, climb up the ladder and be ambitious. I have seen many men who, when they reached their forties or even their fifties, really sagged if they were not promoted, and no longer looked like real human beings... For women, their situation is not so bad. When they reach that age, they are usually married and become motherly and loving. Even though some are not married, they remain loving... I once asked a woman teacher to quit or change to part-time as she was slack at work. She was a mother of two: one was a newborn and the other had just entered primary school. She was always very tired. She told me she woke up at 4 in the morning to do the marking, and therefore made many mistakes. I was very sympathetic, but I also told her frankly, 'You are a teacher, and you are a mother, so *you need to make a choice*. At this stage, if your family is more important to you and you cannot spare enough time for your work, then *you have to choose*. Go part-time or quit.' I didn't ask her to leave; I just analysed the situation for her.
>
> (emphasis added)

We use Alice as an illustration, not because she is the most sexist principal. On the contrary, she is the only principal who has implemented a policy to promote the work–family balance of school staff. Genuine concern for her staff notwithstanding, her gender views remain very conventional. Because of her stereotypical gender views – men need to be ambitious and career oriented, while women are necessarily motherly and family and children oriented – her advice to teachers has inevitably reproduced the legitimacy of a gendered division of labour in both the workplace and families. Furthermore, such gender views also explain why she only considers married women responsible and expects them to find their own solutions when their work–family balance seems to fail. A caring approach itself does not appear sufficient to bring real balance at home if society or school leaders have not also developed a gender equity discourse or perspective.

## Conclusions

There is no doubt that opportunities for women to enter school leadership in primary teaching have improved. It is also undeniable that blatant sexist practices have become less common in schools and in Hong Kong society in general. However, we remain wary about the equalisation of gender relations. As their work narratives demonstrated, our women principals are yet to transcend the traditional requirements of femininity and gender role expectations. Remarkable strengths and commitment notwithstanding, we have not seen any women actively promote the need for career strategies or planning. Instead, they denounce these as instrumental and calculative, and attribute their success to personal qualities such as being dutiful, obedient, diligent, teachable, modest, agreeable, hard-working, loyal and committed. Admirable though these qualities are, when examined critically, they are akin to the conventional requirements and expectations of femininity, and therefore represent some desirable, and limiting, gender scripts available to women, professionals included, in Hong Kong. It is possible that the performance of these Chinese femininities may help women win nurturing, protection, trust, praise, opportunities to demonstrate their strength and even promotion opportunities. Nevertheless, it is worrying that when subscribing to these discourses, whether of dutiful daughters or loyal workers, women are also encouraged to be selfless, sacrificial, others oriented and even passive and submissive in their career development. A more empowering discourse for professional and accomplished women has not yet been found. Moreover, when all our female principals, married or single, still believe that women, employed or not, are the main care providers at home, or that work–family balance is a matter of individual decision or personal trade-off, we have strong reasons to suspect that a gendered division of labour and gender stereotypes are still being propagated in our schools. Our analysis has clearly indicated the importance of examining the work narratives of accomplished women amidst the rise of female school leadership. That said, we are also mindful of the existence of possible generational differences between our middle-aged principals and younger women, or occupational dissimilarities between women in primary teaching and those in other professions. For these we certainly need further research.

## Notes

1. This study was supported by a grant from the Research Grant Council of Hong Kong. The project title is 'Gender and leadership: Life histories of female and male primary school principals in Hong Kong' and the reference number is HKIED840209.
2. I am grateful to my team members, Po King Choi and George Ngai, and research assistant, Alison So, for providing valuable advice and assistance to this research project.

3. To protect the anonymity of our 'storytellers', some of their personal information has been altered and pseudonyms are used.
4. Bi-sessional schooling was a practice that allowed one school to use the premises in the morning and another in the afternoon. It was an exigent measure introduced in the 1950s to accommodate the rocketing schooling population. However, the practice became obsolete in the early 2000 because of the declining school population. All primary schools in Hong Kong are now whole-day, usually starting at around 8 am and finishing around 3 pm.

## References

Bell, C. and Chase, S. (1995) 'Gender in the theory and practice of educational leadership', *Journal for a Just and Caring Education*, 1(2), 200–22.
Blackmore, J. (1999) *Troubling women: Feminism, leadership and educational change* (Buckingham, UK: Open University Press).
Blackmore, J. (2002) 'Troubling women: The upsides and downsides of leadership and the new managerialism', in C. Reynolds (ed.) *Women and school leadership: International perspectives* (Albany, NY: SUNY Press).
Bloom, L. R. and Munro, P. (1995) 'Conflicts of selves: Nonunitary subjectivity in women administrators' life history narratives', in J. A. Hatch and R. Wisniewski (eds.) *Life history and narrative: Questions, issues and exemplary work* (London: Falmer Press).
Boulton, P. and Coldron, J. (1998) 'Why women teachers say "stuff it" to promotion: A failure of equal opportunities', *Gender and Education*, 10(2), 149–61.
Chan, A. K. W. (2011) 'Feminizing and masculinizing primary teaching: A critical examination of the interpretive frameworks of male principals in HK', *Gender and Education*, 23(6), 745–59.
Chan, A. K. W. (2012) 'From "civilising the young" to a "dead-end job": Gender, teaching, and the politics of colonial rule in Hong Kong (1841–1970)', *History of Education*, 41(4), 495–514.
Chan, A. K. W., Ngai, G. S. K. and Choi, P. K. (forthcoming) 'Contextualizing the career pathways of women principals in Hong Kong: A critical examination', *Compare: A Journal of Comparative and International Education*.
Chase, S. (1995) *Ambiguous empowerment: The work narrative of women school superintendents* (Amherst, MA: University of Massachusetts Press).
Chase, S. (2005) 'Narrative inquiry: Multiple lenses, approaches and voices', in N. Denzin and Y. Lincoln (eds.) *The Sage handbook of qualitative research* (Thousand Oaks, CA: Sage).
Chisholm, L. (2001) 'Gender and leadership in South African educational administration', *Gender and Education*, 13(4), 387–99.
Coleman, M. (2002) *Women as headteachers: Striking the balance* (Stoke-on-Trent, UK: Trentham Books).
Coleman, M. (2007) 'Gender and educational leadership in England: A comparison of secondary headteachers' views over time', *School Leadership and Management*, 27(4), 383–99.
Cubillo, L. and Brown, M. (2003) 'Women into educational leadership and management: International differences?', *Journal of Educational Administration*, 41(3), 278–91.

Cushman, P. (2008). 'So what exactly do you want? What principals mean when they say "male role model" ', *Gender and Education*, 20(2), 123–36.

Davis, A. and Johansson, O. (2005) 'Gender and school leadership in Sweden', in J. Collard and C. Reynolds (eds.) *Leadership, gender and culture in education: Male and female perspectives* (Maidenhead, UK: Open University Press).

Deem, R. (2003) 'Gender, organizational cultures and the practices of manager-academics in UK universities', *Gender, Work and Organization*, 10(2), 239–59.

Duncan, J. (1996) 'For the sake of the children as the worth of the teacher? The gendered discourses of the New Zealand national kindergarten teachers' employment negotiations', *Gender and Education*, 8(2), 159–70.

Education and Manpower Bureau (1991–1992) *Statistics on primary and secondary school teachers* (Hong Kong: Statistics Section, Education Department).

Education and Manpower Bureau (2003–2004) *Statistics on primary and secondary school teachers* (Hong Kong: Statistics Section, Education Department).

Education and Manpower Bureau (2011–2012) *Statistics on primary and secondary school teachers* (Hong Kong: Statistics Section, Education Department).

Evetts, J. (1994) *Becoming a secondary headteacher* (London: Cassell).

Fennell, H. A. (2008) 'Walking a fine balance: The life history of a woman principal', *Journal of Women in Educational Leadership*, 6(2), 93–113.

Ford, S. (2007) 'Women and leadership: The big picture', *The annual workshop of pushing the boundaries: Women and leadership*, 9 June, The University of Hong Kong.

Goldring, E. and Chen, M. (1994) 'The feminization of the principalship in Israel: The trade-off between political power and cooperative leadership', in C. Marshall (ed.) *The new politics of race and gender* (Washington, DC: Falmer Press).

Goodson, I. and Sikes, P. (2001) *Life history research in educational settings: Learning from lives* (Buckingham, UK: Open University Press).

Grogan, M. (1999) 'A feminist poststructuralist account of collaboration: A model for the superintendency', in C. C. Brunner (ed.) *Sacred dreams: Women and the superintendency* (Albany, NY: SUNY Press).

Ho, L. (2013) 'Four women blaze trail in Hong Kong politics', *SCMP*, 7 February, http://www.scmp.com/news/hong-kong/article/1144741/trailblazers-women-hong-kong-politics (Accessed 3 June 2013).

Hoff, D. and Mitchell, S. N. (2008) 'In search of leaders: Gender factors in school administration', *Advancing Women in Leadership Journal*, 27, 1–18.

Hong Kong Census and Statistics Department (2011) *Hong Kong annual digest of statistics 2011* (Hong Kong: Hong Kong Government).

Hoyle, E. (1969) *The role of the teacher* (London: Routledge).

Kruger, M. L. (1996) 'Gender issues in headship: Quality vs. power?', *European Journal of Education*, 31(4), 447–61.

Lam, M. (2004) 'The perception of inequalities: A gender case study', *Sociology*, 38(1), 5–23.

Lee, E. W. Y. (2003) *Gender and change in Hong Kong: Globalization, postcolonialism, and Chinese patriarchy* (Vancouver, BC: University of British Columbia Press).

Limerick, B. and Lingard, B. (1995) *Gender and changing educational management* (Rydalmere, NSW: Hodder Education).

Lortie, D. C. (1969) 'The balance of control and autonomy in elementary school teaching', in A. Etzioni (ed.) *The semi-professions and their occupations: Teachers, nurses and social workers* (New York: Free Press).

Luke, C. (1998) 'Cultural politics and women in Singapore higher education management', *Gender and Education*, 10(3), 245–63.

Luke, C. (2004) ' "I got to where I am by my own strength": Women in Hong Kong higher education management', in A. K. W. Chan and W. L. Wong (eds.) *Gendering Hong Kong* (Hong Kong: Oxford University Press).

Mahony, P., Hextall, I. and Menter, I. (2004) 'Threshold assessment and performance management: Modernizing or masculinizing teaching in England?', *Gender and Education*, 16(2), 131–49.

McLay, M. (2008) 'Headteacher career paths in UK independent secondary coeducational schools: Gender issues', *Educational Management Administration and Leadership*, 36(3), 353–72.

Miller, J. (1996) *School for women* (London: Virago).

Moller, J. (2005) 'Old metaphors, new meanings: Being a woman principal', in C. Surgue (ed.) *Passionate principalship: Learning from the life histories of school leaders* (London: RoutledgeFalmer).

Morriss, S., Low, G. T. and Coleman, M. (1999) 'Leadership stereotypes and styles of female Singaporean principals', *Compare*, 29(2), 191–202.

Oplatka, I. (2006) 'Women in educational administration within developing countries: Towards a new international research agenda', *Journal of Educational Administration*, 44(6), 604–24.

Ozga, J. (1993) *Women in educational management* (Milton Keynes, UK: Open University Press).

Pearson, V. and Leung, B. K. P. (1995) *Women in Hong Kong* (Oxford: Oxford University Press).

Reynolds, C. (2002) 'Changing gender scripts and moral dilemmas for women and men in education, 1940–1970', in C. Reynolds (ed.) *Women and school leadership: International perspectives* (Albany, NY: SUNY Press).

Risessman, C. (1993) *Narrative analysis* (London: Sage).

Risessman, C. (2002) 'Analysis of personal narratives', in J. F. Gubrium and J. A. Holstein (eds.) *Handbook of interview research: Context and method* (Thousand Oaks, CA: Sage).

Salaff, J. (1995) *Working daughters of Hong Kong: Filial piety or power in the family?* (New York: Columbia University).

Shakeshaft, C. (1987) *Women in educational administration* (Newbury Park, CA: Sage).

Shakeshaft, C. (2006) 'Gender and education management', in C. Skelton, B. Francis and L. Smulyan (eds.) *The Sage handbook of gender and education* (London: Sage).

Skrla, L. (1999) 'Masculinity/femininity: Hegemonic normalizations in the public school superintendency', Paper presented at the annual meeting of the American Educational Research Association, Montreal, QC.

Smulyan, L. (2000a) *Balancing acts: Women principals at work* (Albany, NY: SUNY Press).

Smulyan, L. (2000b) 'Feminist cases of nonfeminist subjects: Case studies of women principals', *International Journal of Qualitative Studies in Education*, 13(6), 589–609.

Sperandio, J. (2010) 'Modeling cultural context for aspiring women educational leaders', *Journal of Educational Administration*, 48(6), 716–26.

Stufft, D. and Coyne, K. (2009) 'Educational leadership: Where are the women?', *Advancing Women in Leadership Journal*, http://www.advancingwomen.com/ awl/Vol29_2009/Derry _L_ Stufft.pdf (Accessed 3 June 2013).

Tropp, A. (1959) *The school teachers: The growth of the teaching profession in England and Wales from 1800 to the present day* (London: William Heinemann).

Women's Commission (2010) 'What do women and men in Hong Kong think about the status of women at home, work and in social environments?', http:// www.women.gov.hk/colour/en/research_statistics/research_status_of_women. htm (Accessed 3 June 2013).

Young, M. and McLeod, S. (2001) 'Flukes, opportunities, and planned interventions: Factors affecting women's decisions to become school administrators', *Educational Administration Quarterly*, 37(4), 462–502.

Young Women's Christian Association (2008) *Gender division of labour in child-caring: A survey report in HK* (Hong Kong: Young Women's Christian Association).

# 10

# Panacea and Liberator: Racial Formation and the Black[1] Teacher in the United States

*Anthony L. Brown and Keffrelyn D. Brown*

African American teachers in the United States have remained enmeshed within two intervening discourses. In one sense, African American teachers have consistently been part of the wider racial discourse of African American social change. Just as Black leaders, activists and ministers have played a vital role in the racial politics of African Americans in the United States, the Black teacher as well has remained linked to the racial imagination of African American equity and social justice. In another sense, Black teachers' experiences have been framed by the wider racial politics in the United States. The contexts of race and schooling have helped to shape the discourse about the necessity for Black teachers in schools. Thus the contingent histories of race have made the Black teacher a proxy for wider ideological or racial interests.

Drawing from Omi and Winant's (1994) *racial formation theory*, in this chapter we argue that contingent socio-historical rules of race have helped to define how the Black teacher was discussed in schools and society. Omi and Winant (1994) define *racial formation* as 'the sociohistorical process by which racial categories are created, inhabited, transformed, and destroyed' (p. 55). In this sense, we argue that Black teachers in the United States were conceptualised in the sociohistorical process by which race and racial categories have taken shape. Our chapter examines the historical and contemporary racial discourses of the African American teacher in the United States. We first discuss the varied political and cultural contexts of Black teachers from the early 19th century through the late 20th century. The needs for Black teachers emerged during different temporal and spatial contexts. In this context, pedagogy was either viewed as vitally necessary to repudiate African

American student underachievement or positioned as either insignificant or a barrier to Black educational and social growth. In this chapter, we explore the context of this ambivalence towards the Black teacher in the United States. We also show how, at varying times, the interests for Black teachers converged with multiple interests in the United States.

We also highlight how varied ideological interests have converged within the recent discourse to recruit and retain Black teachers in the United States. We specifically discuss how the call for Black male teachers has remained inscribed within two competing metaphors – Black male teacher as the 'panacea' to fix urban problems and Black male teacher as 'liberator' of Black injustices. This chapter explicates the varied ways such metaphors inform the political and racial discourse about Black teachers in the United States. We compare the problems and possibilities of this discourse to contemporary discussions about recruiting, certifying and retaining more African American teachers in the United States.

## Early American discourse and the Black teacher

Numerous scholars of African American education have documented the racial politics of the Black teacher during the late 19th and early 20th century (Anderson, 1988; Fultz, 1995a, 1995b). During this period the Black teacher was the face of educational reform. The Black teacher was discussed in the context of school development, school curriculum, student development and the wider political space as a symbol of racial progress. For example, in the early 1800s, the Black teacher became central to the discussion about educational change in the state of New York when African American educators, community leaders and parents advocated for school officials to hire African American teachers to teach African American students (Mabee, 1979; Rury, 1983). It was during this time that the earliest discourse emerged about how the Black teacher could serve as a role model or as pillar for 'moral righteousness' and social uplift to Black youth. Such discussions about the Black teacher would emerge again in the 1980s and 1990s and even within present-day educational reforms for Black males.

### Arguments for African American teachers, 18th and 19th centuries

Historian John Rury (1985) explains that during this period, directly after the American Revolution, a nascent movement surfaced with the intent of abolishing slavery in the North. There were two ideological beliefs that undergirded the abolitionist movement. The first was the abolishment of slavery in the United States and the second was the belief that the movement would operate as the 'moral and political guardians' of the local free Black population in the north-east. This was the focus of the New York Manumission Society. While the initial goals of the society were to protect the human rights of free African Americans from local acts of racism, it gradually shifted its focus onto ways of controlling the behaviour of free African Americans. Rury (1985) illustrates this point:

> At its third meeting, in May, 1785, the Manumission Society ordered its standing committee to 'Keep a watchful eye over the conduct of such Negroes as have been or may be liberated; and... to prevent them from running into immorality or sinking into idleness'.
>
> (p. 233)

This committee advised against free African Americans allowing slaves or servants into their homes or to engaging in 'fiddling, dancing or any other noisy behavior' (Rury, 1985, p. 234). The focus of the society was to socialise the recently manumitted[2] African Americans to a standard of moral conduct that was consistent with the White elite communities of New York. Thus, the society opened schools that would educate a select few African American leaders that could meet the objective of controlling the so-called 'immorality' of African Americans. Here Rury (1985) outlines the purpose of the African Free School (AFS):

> Moral education remained the essential purpose of the African Free School throughout its initial twenty-five years. Rules concerning matters of appearance, conduct to and from school, behavior in class, as well as respect for property and 'our Great Maker's awful name were rigidly enforced'. If they learned nothing else, the students at this school would have a clear understanding of the moral expectations they faced upon graduation.
>
> (p. 236)

As a way to support this vision, the society hired only White teachers to work in the AFS. It was during this period that the Black teacher (even those educated at the AFS) was not considered in relation to the vision of African American educational reform. What was implied from this period is that White elite teachers were best suited to educate the recently freed Blacks.

During this period, however, there also was an emerging debate about whether Black teachers would better serve the mission of educating the African American child. For instance, in 1805, members at the American Convention of Abolitionist Societies argued that Black children could benefit from working with African American teachers. Convention members hailed that instruction by African American teachers would 'kindle a spirit of] emulation' in Black children (Mabee, 1979, p. 93). In addition, historian John Rury (1983) found that Black parents consistently declared to the Manumission Society the importance of Black teachers educating their children. Through the late 1800s and 1900s there were countless arguments made after Reconstruction for the importance of Black teachers educating Black children (Blackshear, [1902] 1969; Mabee, 1979). This quote from noted African American educator E. L. Blackshear ([1902] 1969) highlights a common discourse about how African American teachers could best serve the specific needs of Black children:

> The colored teacher has been a herald of civilization to the youth of his people. His superior culture and character have acted as a powerful stimulus to the easily roused imagination of the colored youth, and the black boy feels, the presence of the black 'professah', to him the embodiment of learning, that he too can be 'something'. At first he does not know what that something is, but he determines to be 'somebody' and to make a place and a standing for himself in the world.
>
> (p. 337)

In some respects, this quote reflects an underlying belief about the role and capacity of the Black teacher that has persisted in the present. However, as we argue in this chapter, the rules of race and the contingent histories of educational reform for African Americans would have a lasting impact on Black teachers through most of the 20th century.

### The Black teacher in the Jim Crow era

After the Reconstruction period in the United States, the concerns of Black education were of great significance. During this period, through the impetus of industrialisation, philanthropists were poised to develop schools to train African Americans for the growing demands of labour. However, such schools also served as institutions to train African American teachers who would eventually serve the needs of African American students. The training of the Black teacher would prove invaluable given the demands of the woefully under-served Black schools in the segregated South. The context of the Black teacher was framed by a racial order where Black education was segregated and underfunded – yet overwhelmingly housed with Black teachers. Unlike the Manumission Society which saw White teachers as necessary to educational reform, Black teachers in the Jim Crow South would become emblematic of racial progress for African Americans. However, by the early 1900s, numerous African American scholars and activists began to ask very pointed questions about the pedagogical training of African Americans (Caliver, 1933; Fultz, 1995a).

African American educators insisted that teacher training for Black teachers would provide more 'competent professionalism' and 'improved instruction' (Fultz, 1995a, p. 205). For example, Fultz (1995a) found that several Black state teacher associations, including the National Association of Teachers in Colored Schools, 'carried the banner of improved training and instruction' (p. 205). Sociologists and educational scholars adamantly insisted that African American colleges provide rigorous instruction and professionalism to assist in the advanced training of Black teachers (Caliver, 1933). For example, Charles Johnson argued that 'These poorly trained teachers ... will inflict the accumulated deficiencies of the system in which they have been trained upon their pupils, and so perpetuate it' (Fultz, 1995a, p. 197). Educational scholar Ambrose Caliver (1933), who conducted one of the first comprehensive studies about the education and training of African American teachers, also suggested that African American education could not progress without the rigorous training of Black teachers. The following are a few of his recommendations:

- Teacher-preparing institutions for Negroes should raise their entrance requirements, making them more selective, and should improve their admission procedures in order to assure to the teaching profession recruits with better background and preparation.
- More attention should be given by school officials to the qualifications and certification of Negro applicants, and appointments should be made solely on merit.

(Caliver, 1933, pp. 117–18)

So, while there was strong advocacy for Black teachers' social practices (such as community leadership and role modelling), African American educators consistently argued that improved educational outcomes *must* equally occur through sound educational training and professionalism.

Much of the early debates and discussions about the roles and responsibilities of African American teachers emerged out of larger political concerns for racial and social justice. While racial and cultural identification was a central argument made for the placement of Black teachers in African American classrooms, several African American educators and scholars expressed concern about the instructional training of Black teachers to meet the educational needs of African American children. Fultz (1995a) argues, '[T]he fate of the race depended on the types of schools it had, the types of schools Blacks possessed depended on the quality of the teacher available to them, and the quality of the teachers depended upon sterling character and professional training' (p. 197). In summary, while the historical contexts of the debate for Black teachers has changed since the early 1900s, more recent educational literature reveals the enduring discussions about whether Black teachers could best serve the educational needs of African American students.

## The Black teacher in the post-*Brown* era

While the 1940s and 1950s helped to engage the discussion about the proper teacher training of Black teachers, a new racial order would have an indelible mark on the Black teacher. In essence, the Black teacher would become an unintended causalty to a convergence of interests between the desires of African Americans to dismantle segregation and the growing interests of the US government to intentionally alter its image to reflect a more egalitarian democracy (Bell, 1980).

As numerous legal and educational scholars have noted, the most significant unintended outcome of *Brown v. Board of Education*[3] was its inability to produce lasting changes to the conditions for African American schooling (Fultz, 2004; Grant, 1995; Guinier, 2004). Another significant outcome was the systematic removal of close to 90 per cent of the Black teaching force. Again, this illustrates that the rules of race in the 1950s would help ultimately define the fate of Black teachers.

By the 1960s, however, a new discourse emerged about African Americans that would eventually set the context for a renewed discussion about the cultural efficacy of the Black teacher. During this time numerous social scientists began to examine the impact that racism and poverty had on the social and psychological development of African American students (Pettigrew, 1964; Riessman, 1962; Rohrer and Edmonson, 1960; Silberman, 1964). While researchers examined the social forces that shaped African American achievement, much of this discourse relied on cultural deficit theories to explain the social and education experiences of African American students (Moynihan, 1967; Riessman, 1962). Scholars routinely examined the cycle of norms, behaviours and internal relations of the Black family structure in order to understand the cause of underachievement (Moynihan, 1967; Pettigrew, 1964; Riessman, 1962).

Several scholars advanced new theories for understanding the educational context of African American students (Banks and Grambs, 1972; Gouldner, 1978; Rist, 1973). This work challenged deficit theories, arguing that teacher's perceptions and expectations of African American students had a huge impact on academic outcomes (Abrahams and Gay, 1972). Banks and Grambs (1972), for example, asserted that *White racism* had profoundly influenced African American students' self-concept. For Banks and Grambs, *self-concept* was defined as how one understands identities in relation to 'significant others'. Banks and Grambs (1972) stated,

> Since whites are the dominant and 'significant others' in American society, and black children derive their concepts of themselves largely from white society and its institutions, we are not going to progress significantly in augmenting the black child's self-concept until we either change the racial attitudes and perceptions of White Americans or create new 'significant others' for black children.
>
> (p. 8)

Banks and Grambs (1972) further argued that *White racism* or the *devaluation of Blackness* had a direct impact on how teachers made decisions in the classroom. Furthermore, they claimed that teachers who subscribed to the *devaluation of Blackness* would invariably accept deprivation theories, which presumed that specific ethnic or racial groups had 'irreversible cognitive deficits'.

Similar to Banks and Grambs (1972), Gay (1975) argued that until educators understood the cultural differences of African Americans, they would continue to pathologise and stereotype their culture and thus devalue their academic potential. Furthermore, in order to better understand the cultural viewpoints of students, teachers had to understand that African American children carried perspectives about them that had direct implications to what happened in the classroom. Here Gay (1975) made an argument for a more culturally specific orientation to teaching:

> Without conscious awareness of these differences, and the knowledge necessary to use them advantageously, cultural conflict between white teachers' and Black students' expectations are inevitable. These conflicts, if unresolved, are likely to cause frustrations and alienation

for both students and teachers and to interfere with the effectiveness of the instructional process. To avoid homogenizing Blacks and other culturally different children, and to maximize their opportunities for quality education, teachers must make 'school living' more compatible with 'home living'.

(p. 30)

For Gay (1975) this type of culturally responsive teaching was vital to understanding the education process.

This challenging narrative helped set the stage for subsequent studies in the 1980s and 1990s which more closely explored the cultural aspects of teaching, specifically addressing the education experiences of African American students (Foster, 1987; Irvine and Irvine, 1983; Shade and Edwards, 1987). At the centre of such discussions was the cultural and ideological efficacy of the Black teacher in helping to reach the underachieving Black student. The Black teacher would surface again in relation to pending concerns about the Black-White achievement gap and the ongoing ideological politics of African Americans' consideration of whether African American social actors (for example, mayors, teachers, doctors and lawyers) were best suited to represent African American issues.

## An emerging field: The Black teacher in research

By the early 1990s, following the work of previous multicultural education scholarship, numerous studies emerged specifically examining the cultural and political aspects of Black teachers' pedagogical practices (Foster, 1991a, 1991b; Irvine, 1990a, 1990b; King, 1991; Ladson-Billings, 1991, 1994). These studies were primarily concerned with how Black teachers' pedagogical practices influenced the educational achievement of African American students.

Much of the late-20th-century scholarship about effective Black teachers of Black children has focused on two central dimensions to pedagogy – a cultural dimension and a political/ideological dimension. The cultural dimension sought to explicate the cultural aspects of the African American experience by providing a cultural context to the collective experiences of African Americans and the African diaspora. This scholarship offered several exemplars of effective Black teachers and their adherence to an in-depth understanding of African American culture, history and politics. In addition, this work expressed how knowledge acquisition was culturally responsive and how Black teachers drew from both dominant and culturally specific orientations to learning. These studies revealed how Black teachers served as agents of social and political change. Common across the extant scholarship on Black teachers is the ideological belief that successful Black teachers of Black children possessed (1) an ethic of caring; (2) a deep understanding of the social, historical and political lives of Black children; and (3) an understanding of the link between culture and knowledge acquisition (Irvine, 1990a, 1990b; King, 1991; Ladson-Billings, 1991).

Moreover, this body of research found that Black teachers who possessed such qualities would have a direct impact on the academic achievement of African American children (Delpit, 1995; Foster, 1994; Irvine, 1990a, 1990b, 2003). While some of this work has tended to focus on the cultural aspects of pedagogy, by situating culture as the central mechanism for social change, some of this work has also focused on the nexus between culture and critical/political aspects of pedagogy (for example, critical pedagogy, emancipatory pedagogy, liberatory pedagogy, critical race theory and Black feminism) and explicitly addressed the critical/political orientations to pedagogy (Ball, 2000; Henry, 2006; King, 1991; Ladson-Billings, 1994; Lynn, 2002).

The cultural orientation to pedagogy emphasised the symbolic and aesthetic connection between the roots of African American behaviours and dispositions as they related to the cultural foundations of African norms and culture. Within studies on the pedagogy for Black children, there has been a specific focus on rhythm, expression, knowledge acquisition and learning environment as key elements to the Black child's learning experience (Akoto, 1994; Delpit, 1995; Hale-Benson, 1982; Hilliard, 1992, 1995; Irvine, 1990a, 1990b). In addition, this work sought to restructure the curriculum by infusing the contributions of African Americans and the historical legacies of Africans predating the 1600s (Hilliard, 1992, 1995). Irvine's (1990a) 'synchronization theory' insisted that teachers must value, understand and incorporate the experiences and culture of the child in order to be effective in the classroom. Irvine (1990a) found that teachers must understand how African American cultural distinctiveness is rooted in concepts of Afrocentricity. For example, Irvine (1990a) argued that African American children possess the following culturally distinct qualities:

> First depth of feeling is evidenced by black children's highly charged, noisy, and emotional expressions. The second aspect – naturalistic attitudes – refers to blacks' aversion to formality, their frankness of manner, their casualness in social transaction, their contempt

for artificiality, and their acceptance, without guilt or shame, of their sensuality and sexuality. Style – the third characteristic – is the manner in which blacks present and display their uniqueness. Fourth is the poetic and prosaic vernacular, in which peculiarly black speech rhythms, voice inflections, and tonal patterns are used. Finally, expressive movement is the heavy dependence on dance and music in everyday activities.

(pp. 25–6)

Irvine (1990a) further found that teachers who possess this understanding will have higher expectations for students and will create a learning environment conducive for African American students to achieve academically. She also argued that unfortunately, because of the decrease in African American teachers, there is a greater likelihood that African American students will continue to be misunderstood resulting in 'hidden conflict, hostility, infrequent instruction, detachment, and negative teacher and student expectations' (Irvine, 1990a, p. 42). Similar to Irvine, Foster (1991c) argued that successful African American teachers of African American children possessed a *cultural responsiveness* which fostered a community environment for learning. Here one of the teachers in Foster's (1991c) study on Black teachers explains that appropriate pedagogy for African American students must not be limited to academics:

I always point out those examples of other things that they can do and things that they can be, so I think that's probably what I give them – high and different expectations. I tell them that I really want them to learn to think by themselves and I want them to learn how to find things out. I think it's more important for me to let them know how to find things out than give them everything because learning is a lifelong thing. I want them to be able to use it (education) as a lifelong thing and to have a quality life based on knowing something about their history and literature.

(p. 285)

Foster (1991c) further found that although some African American teachers in her study did not overtly mention whether African American culture informed their work, their work implicitly reflected norms often recognised in this culture:

As you will notice if you walk into my classroom, or you'll notice that soon after, if not right away, everyone is involved. I don't believe in standing in front of a class and expounding on something forever. I like for everyone to be involved. I don't believe in rappin', I mean not like the rap song, but to me you have to discuss something meaningfully.

(p. 296)

While much of the literature about Black teachers has focused on the cultural dimensions to their pedagogical practice (Foster, 1991c; Irvine, 1990b, 2003), some of this body of work has also focused more closely on the political/ideological aspects to pedagogy (Beauboeuf-Lafontant, 2002; King, 1991; Ladson-Billings, 1994; Ladson-Billings and Henry, 1990; Lynn, 2002).

This work explored more closely how teachers critically challenged power relations in schools (Ball, 2000; King, 1991; Ladson-Billings, 1994; Ladson-Billings and Henry, 1990). In their study of Black female teachers in the United States and Canada, Ladson-Billings and Henry (1990) argued that teachers can 'incite creative and powerful strategies to overcome oppressive forces' (p. 75), or engage in what they call *liberatory pedagogy*. King (1991) similarly argued that Black teachers who understood student alienation and power relations within the school and community incorporated what she called *emancipatory pedagogy*. King (1991) stated,

> The struggle is about whether education is for social transformation or system maintenance. Through their self-affirming resistance, these teachers are choosing education for personal and social emancipation for their students. In so doing, they position themselves squarely on the 'front lines' of this continuing struggle.

(pp. 260–1)

One important aspect to *emancipatory pedagogy* is the ability of the teacher to create liberating and empowering school knowledge. As King (1991) explained, '[C]ritical thinking is thinking critically about liberating, antiracist, and antielitist content' (p. 255). She further asserted that the teacher must have the ability to counteract distortions in the curriculum and the school knowledge. The teachers in King's (1991) study talked about 'exploding myths' about history, current events and society. Here one of the teachers from King's (1991) study discussed how 'exploding myths' is achieved through the curriculum:

> We spent a lot of time on who did the work on the California missions and who got the credit. Even the films couldn't hide the fact

that Indians were making the bricks and the priests were just sitting around.

(p. 256)

King (1991) also found that teachers who constantly sought opportunities to counter distorted images in the curriculum engaged in an *emancipatory pedagogy*.

Ladson-Billings' (1991, 1994) work also offers a political dimension to pedagogy, or what she defines as *culturally relevant pedagogy* (p. 237). According to Ladson-Billings (1994), critical pedagogy played an important role in the theoretical development of *culturally relevant pedagogy*:

Pedagogy refers to a deliberate attempt to influence how and what knowledge and identities are produced within and among particular sets of social relations. It can be understood as a practice through which people are incited to acquire a particular 'moral character'. As both a political and practical activity, it attempts to influence the occurrence and qualities of experiences that will organize and disorganize a variety of understandings of our natural and social world in particular ways... Pedagogy is a concept that draws attention to the processes through which knowledge is produced.

(p. 14)

From this conception of pedagogy, Ladson-Billings (1991, 1994) argues that the culturally relevant pedagogue identifies the dimensions of power which define relationships in schools for African American students. In addition, teachers who possess this in-depth understanding of different contexts which shape African American students' educational experiences also have an ability to challenge and disrupt existing power relations. The following interview involving an African American teacher reveals this *critical* dimension to the teaching of African American students:

I've taught all kinds of kids, rich ones, poor ones, white ones, black ones. Some of the smartest youngsters I've worked with have been right here in this community, but a lot of the time they don't believe in themselves. School saps the life out of them. You want to see intelligence walking around on two legs? Just go into a kindergarten class. They come to school with fresh faces, full of wonder. But by third grade you can see how badly school has beaten them down. You can really see it in the boys. I sometimes ask myself just what it is we're doing with these children.

(Ladson-Billings, 1994, p. 89)

This example illustrates the teacher's understanding of how schools operate to reproduce low expectations and low academic standards for African American students and males in particular. In recent years, several other studies have continued to explore how successful African American teachers of African American children address aspects of power within a school context (Agee, 2004; Beauboeuf-Lafontant, 2002; Brown, 2012; Dixson, 2003; Howard, 2001; Lynn, 2002, 2006). Some of this work has specifically examined African American male teachers.

The literature about African American male teachers is quite limited and narrow in scope as much of the scholarship about African American teachers has focused on African American women. Although there have been studies and teacher narratives that have featured African American male teachers, few of these studies have specifically explored the implications of having an African American male teacher in the classroom. One of the obvious reasons for this lack of attention is due to the small number of African American male teachers in the profession. Part of this could be explained by what Michael Fultz (1995b) referred to as the 'feminisation' of the teaching profession, where he found that between 1890 and 1930, because of the broader professional opportunities given to African American men, the total percentage of African American male teachers decreased from 28.7 in 1890 to 13.8 in 1930. An additional factor might be the significant numbers of African American teachers who were dismissed to accommodate desegregation mandates after the *Brown* decision (Fultz, 2004; Irvine and Irvine, 1983). More recently, attempts have been made to remedy such outcomes through targeted efforts to recruit African American males to the teaching profession (Holman, 1996; Smiles, 2002).

There also have been considerable policy and education reform efforts that have explored how to recruit and retain more African American men to the profession (Brown and Manwell-Butty, 1999; Holland, 1991; Holman, 1996; Lewis, 2006; Smiles, 2002). Much of this work has focused on role model theories as a rationale to bring more African American male teachers to the profession. Role model theories maintain that a teacher or mentor of the same gender or race of students can serve as a model or image for those students to emulate and follow (Odih, 2002; Zirkel, 2002). It has been suggested that when African American male students engage in positive day-to-day interactions with an African American male, teachers can positively reform these students' social and education identities (Holland, 1991). Consequently, through this type of socialisation, it is believed that the African American male possesses a higher likelihood of achieving academic success. However, much of this literature addresses the role-modelling process in theory and rarely draws from actual classroom interactions of African American male teachers and African American male students.

From the 1990s onwards, however, researchers have begun to explore the practices and experiences of African American male teachers. Drawing from personal narratives and interview data, this work discusses the experiences and practices of African American male teachers. Although some studies such as Michelle Foster's (1997) *Black Teachers on Teaching* focused on Black teachers in general, some of the teacher narratives offer insights into the education philosophies and practices of African American males. Although there is a rather thin body of research specifically about African American male teachers, some education researchers have attempted to focus exclusively on the theory and practice of Black male teachers (Lynn, 2000, 2002, 2006; Pang and Gibson, 2001). Within these studies, the following themes surfaced: (a) African American male teachers acknowledge, understand and infuse in their pedagogical practice the racial context of African Americans; (b) African American male teachers possess a moral, political, spiritual and philosophical belief that guides their practice; and (c) African American male teachers understand the subject position of African American male students in relation to their own personal experiences.

The expectations of the African American male teacher, however, are not exclusively situated within education discourse, but are also part of larger political discussions about viable strategies for addressing the social and educational realities of African American males (Legette, 1999). For example, numerous African American political organisations, fraternities and legislators have positioned African American men as the single most important role model for Black children (Legette, 1999). This was particularly visible in the political discourse of 1992 Million Man March, where African American leaders called for African American men to take greater responsibility at rectifying the political and social struggles of the Black community, with special attention given to the needs of Black males (Dawson, 2001). Thus the African American male teacher represents a central strategy or course of action necessary to remedy the social and educational realities of African American male youth. This, however, was also compelling to school districts concerned with how to meet the needs of African American students. In this sense, the Black male teacher was seen as a 'surrogate father' for Black male students. Several recent studies have questioned some of the essentialising perspectives about Black teachers by highlighting the varied ideological and subject positions of Black men as teachers in schools (Brockenbrough, 2012; Brown, 2009; Rezai-Rashti and Martino, 2010). The intent of this work has been to trouble the common-sense discourses about the Black male teacher as a flat, one-dimensional role model.

## Black teacher: Discussion and implications

The Black teacher is inextricably tied to the politics of race. The earliest conversations in the 1800s about the Black teacher resulted in free Blacks questioning White authorities about why Black teachers were not hired to work in all Black schools. However, implicit to this period was a prevailing belief that Black teachers were not necessary to foster social change for the recently manumitted African Americans. The Black teacher would remain enmeshed within the ideological politics of race in subsequent centuries, as the question would consistently resurface about the efficacy of the Black teacher to meet the needs of the Black student. Indeed, these concerns would again surface after Reconstruction and through the early 20th century, when the African American teacher was consistently discussed within the context of racial uplift. The Black teacher was *the* image of moral righteousness for African Americans. But again, the prominence and significance of the Black teacher was mostly significant within the racial context of a Jim Crow racial society which placed Black students, Black curriculum and Black teachers in the strident boundaries of racially segregated society in the United States. Then, as the rules of race changed in an increasing racially desegregated US society, the Black teacher was systematically removed from classrooms. Ironically, in the decades after the passing of *Brown*, the Black teacher became a growing policy concern of historically under-served schools.

In keeping with Omi and Winant's (1994) notion of *racial formation theory*, as the rules of race changed, so did the context of the Black teacher. In recent years, the Black teacher, and Black male teacher in particular, has resurfaced again. While this period of public discourse differs from the other periods historically, it also highlights how the formation of 'race' implicitly constructs the subject position of the Black teacher. In this context the Black male teacher serves as *the* educational reform of the underachieving Black boy, while also operating as a proxy for race and gender political imaginations for Black social change. So, why is this history of the Black teacher important?

There are two problems with situating Black teachers solely in the ideological imagination of Black liberation or as panacea to looming urban problems. We should first note that our critique of each of these conceptions of the Black teacher is not to negate the work of previous scholarship which noted the efforts of the Black teacher (Foster, 1997; Siddle-Walker, 2001). However, we wish to offer some theoretical clarity or nuance to the existing discourse of the Black teacher. Let us start with the metaphor of the Black teacher as liberator of Black people. While there are numerous cases in history and in the present where Black teachers' pedagogy would be deemed transformative and liberatory, there is no single ideological perspective that defines what this looks like. Throughout most of the 20th century and continuing into more recent debates about the role of Black teachers, different ideological visions have been used to explain and imagine their role and expectations. While it is for certain that during the early 1900s several African American educators shared similar conceptual beliefs about the Black teacher serving as a 'representative of the race', different education visions called for the Black teacher to embody and reflect varying beliefs and practices. For example, under W. E. B. DuBois' (1902) education vision, education should provide more than the practical knowledge for job training, and this meant that the Black teacher needed to offer political knowledge necessary to agitate the existing social order. During the late 1960s and early 1970s, Black nationalists imagined very different conceptual and practical meanings about the purpose of the Black teacher than did integrationists during this same period, arguing that the Black teacher's role was less about helping the Black child integrate into US society, but more to foster self-determination and Black pride (Campbell, 1970).

These differences, albeit subtle, about the role and expectations of the Black teacher exist within contemporary discourses about the Black teacher. For example, while a cultural nationalist orientation would see the Black teacher as a *cultural representative* of a unified African cultural norm (Akoto, 1994), conversely, a more *critical* orientation might imagine the Black teacher as an agent to de-essentialise stable cultural norms used to fasten in place a permanent identity about African American students. Brown's (2009, 2012) work on Black male teachers, for example, has highlighted the significance of understanding the nuanced perspectives and experiences Black teachers bring to the classroom.

In this sense, we argue that the Black teacher cannot be thought of or positioned as a cultural monolith.

Discourses of Black teacher as the panacea for urban problems also require re-conceptualisation. While we agree with the existing literature that Black teachers who possess culturally responsive and culturally relevant pedagogies can mitigate many issues in schools, we argue that the pedagogical skill of the Black teacher often gets lost within broader public discussions about recruiting and retaining these teachers. Indeed, what scholars have consistently noted about the literature on Black teachers is not just who they are as Black people, but what they do pedagogically (Brown, 2009; Foster, 1997). To reduce the Black teacher to a socio-psychological dimension, where their pedagogy and work is relegated to an image or symbol of achievement for the Black child to model after, profoundly undermines the kinds of training, professionalism and development successful Black teachers of Black students have and continue to employ. In many respects the discourse around Black teachers as role models and mentors is a subtle critique of the Black family and Black community, in that it presumes Black student underachievement is the result of problematic dynamics of the Black family and society, and not directly aligned with the decades of school neglect and the long-term structural and institutional practices of race which have both produced and sustained inequitable learning opportunities.

As we have shown in this chapter, the Black teacher was never separate and apart from the rules of race. This perspective is quite important to current discussions about Black teachers. The most significant concern is that Black teachers in the United States have remained inscribed by both racial politics and educational reform. The Black teacher becomes a ready-made construct, called to the teaching profession to only teach specific students and to address particular kinds of educational problems, or what Brown defines as a *pedagogical kind*, that is 'a type of educator whose subjectivities, pedagogies, and expectations have been set in place prior to entering the classroom' (2012, p. 299).

An alternative approach to this discourse is to first think about Black teachers in relation to the teacher education they received, and then of the context in which their histories, experiences and ideological perspectives could inform the educational experiences of Black students. In other words, the Black teacher must be conceptualised as a person in need of rigorous training and preparation and not simply as an *a priori* construct of potential Black political change and urban educational utility.

## Notes

1. Definitions of 'Black' and other ethnic groups vary considerably across countries. Black and African American will be used interchangeably throughout this chapter.
2. Manumission is usually defined as the act of a slave owner freeing his or her slaves.
3. The *Brown v. Board of Education* of 1954 helped to challenge and dismantle the legal precedent of racial segregation established by the 'separate but equal' clause of the 1896 *Plessy v. Ferguson* case.

## References

Abrahams, R. and Gay, G. (1972) 'Talking Black in the classroom', in R. Abrahams and R. Troike (eds.) *Language and cultural diversity in American education* (Englewood Cliffs, NJ: Prentice Hall).

Agee, J. (2004) 'Negotiating a teaching identity: An African American teacher's struggle to teach in test-driven contexts', *Teachers College Record*, 106(4), 747–74.

Akoto, A. (1994) 'Notes on an African-centered pedagogy', in J. Shujaa (ed.) *Too much schooling, too little education: A paradox of Black life in White societies* (Trenton, NJ: African World Press).

Anderson, J. (1988) *The education of Blacks in the South, 1860–1935* (Chapel Hill, NC: University of North Carolina).

Ball, A. (2000) 'Empowering pedagogies that enhance the learning of multicultural students', *Teachers College Record*, 102(6), 1006–34.

Banks, J. and Grambs, J. (1972) *Black self-concept: Implications for education and social science* (New York: McGraw-Hill).

Beauboeuf-Lafontant, T. (2002) 'A womanist experience of caring: Understanding the pedagogy of exemplary Black women teachers', *Urban Review*, 34(1), 71–86.

Bell, D. (1980) '*Brown v. Board of Education* and the interest-convergence dilemma', *Harvard Law Review*, 93, 518–33.

Blackshear, E. L. ([1902] 1969) 'What is the Negro teacher doing in the matter of uplifting the race?', in D. W. Kulp (ed.) *Twentieth century Negro literature* (New York: Arno), 334–8.

Brockenbrough, E. (2012) 'Emasculation blues: Black male teachers perspectives on gender and power in the teaching profession', *Teachers College Record*, 114(5), 1–43.

Brown, A. L. (2009) ' "O brotha where art thou?" Examining the ideological discourses of African American male teachers working with African American male students', *Race Ethnicity and Education*, 12(4), 473–93.

Brown, A. L. (2012) 'On human kinds and role models: A critical discussion about the African American male teacher', *Educational Studies*, 48(3), 296–315.

Brown, J. W. and Manwell-Butty, J. (1999) 'Factors that influence African American male teachers' education and career aspirations: Implications for school district recruitment and retention efforts', *Journal of Negro Education*, 68(3), 280–92.

Caliver, A. (1933) 'The Negro teacher and a philosophy of Negro education', *Journal of Negro Education*, 2, 432–47.

Campbell. L. (1970) 'The Black teacher and Black power', in N. Wright (ed.) *What Black educators are saying* (New York: Hawthorn Books).

Dawson, M. (2001) *Black visions: The roots of contemporary African-American political ideologies* (Chicago: University of Chicago Press).

Delpit, L. (1995) *Other people's children: Cultural conflict in the classroom* (New York: New Press).

Dixson, A. (2003) ' "Let's do this!" Black woman teacher's politics and pedagogy', *Urban Education*, 38(2), 217–35.

DuBois, W. E. B. (1902) 'Of training of Black men', *Atlantic Monthly*, http://www. theatlantic.com/unbound/flashbks/blacked/dutrain.htm (Accessed 15 July 2013).

Foster, M. (1987) 'It's cookin' now: A performance analysis of the speech events of a Black teacher in an urban community college', *Language in Society*, 18(1), 1–29.

Foster, M. (1991a) 'The politics of race: Through African American teacher's eyes', *Journal of Education*, 172, 123–41.

Foster, M. (1991b) 'African American teachers and the politics of race', in K. Weiler (ed.) *What schools can do: Critical pedagogy and practice* (Buffalo, NY: SUNY Press).

Foster, M. (1991c) 'Just got to find a way: Case studies of the lives and practice of exemplary Black high school teachers', in M. Foster (ed.) *Readings on equal education, Volume 11: Qualitative investigations into schools and schooling* (New York: AMS).

Foster, M. (1994) 'Educating for competence in community and culture: Exploring the views of exemplary African-American teachers', in S. Shujaa (ed.) *Too much schooling, too little education* (Trenton, NJ: African Free Press).

Foster, M. (1997) *Black teachers on teaching* (New York: New Press).

Fultz, M. (1995a) 'Teacher training and African American education in the South, 1900–1940', *Journal of Negro Education*, 64, 196–210.

Fultz, M. (1995b) 'African-American teachers in the South, 1890–1940: Growth, feminization and salary discrimination', *Teacher College Record*, XCVI, 544–68.

Fultz, M. (2004) 'The displacement of Black educators post-*Brown*: An overview and analysis', *History of Education Quarterly*, 44, 11–45.

Gay, G. (1975) 'Cultural differences important in education of Black children', *Momentum*, VI, 30–3.

Gouldner, H. (1978) *Teacher's pet, troublemakers, and nobodies: Black children in elementary school* (Westport, CT: Greenwood).

Grant, C. (1995) 'Reflections on the promise of *Brown* and multicultural education', *Teachers College Record*, 96(4), 707–21.

Guinier, L. (2004) 'From racial liberalism to racial literacy: *Brown v. Board of Education* and the interest-divergence dilemma', *Journal of American History*, 91(1), 92–118.

Hale-Benson, J. (1982) *Black children: Their roots, culture, and learning styles* (Baltimore, MD: Johns Hopkins).

Henry, A. (2006) 'Black-feminist pedagogy: Critiques and contributions', in W. Watkins (ed.) *Black protest thought and education* (New York: Peter Lang).

Hilliard, A. (1992) 'Behavioral style, culture, teaching and learning', *Journal of Negro Education*, 61(3), 370–7.

Hilliard, A. (1995) *The maroon within us: Selected essays on African American community socialization* (Baltimore, MD: Black Classic Press).

Holland, S. (1991) 'Positive role models for primary-grade Black inner-city males', *Equity and Excellence*, 25, 40–4.

Holman, M. (1996) 'Wanted Black males', *Black Collegian*, 26(2), 66.

Howard, T. (2001) 'Powerful pedagogy for African American students: A case of four teachers', *Urban Education*, 36, 179–202.

Irvine, J. J. (1990a) *Black students and school failure: Policies, practices, and prescriptions* (New York: Greenwood).

Irvine, J. J. (1990b) 'Beyond role models and examination of cultural influences on the pedagogical perspectives of Black teachers', *Peabody Journal of Education*, 66, 51–63.

Irvine, J. J. (2003). *Educating teachers for diversity: Seeing with the cultural eye* (New York: Teachers College Press).

Irvine, R. and Irvine, J. J. (1983) 'The impact of the desegregation process on the education of Black students: Key variables', *Journal of Negro Education*, 52(4), 410–22.

King, J. (1991) 'Unfinished business: Black student alienation and Black teachers' emancipatory pedagogy', in M. Foster (ed.) *Readings on equal education, Volume 11: Qualitative investigations into schools and schooling* (New York: AMS).

Ladson-Billings, G. (1991) 'Returning to the source: Implications for educating teachers of Black students', in M. Foster (ed.) *Readings on equal education, Volume 11: Qualitative investigations into schools and schooling* (New York: AMS).

Ladson-Billings, G. (1994) *The dreamkeepers: Successful teachers of African American children* (San Francisco, CA: Jossey-Bass).

Ladson-Billings, G. and Henry, A. (1990) 'Blurring the borders: Voices of African liberatory pedagogy in the United States and Canada', *Journal of Education*, 172(2), 72–88.

Legette, W. (1999) 'The crisis of the Black male: A new ideology in Black politics', in A. Reed (ed.) *Without justice for all: The new liberalism and our retreat from racial equality* (Boulder, CO: Westview).

Lewis, C. (2006) 'African American male teachers in public schools: An examination of three urban districts', *Teachers College*, 108 (2), 224–45.

Lynn, M. (2000) 'Raising the critical consciousness of African American students in Baldwin Hills: A portrait of an exemplary African American male teacher', *Journal of Negro Education*, 68(1), 42–53.

Lynn, M. (2002) 'Critical race theory and the perspectives of Black men teachers in the Los Angeles public schools', *Equity and Excellence in Education*, 35(2), 119–30.

Lynn, M. (2006) 'Dancing between two worlds: A portrait of the life of a Black male teacher in south central LA', *International Journal of Qualitative Studies in Education*, 19(2), 221–4.

Mabee, C. (1979) *Black education in New York State: From colonial to modern times* (Syracuse, NY: Syracuse University Press).

Moynihan, P. (1967) 'The Negro family: The case for national action', in R. Rainwater and W. Yancey (eds.) *The Moynihan report and politics of controversy* (Cambridge, MA: MIT Press).

Odih, P. (2002) 'Mentors and role models: Masculinity and the education "under-achievement" of young Afro-Caribbean males', *Race Ethnicity and Education*, 5(1), 91–105.

Omi, M. and Winant, H. (1994) *Racial formation in the United States: From the 1960s to the 1990s* (New York: Routledge).

Pang, V. and Gibson, R. (2001) 'Concepts of democracy and citizenship: Views of African American teachers', *Social Studies*, 92(6), 260–6.

Pettigrew, T. (1964) *Profile of the Negro American* (Princeton, NJ: D. Van Nostrand).

Rezai-Rashti, G. M. and Martino, W. J. (2010) 'Black male teachers as role models: Resisting the homogenizing impulse of gender and racial affiliation', *American Educational Research Journal*, 47(1), 37–64.

Riessman, F. (1962) *The culturally deprived child* (New York: Harper and Row).

Rist, R. (1973) *Urban school: A factory of failure* (Cambridge, MA: MIT Press).

Rohrer, J. and Edmonson, M. (eds.) (1960) *The eighth generation: Cultures and personalities of New Orleans Negroes* (New York: Harper and Brothers).

Rury, J. (1983) 'The New York African Free School, 1827–1836: Conflict over community control of Black education', *Phylon*, 44(3), 187–97.

Rury, J. (1985) 'Philanthropy, self help, and social control: The New York Manumission Society and free Blacks, 1785–1810', *Phylon*, 46(3), 231–41.

Shade, B. J. and Edwards, P. (1987) 'Ecological correlates of the educative style of Afro-American children', *Journal of Negro Education*, 56(1), 88–99.

Siddle-Walker, V. (2001) 'African American teaching in the South: 1940–1960', *American Education Research Journal*, 38, 751–79.

Silberman, C. (1964) *Crisis in Black and White* (New York: Random House).

Smiles, R. (2002) 'Calling all potential misters', *Black Issues in Higher Education*, 19(17), 26–8.

Zirkel, S. (2002) 'Is there a place for me? Role models and academic identity among White students and students of color', *Teachers College Record*, 104(2), 357–76.

# 11
# The Limits of Role Modelling as a Policy Frame for Addressing Equity Issues in the Teaching Profession

*Wayne Martino*

## Introduction

In this chapter, I focus on the policy implications of male teacher shortage and recruitment in terms of addressing fundamental equity issues in the teaching profession. These equity issues have been highlighted in response to the question of male teacher shortage and continue to provoke considerable debate, as I will illustrate in this chapter with specific reference to discourses about the 'endangered male teacher' and the policy implications of this in Canada and specifically Ontario (Abraham, 2010a, 2010b, 2010c). Concerns about male teacher shortage have been expressed in terms of two fundamental discourses or policy narratives: (i) the need for more male role models which ties in with anxieties about *absent fathers* and the increasing prevalence of single-parent families (Brockenbrough, 2012a; Harnett and Lee, 2003; Hutchings et al., 2008; Maylor, 2009; Pepperell and Smedley, 1998) and (ii) the question of striking a more representative gender balance in the teaching profession, a position that is underscored frequently by limited notions of equity which fail to engage with important considerations about the status of women's work, racial inequality and male privilege (Brockenbrough, 2012b; Drudy, 2008; Drudy et al., 2005; Griffiths, 2006; Martino, 2008; Moreau et al., 2007; Riddell and Tett, 2010; Thornton and Bricheno, 2006; Williams, 1993). While I direct considerable attention to the limits of role modelling in this chapter, the two discourses are often intertwined in dominant policy narratives about male teacher shortage, particularly in relation to understanding the *policy habitus* of boys' education in which questions of 'failing boys' have become inextricably linked to the phenomenon of the increasing feminisation of schooling (Carrington and McPhee, 2008; Carrington et al., 2008; Skelton, 2002).[1] As I illustrate in this chapter, such policy narratives, which are often provoked by anxieties about feminisation and the need for more male role models, are premised on a degree of 'conceptual *naïveté*', and rely on arguments that are grounded in simplistic notions of gender and race matching-identification between student and teacher (Skelton and Francis, 2009, p. 119; see also Carrington et al., 2007; Francis et al., 2008; Martino and Rezai-Rashti, 2012a). Riddell and Tett (2010) also identify some tensions between modernist and post-structuralist accounts of sex and gender as they pertain to debates about gender balance in teaching. The former, they argue, tend to rely on rather rarefied conceptions of 'man' and 'woman' as social categories and treat bodies in fairly unproblematic terms by simply working in the policy domain to ensure equity by increasing the numbers of male teachers in order to strike a more representative and gender balanced teaching profession. Such policy initiatives simply translate into putting more male bodies in schools. They do not necessarily address the politics of gender and race and, hence, eschew a consideration of broader systemic and historical forces and norms at play that lead to a devaluation and rejection of teaching as women's work (Martino and Rezai-Rashti, 2012a; Williams, 1993).

Riddell and Tett (2010), however, also draw attention to the limitations of feminist post-structuralist accounts at the heart of debates about male teacher shortage, which question the binary categorisation of sex–gender configurations, and focus on how gender is performed and not necessarily foundational to one's biological sex. Such epistemological tensions have resulted, these scholars argue, in a decoupling of sex and gender which has created a divide between policy-makers who deny that the sex of the teacher is irrelevant, and academics who question 'the utility of binary categories of "man" and "woman" [in] suggesting that gender is performed and may have little to do with the body of the person who is involved in the particular performance' (Riddell and Tett, 2010, p. 464). Rather, Riddel and Tett argue for a position which acknowledges that *bodies matter* in terms of gender performance and the extent to which it is constrained by available norms and conditions governing what are considered to be acceptable or viable expressions of masculinity and femininity (Butler, 1993). Such discussions clearly highlight the need for further reflection on the onto-epistemological concerns governing both policy-making and the theoretical frameworks informing empirical research in the field of gender and education (Martino et al., 2013).

As I illustrate in this chapter through a discussion of male teacher shortage in the Ontario context, what is still needed is a degree of critical reflexivity with regard to the analytic frames of reference for defining and making sense of the problem, as well as some consideration, on behalf of policy-makers, of the significance of the historical legacy of the politics of teaching as *women's work*. I first direct attention to the specific policy context of Ontario as a case in point to illustrate how questions of striking a more gender-balanced profession continue to get implicated in certain neoconservative frames of reference for which there is a questionable empirical basis. I then devote some attention to the role of the Canadian media in driving such policy agendas, as an illustrative case. Finally, I draw on some of the research I conducted with my colleague Goli Rezai-Rashti to highlight key issues related to male teacher recruitment and privilege in the education system in Toronto.[2]

## Attracting men to teaching in the Ontario context

There is certainly no official policy in Ontario regarding male teacher shortage and attracting men to the profession, but there is clearly a media-generated and media-fuelled discourse and also evidence of a range of stakeholders concerned to influence and drive policy in this particular direction. For example, in 2004, a consortium of stakeholders comprising the Chief Executive Office from the Ontario College of Teachers, the Director of Education from the Trillium Lakelands District School Board, the Director of Education for the School Board District Central South West and the Director of English Language, School of Education, Laurentian University, released a report entitled *Narrowing the Gender Gap: Attracting Men to Teaching* (Bernard et al., 2004). What is immediately apparent, just from the title, is the invocation of a crisis through inciting a discourse of 'gap talk'. Gillborn (2008), for example, argues that 'talk of "closing" and/or "narrowing" gaps operates as a discursive strategy whereby statistical data are deployed to construct the view that things are improving and the system is moving in the right direction' (p. 65). In this particular case, the notion of narrowing the gap is used to incite a sense of moral concern and urgency about the need to address the problematic of male teacher shortage. This effect is achieved through citing statistics which reveal that there is a declining number of male teachers entering teaching and, hence, an increasing feminisation of the profession. The goal behind the production of the report is to develop a 'philosophical framework for a practical response to the perceived need to attract men to the teaching profession' (p. 2).

The report involves a review of literature and practices in other jurisdictions designed to address male teacher shortage and also an empirical component involving results from both an online survey of male university students and focus group interviews with male high school students, early and second career teachers, senior administrators and certain education stakeholders. The results reported indicated that male high school students were not attracted to teaching because of its low salary and status, as well 'as lack of male teacher role models' (p. 2). However, male high school teachers also indicated that 'initial salaries were too low', and that there was more need for 'male visibility in promoting teaching'. This viewpoint appeared to be confirmed by senior administrators and other education stakeholders, who also mentioned teacher status as an issue and the need for 'more aggressive marketing' and mentoring programmes for male teachers in the profession (p. 2).

The whole report frames male teacher recruitment as an urgent matter that requires serious attention as an equity issue and matter of ongoing public concern (p. 4). The problem, as I will illustrate, is its failure to engage with the substantive literature in the field and with critical frameworks for addressing the politics of occupational segregation. This literature tends to highlight the ways in which the interests of men entering the profession continue to be served and raises some serious questions about the rationality of affirmative action driving the politics of policy-making related to male teacher shortage (Bagilhole and Cross, 2006; Lupton, 2000; Moreau et al., 2007). In other words, rather than couching the question of increasing male teacher representation in terms of promoting more progressive forms of masculinity which do not rely on the devaluing of nurturing capacities (Griffiths, 2006), the report tends to cite and reiterate the familiar discourses of role modelling and male teachers/boys as victims requiring affirmative action. For example, the Ontario Minister for Education at the time is quoted as linking 'male teacher shortage to the poor academic performance levels of boys and young men in Ontario classrooms', and, hence, to the 'lack of male role models in teaching positions' (p. 5). The report actually calls for the Ministry of Education to investigate the 'correlation between academic achievement of boys and the presence of male teachers in Ontario classrooms' (p. 3), but rejects empirical research from the standpoint of students themselves, which has questioned such positions about the influence of male teachers as role models (Lahelma, 2000; Lingard et al., 2002).

Later and more current research has actually refuted a correlation between the gender of the teacher and student achievement and motivation, specifically with regard to attainment in reading literacy (see Lam et al., 2010; Sokal et al., 2007). In addition, research on the role of the gender of the teacher in motivating students of the same sex found no empirical basis for the contention that boys are better motivated by male teachers (Marsh et al., 2008; Martin and Marsh, 2005). Other research in the United Kingdom has found that the teacher's gender is considered to be largely immaterial (Carrington and McPhee, 2008; Carrington et al., 2007, 2008). Recent research in Malaysia revealed that both boys and girls do better when taught by female teachers (Hoque et al., 2010). Our own research in urban schools in Toronto with elementary school students found that the gender of the teacher was not considered to be a significant determinant of student achievement or motivation. The students indicated that what mattered was good teaching. Good teaching was defined explicitly in terms of the capacity of the teacher to engage students positively in learning, provide intellectually stimulating and engaging curriculum, build productive relationships based on mutual respect and reciprocity and manage classroom situations effectively to ensure fair treatment and clear boundaries (Martino and Rezai-Rashti, 2012a). A major study conducted by researchers in Germany, published recently in the *European Sociological Review*, found 'virtually no evidence of a benefit from having a same-sex teacher, neither for boys nor for girls', and concluded that 'the popular call for more male teachers in primary schools is not the key to tackling the growing disadvantage of boys' (Neugebauer et al., 2011, p. 669). Such empirical findings are also supported by researchers in the United States and Australia, who have investigated extensively the pedagogical conditions and factors that contribute to effective classroom learning (see Darling-Hammond, 1997; Hayes et al., 2006; Lingard et al., 2003; Newman and Associates, 1996). This research, some of it published before the report was compiled, highlights the problematic of what is to count as evidence and equity in education policy-making, particularly as it relates to male teacher shortage. As Luke et al. (2010) argue, this problematic requires careful examination of 'different approaches to evidence and [the need] to focus on how each reflects particular ways of defining, explaining, and framing inequality and equality in educational policy and practice' (p. vii).

Statistics abound in the report, which highlights that there has been 'a noted decline in the number of men entering the teaching profession' (p. 6) – only 30 per cent of Ontario's teachers are male. In addition, it is stated that only 26 per cent of applicants to pre-service education programmes are men. The Ontario case is one which is mirrored not only across Canada but also in the United States and many other OECD countries. In fact, the remainder of the report is devoted to presenting comparative statistics from other countries to support the position that a crisis of male teacher shortage applies, not only in Canada, but across the globe. Once again, the reference to declining numbers of male teachers entering the profession in other nations such as Australia, New Zealand, the UK and the United States serves to highlight the magnitude and extent of the problem.

Barriers that account for such low numbers, as identified in the report, include the poor status of teaching as an undervalued occupation in which teachers are 'badly overworked' and 'sadly underpaid' in comparison to 'other more glamorous or status-rich professions' (p. 5). In addition, the report indicates that there is a pervasive culture which is suspicious of male teachers working with children, and which endorses the perception that they are less nurturing than their female counterparts. Such framing of male teachers implicates them as victims of a culture which is denying or hindering their access to a profession, and is couched in terms which paint them merely as victims of broader systemic forces at play, thereby constituting a problem that requires affirmative action policy intervention. In short, by simply advocating the need to attract more men to careers in teaching, without attending to the politics of hegemonic masculinities and the cultural devaluation of women's work, the report resorts to endorsing a crude form of affirmative action as a basis for policy intervention which relies simply on importing male bodies into classrooms and schools (see also Chapter 6). It is not to argue that the sex of the teacher is simply unimportant, but to highlight the extent to which such a rationality of affirmative action, as a basis for policy intervention, detracts attention away from the politics of gender relations and embodiment involving the participation and recruitment of male teachers. The *Narrowing the Gender Gap* report, therefore, represents an exemplary instance of the failure of policy-makers to take into consideration the historically contingent and specific norms governing the embodiment and performativity of various masculinities and the potential for male teachers to offer more progressive alternatives and democratised expressions of masculinity (Martino, 2012).

This position is consistent with the feminist insights proffered by Griffiths (2006) and others such as Francis (2008). The former argues that 'schools would benefit from having both men and women, in all their cultural diversities, but only in so far as the profession is able to create a culture that values difference' (p. 388). Francis is also at pains to highlight, not so much that the sex of the teacher does not matter, but that its comprehensibility and what counts as a proper or viable expression of embodied masculinity is imbued with politics and, therefore, cannot be reduced to simply a matter of biological sex as an essentialised phenomenon. In other words, 'its categorization does not lie in the body' but in how male teachers' bodies signify in their performativity (p. 110). It is in this sense that such empirical work cannot be simply pitted against a dominant policy position that supports or endorses the body over another policy stance which simply refutes its materiality, as suggested by Riddell and Tett (2010). Francis (2008) herself argues that 'we cannot ignore the influence of embodiment', an epistemological position that is also endorsed by feminists such as Paechter (2007). The problem is not so much those who espouse such positions regarding gender fluidity and performativity, but rather a dominant policy frame that resorts to relying on familiar tropes of essentialised male embodiment as a basis for affirmative action which, for the most part, is encapsulated by appropriating and invoking the familiar discourse of male teachers as role models.

The empirical data derived from the studies undertaken by the stakeholders who compiled the report support dominant beliefs about the need for male teachers as role models on the basis that they are essentially different. For example, male students who were interviewed indicated that 'men and women think and teach differently', and that 'men and women are different by nature and as a result have different teaching styles' (p. 14). Many of the male students also cast themselves as the 'primary wage earner', and indicated that they preferred other more high-status professions, which afforded a higher income, such as law, medicine, aviation, engineering and business. It is stated that some even indicated that they 'wanted work that was more physical – firefighter, police officer, ambulance attendant, actor', and that some boys perceived elementary school teaching as 'a feminine, care-giving profession' which was not suited to men in general (p. 15). The teachers interviewed also highlighted the need for 'positive role models' and 'active mentoring', citing the 'reality of female-headed households in the lives of boys', as well as the 'pervasiveness of male TV violence' as a justification (p. 16). They also indicated that there was a difference 'between men and women in the administration of discipline' (p. 17). In addition, it is noted that female teacher candidates tend to do better academically than their male counterparts, and, in this sense, are at an advantage in gaining acceptance into teacher education faculties where entry requirements in Canada are, in contrast with what happens in other countries, quite stringent due to quotas imposed by the government (see also Chapter 3).

What is significant is that the assumptions and masculinity politics underpinning many of the above assertions remain unproblematised in the report. Moreover, there is a sort of common-sense logic behind the justification for the supposed significance of an embodied male presence in school communities. The fundamental rationality of role modelling which underscores the entire policy impetus and justification for male teacher recruitment is encapsulated by the following quotes which are highlighted in bold and large print, and positioned strategically throughout the report to capture the reader's attention:

'Male teachers are often "dad for the day" with boys from single parent (female) families, so a male teacher may be the only male that boys from those families can talk to'

(p. 9)

'It is important to have men in teaching because, like a father in a home, a male influence is important in life'

(p. 15)

'Men in schools can be "anchors in the storm" especially for male students'

(p. 17)

These quotes serve to capture essentially the justificatory basis for role modelling as a driving force behind the policy to recruit more male teachers in Ontario schools.

## Role modelling as a 'regime of truth'

Scholars such as Britzman (1993), however, point to serious deficiencies in frameworks which resort to role modelling as a basis for explaining and accounting for the influence of teachers, on the basis of the singularity of their gender and/or race. Such positions lend themselves to a certain idealisation, oversimplification and degree of *naïveté* about the heteronormative imperatives governing dominant conceptions of what is considered to be an acceptable male role model for boys in schools (see King, 2004; Silin, 1997). Britzman draws attention to the extent to which discourses of role modelling are implicated in sex role socialisation theories, which are invested in establishing identities in normative and fixed terms:

> ...sex role socialization theory, because it is so firmly grounded in traditions of essentialism and its push to present identity as stable, cannot offer teachers and students insight into either deep emotional investments people make in normative actions and in committing themselves to living traditional roles, or the deep conflict that emerges when one attempts to lives these roles.

(p. 35)

Thus the problem of relying on role modelling as a policy frame is that it fails to take into account the complexity of identificatory relations and practices and the tensions involved in how one negotiates one's relationality and the norms governing how one relates to oneself and to others.

It is not that bodies do not matter but, as Butler (1993) highlights, 'which bodies come to matter and why', given the regulatory 'constraints by which bodies are materialized as sex' (p. ix): '...bodies only appear, only endure, only live the productive constraints of certain highly gendered regulatory schemas' (p. xi). And this is essentially the problem of role modelling as a basis for governing policy framing around male teacher shortage, as certain sorts of males are invoked or imagined as suitable, often in accordance with stereotypical traits of what constitutes the regulatory constraints of heteronormative masculinity. As Britzman illuminates, adherence to role modelling as a regime of truth for understanding the influence of teachers is 'to bring to the fore one's own investments in maintaining stereotypical appearances, naturalizing heterosexuality as the only sexuality, and in continuing gendered practices without admitting their stultifying and contradictory effects' (p. 40).

What gets left out of policy frames which rely on role modelling as a moral regulatory schema is any specification regarding exactly what sort of masculinities men are required to model or rather as Britzman reiterates 'exactly what are roles modeling?': 'The point is that, although role models always model a particular version of morality, the way they are handled prevents any critical discussion of how morality becomes constituted' (p. 38). It is in this sense that a more sophisticated rendering of bodies is required when attending to policy matters related to the recruitment of male teachers. What is needed are conceptual frameworks which interrogate the essentialist regimes of truth and moral hetero-regulatory frames which govern thinking about role modelling and bodies. As Butler (1993) argues: 'Sex is, thus, not simply what one has, or a static description of what one is: it will be one of the norms by which the "one" becomes viable at all, that which qualifies a body for life within the domain of cultural intelligibility' (p. 2).

Britzman (1993) overall raises important questions about role modelling as a grid of cultural intelligibility for reducing the 'meaning of gender... to the category of sex-role stereotyping' and, consequently, advocates for the need 'to move beyond singularity, taking into account the reality that each of us embodies a wide range of categorical commitments such as race, sexuality, generation, class, and so on; the shifting meanings of these social markers arrange the experience of gender' (p. 26). However, as I have illustrated in this chapter with the specific case of *Narrowing the Gender Gap*, and in my previous research, role modelling needs to be understood in the Foucauldian sense, as 'a regime of truth' through which certain power/knowledge relations are mobilised to constitute male teacher shortage as a particular object of policy-making. For example, the male teacher subject gains a particular currency by relying on certain bodies of disciplinary knowledge about sex-role socialisation and sex differences as a means by which to enforce a certain normalisation of gendered bodies. Foucault (1980), for example, claims that

> Truth is centred on the form of scientific discourse and the institutions which produce it; it is subject to constant economic and political incitement (the demand for truth, as much for economic production as for political power); it is the object, under diverse forms, of immense diffusion and consumption (circulating through apparatuses of education and information whose extent is relatively broad in the social body, not withstanding certain strict limitations); it is produced and transmitted under control, dominant, if not exclusive, of a few great political and economic apparatuses (university, army, writing, media); lastly it is the issue of a whole political debate and social confrontation ('ideological struggles').
>
> (pp. 131–2)

As I have already illustrated, various institutions such as school boards, ministries or state departments of education and teacher licensing bodies such as the Ontario College of Teachers have attempted to steer policy regarding male teacher recruitment through authorising certain truths about male teachers in their capacities to serve as role models.

This policy steering needs 'to be understood as a system of ordered procedures for the production, regulation, distribution, circulation and operation of statements' (Foucault, 1980, p. 133). It is in this sense that enunciations about male teachers as role models have a constitutive and regulatory effect in governing the way in which male teachers can be thought about as particular objects, not only of the gaze of policy-makers, but also of journalists, as I will further illustrate in the following section.

## 'The endangered male teacher': An object of moral concern in the Canadian media

The role of the media in influencing and steering policy-making, particularly with regard to matters related to boys' education and male teacher recruitment, has been significant. Attention by the media to the shortage of male teachers has contributed significantly to fuelling a *moral crisis* about the dearth of male teachers and the increasing feminisation of the teaching profession, with its particular impact on boys' developing masculinities and engagement in learning. The problem is attributed to both the preponderance of female teachers in elementary schools and to the increasing influence of single-parent mother households. The proliferation of such discourses is widespread and has global significance in terms of their circulation through media outlets which cut across national boundaries, extending their influence on policy-making in the field of education. Such *mediascapes* are connected to certain *ideoscapes* of 'recuperative masculinity politics' (Lingard and Douglas, 1999), and are clearly related to the proliferation of particular master narratives, which have certain regulatory effects in terms of inscribing the heteronormative limits for invoking the legitimised male teacher subject as an object of policy-making in education (see Appadurai, 1990). It is in this sense that male teacher shortage needs to be understood as emerging within a particular *policy habitus* of boys' education which is characterised by a specific *logics of practice* that under-scores 'the dispositional tendencies' of policy-makers (Lingard et al., 2005). These tendencies are connected to a broader 'recuperative masculinity politics' involving the mobilisation of backlash discourses about the inimical effects of feminisation on male teachers' and boys' lives in schools. It is in this sense that the problem of male teacher shortage is set against a particular policyscape (Ball, 1998), in which the interplay of the national and global forces are mobilised around the recuperative masculinity interests of proliferating a particular social imaginary about male teachers and boys as the 'new disadvantaged', through the mediatisation of policy production (Lingard and Rawolle, 2004; Martino and Rezai-Rashti, 2012b).

Particular evidence of such a policyscape exists in the Canadian context with the national newspaper *The Globe and Mail* identifying 'failing boys' as one of the most pressing challenges (along with the problems afflicting Canada's publicly funded health-care system and the future of the military post-Afghanistan) facing the nation in the next decade and beyond (Abraham, 2010a). A whole week was dedicated to reporting on each of the identified challenges throughout the year, with specific attention being devoted to the topic of 'the endangered male teacher' as part of the 'failing boys' featured focus (Abraham, 2010b). The feature on male teachers immediately invokes discourses of male teachers as an 'endangered species' in terms of their diminishing numbers, indicating that in many schools 'his numbers can be counted on a single hand'. While certain academics are quoted in the article as sources of authority, they are used to paint a picture of male teachers as 'disadvantaged' in a profession that is considered to be 'a nurturing feminine domain, underpaid, over-worked, low in social status and – for a male – stigmatized'. The sense of a *moral crisis* is provoked through emphasising details about 'their numbers dwindling to less than 20 percent nationally' as a basis for establishing the urgent need to fix the gender imbalance afflicting the teaching profession. Such urgency is further sedimented by connecting the 'lack of male role models' to explanations behind 'why boys trail girls in academics'. So immediately it is possible to identify what Foucault (1972) terms as 'the general set of rules' governing the emergence of particular discourses about male teachers and boys as particular sorts of objects and 'the system of their referentials':

> ...that one defines the general set of rules that govern the different modes of enunciation, the possible distribution of the subject positions, and the system that defines and prescribes them;...that one defines the set of rules common to all their associated domains, the forms of succession, of simultaneity...of which they are capable, and the system that links all these fields of coexistence together; lastly...that one can define the general set of rules that govern the status of these statements, the way in which they are institutionalised, received, used, reused, combined together, the mode according to which they become objects of appropriation, instruments for desire or interest, elements for a strategy.
>
> (p. 115)

In the particular case of this media report on male teachers, it is possible to identify the correspondences in the logics of practice that govern the dispositional tendencies of both journalists and policy-makers in terms of the intertwining discourses that clearly come to define both the terms and limits of their object of concern. The strategic deployment of the familiar tropes of male teachers as role models and increasing feminisation requires critical interrogation. Such linking of disparate discourses across various fields serves to solidify and to steer the terms of the debate about male teacher shortage and failing boys in a policy direction which is supportive of some kind of affirmative action. The journalist herself in this particular media report actually acknowledges this when she states that statistics regarding the declining numbers of male teachers entering the teaching profession have given rise to 'a certain urgency' accompanied by 'talk of affirmative action'. This urgency is also linked to a *moral concern* that 'boys increasingly grow up without fathers at home', and so the referentials that define this particular system of thought are brought together in familiar enunciative ways which continue to point to desired policy outcomes. While the article acknowledges that there is no evidence that male teachers actually impact on boys' academic performance and school-related problems, one professor is cited as claiming that female role models in math, science, law and medicine 'worked for girls', and have contributed not only 'to increases in aspirations of girls overall' but also to 'increasing presence in medical school and law school'. This particular professor also believes that 'the same logic' needs to 'apply men serving as models for boys [and girls] in the younger grades'.

What follows are comments from another male academic who has taught elementary teacher candidates for 25 years, and whose assertion about the attrition of 'the vast majority of male graduates' from the teaching profession serves to incite a discourse of moral urgency about the need 'to use affirmative action to ensure that 20 percent of teachers at every school are male'. The article ends with a final comment from this scholar who identifies feminisation as the source of the problem which supposedly leads to female-oriented approach to delivering the curriculum that relies 'too heavily' in the early grades on having students 'sitting still' and stresses 'co-operation over competition'. He asserts that 'females are making the decisions, they're choosing the books, and setting up the class'. This same professor is also quoted as an authoritative source in another report as part of this series on *failing boys* on the medication of boys with attention deficit hyperactivity disorder (ADHD), where he is cited as identifying the decline of male teachers in primary schools and, hence, the preponderance of female teachers as partly to blame for the 'ballooning drug use: "What are we drugging? Female teachers who don't understand [that] boys like to run and jump and shout – that's what boys do" ' (Abraham, 2010c).

What is evident in this particular media domain is the intertwining discourses which are strategically employed by the journalist and which involve various modes of enunciation that connect the decline of male teachers to the problem of feminisation in the form of female teachers' influence on boys' engagement with schooling. However, this domain of 'failing' and 'medicated' boys at school is also linked to the family domain, where discourses about the *absent father* in many single-parent homes also play into the constitution of a familiar meta-narrative about the detrimental effects of feminisation. The *rules* which govern the articulation of this narrative have direct correspondences to policy-generated concerns about male teacher shortage which, as we have witnessed with the *Narrowing the Gender Gap* report, rely on the same or similar terms of reference for justifying affirmative action in terms of recruiting more male teachers to the profession.

## Male teacher recruitment and presence in Toronto schools

While there is clearly a sense of urgency and moral concern about the need for more male teachers in schools, the issue, as I have illustrated above in both the policy and media domains, has been the terms of reference for defining the problem of male teacher shortage. Rizvi and Lingard (2010), in fact, have called for 'an historically informed reflexivity' in the education policy analysis field (p. 51). It is not that gender representation is not important, but it needs to be addressed with some attention and sensitivity to the historical legacy of the politics of doing 'woman's work', and must not involve merely an attempt to re-masculinise the teaching domain in order to ameliorate the supposed inimical effects of feminisation (Martino, 2008). Framing such policy initiatives in these terms denies the broader cultural manifestations of a masculinity politics that continue to serve the interests of men. What is needed is greater attention, on behalf of policy-makers, to the dangers of re-masculinisation of the profession, and to critical questions of how certain hegemonic norms continue to govern the identity work at play in invoking male teachers as certain sorts of role models that rely on the heteronormative imperatives of the singularity of gender and race.

For example, our research in Toronto, which involved interviews with over 70 elementary school teachers and observations in over 20 classrooms, found evidence that, while men are clearly in a minority in terms of their numbers, they are disproportionately represented in leadership positions and privileged in a number of ways, not only in terms of recruitment, but also in terms of opportunities for senior administrative positions. The female teachers we interviewed discussed at length the preferential treatment of male teachers in elementary schools by administrators and parents, while many male teachers themselves acknowledged a degree of male privilege in terms of both gaining entry into elementary teaching, and securing employment by school boards. They were aware that many principals and school boards were actively seeking male teachers as preferred candidates for teaching positions in elementary schools. For example, in one particular high-poverty, high-minority inner-city school, the principal indicated that she actively recruited male teachers and mentioned the recent appointment of a Black male Caribbean teacher (Patrick), which she felt was important given the cultural diversity of the school's population, a commitment to equity and the benefits of race-role modelling, particularly for the Black male students. However, important differences existed in terms of race, culture and religious affiliations between this particular teacher and many of the students at the school, given that most of the student population comprised of Somali-speaking students from Muslim backgrounds. The principal's position on equity and recruitment seemed to be based on an essentialising tendency, resulting in what Cornel West (2005) argues is characterised by a familiar 'homogenizing impulse' which assumes that all Black people are alike. This essentialising tendency results, he asserts, in 'obliterating differences (class, gender, region, sexual orientation) between black people' (p. 36).

The fact that Patrick identified as gay and, in fact, subscribed to some stereotypical beliefs about Muslims in the community, based on their cultural and religious backgrounds, actually led to some tensions for him in his relations with students and the parent community. His fear about his own sexuality and the potential homophobia that he felt he would be subjected to if he were to come out compelled him to remain in the closet. In fact, Patrick indicated that such a denial of his sexuality actually detracted from his ability to be an effective teacher and to serve as a role model for his students. Such an account draws attention to both the limits of representation and role modelling in terms of treating race as a fixed or singular category, and highlights McCarthy's (1998) point that

> one cannot understand race, paradoxically, by looking at race alone. Different gender, class, and ethnic interests cut at right angles to racial coordination and affiliation.
>
> (p. 17)

We also encountered cases of the specific institutionalisation of particular *gender regimes* in elementary schools and a culture of masculinisation (Kessler et al., 1985), which tended to defy simplistic arguments about the impact of feminisation which often gets reduced to a crude question of numbers in terms of dominance of female teachers and the corresponding absence of male teachers. For example, in one particular school, the whole question of male privilege and entitlement was identified by a number of teachers who talked at length about the existence of a 'boy's club', which they believed guaranteed a degree of privilege which was denied to female and non-normative male teachers. The principal, a White male in his late forties, whose office was decorated with hockey memorabilia, such as trophies and photos of hockey teams, was identified as actively supporting a particular group of men. The vice-principal, a Black Caribbean man, was also identified as a key figure in the support which some teachers felt was provided to a specific group of male teachers at the school. This support was not always overt, but was understood in terms of the following: (i) a politics of representation in terms of male authority in the administrative hierarchy of the school – despite the fact that there were more female teachers at the school (there were only seven males), only one woman held a position of administrative leadership in the school (Mahony et al., 2004); (ii) the sense that male teachers were taken more seriously by the male-headed administration than their female counterparts – there was a sense that the same request by a female teacher would not have the same currency as that by a male teacher (male teachers had more access to the administrative hierarchy and were taken more seriously); (iii) a sense that men who were part of this 'club' were being primed for accelerated promotion.

These two cases draw attention to the politics of gender which occur more at the informal level of social relations and interactions in school communities, and the effects of such relations for maintaining and supporting male privilege and entitlement (Moreau et al., 2007). The insights we gained from talking with many teachers and principals in schools about the unofficial privileging and preference given to male teacher hires were confirmed recently with reports in the *Globe and Mail* newspaper earlier this year, indicating that an internal memo released by the Toronto District School Board, one of the most racially and culturally diverse school boards in North America, had stipulated that 'interview be granted to teacher candidates "that meet one or more of the following criteria in addition to being an outstanding teacher: Male, racial minority, French, Music, Aboriginal"' (Hammer and Alphonso, 2013, p. A1). Arguments from the board in terms of such a policy directive on teacher recruitment were justified in terms of a commitment to ensuring a more gender- and race-balanced representative teaching population, given that only 22 per cent of elementary and 23 per cent of high school teachers are visible minorities (a term used in the Canadian census to refer to those who do not belong to the White majority), while 72 per cent of students are visible minorities (p. A12). The journalists also quote statistics indicating that 77 per cent of elementary teachers and 59 per cent of high school teachers are female, but qualify these numbers with the statement that 'many experts blame a shortage of role models for the fact that boys and some minority groups lag behind girls on standardised tests and postsecondary achievement'. This sort of qualification once again hearkens back to the problematic previously explicated in relation to the lack of evidence to support such claims about the impact of male teachers on student achievement and the extent to which discourses of role modelling are easily mobilised in accordance with a particular *game or regime of truth* (Foucault, 1980), which has come to set the terms of reference governing the policy habitus of boys' education. It also raises some questions about the legality of an unofficial policy of male teacher recruitment, or at least a preference for male teachers that was identified by many teachers in our research.[3]

## Implications and conclusion

There are clear implications for deploying role modelling as a policy frame for male teacher recruitment, which have limiting effects in terms of addressing fundamental equity issues in the teaching profession, particularly as they relate to the status of women's work and the politics of masculinity. As I have illustrated, both role modelling and a focus on representation as a basis for justifying male teacher recruitment actually exacerbate equity concerns and eschew important questions related to the cultural devaluation of certain sorts of gendered labour. In fact, such narratives result in the familiar dispositional tendency to embrace re-masculinisation as a basis for policy intervention. While advocating for more male and minority teachers does not necessarily have to align with such a political project of recuperative masculinity politics, such attention to recruitment along these lines needs to engage with epistemological and empirical work which problematises the homogenising tendencies which govern thinking about race- and gender-based role modelling and the politics of representation, as they are embodied by the male and minority teacher.

They also draw attention away from a more careful consideration of the conditions which contribute to teacher attrition and retention particularly in high-poverty, high-minority urban school communities (Ingersoll and May, 2011).

In this sense, policy-makers would do well to steer away from grounding the problem of male teacher shortage in discourses that rely on role modelling or too heavily on a politics of representation. In short, neither representation nor role modelling alone can serve as an adequate basis for addressing and explaining the problem of male teacher shortage. A politics of representation, while important, often relies on liberal notions of affirmative action, and involves simply increasing the number of male bodies, without attending to the significance of the politics of masculinity or rather the power relations that are implicated in its embodiment. Moreover, what such politics means pedagogically speaking, in terms of enhancing the quality of learning and the education of all students, is never addressed. Similarly, relying on role modelling as a policy frame for justifying male teacher recruitment suffers from similar deficiencies in that it is often governed by normalising assumptions and investments in maintaining 'stereotypical appearances' and hegemonic forms of sociality which ignore important questions of sexuality and the contradictory and shifting effects of negotiating one's identity (Britzman, 1993).

In fact, both policy frames tend to be grounded in a sort of identity politics, and fail to address the more redistributive issues that relate to socio-economics and how such forms of disadvantage contribute significantly to poor achievement in schools and high dropout rates. In following Fraser (1997), to limit policy concerns surrounding male teacher shortage to a fundamental politics of recognition in order to draw attention to the marginalisation of and discrimination directed against male teachers is to fundamentally ignore and mis-recognise the historical contingencies of economic conditions that have led to the cultural devaluation of teaching as a profession, and which has served to structure and perpetuate gender-specific modes of occupational exploitation and segregation (Blount, 2005; Martino, 2008). Such histories enable one to understand the residual effects of this cultural devaluation of women's work, as well as the maintenance of male privilege and certain forms of masculinity within the profession itself in terms of the support which is offered to certain sorts of male teachers. It is in this sense that policy related to addressing male teacher shortage needs to be grounded in a 'historically informed reflexivity' (Rizvi and Lingard, p. 51). As Brown (2012), in drawing on Popkewitz (1997), stipulates, what is needed are *methods of analysis* which enable us to 'examine how trajectories of the past help to shape how "ideas and events are constructed"' (p. 300; see also Chapter 10 and Martino, forthcoming). He argues for an analytic focus on Black male teachers which involves a meta-awareness of how the Black male subject is already constituted, and the historical contingency and emergence of such constructions, as a basis for developing a deeper understanding of the politics of their pedagogical practices when working with Black male students. Such historical analyses are also necessary in order to serve as a basis for more sound policy and gender-just approaches to policy-making, particularly as they pertain to male teacher recruitment.

Overall, what is needed is more of an attempt in the policy field to engage with the substantive literature in the field as a basis for addressing a significant policy-research gap when it comes to a consideration of what counts as evidence and equity in the claims that can be made for male teachers and their particular effects in classrooms on student learning generally and specifically on boys. A more long-term focus and commitment to addressing the politics of masculinity, while simultaneously directing attention to the conditions and resources that are needed to foster quality teaching, particularly in high-needs, high-poverty and high-diversity urban schools, would lead to more productive outcomes and politically informed understandings about the sort of role that male teachers need to play in education and more specifically in boys' lives.

## Notes

1. The 'policy habitus' refers specifically to a particular field and interconnected networks of relations and flows of discourses in which policy-making is implicated. As Lingard et al. (2005) explicate, a policy habitus refers to dispositional tendencies of policy-makers which are implicated in specific histories, cultures and structures of thought (p. 764). With regard to boys' education there is clearly particular logics of practice, which I identify in this chapter as having a basis in *recuperative masculinity politics* (Lingard and Douglas, 1999). Such logics of practice are implicated in certain value systems which are identified in terms of connecting discourses of feminisation to the significance of male role models and absent fathers in boys' lives as strategic elements in an orchestrated policy imperative with regard to addressing the problematic of male teacher shortage.
2. This chapter is based on an SSHRC (Social Sciences and Humanities Research Council)-funded grant, entitled 'The influence of male elementary school

teachers as role models' (410-2006-115381). It is also derived from an invited address at the International Conference on Teachers and School Administrators: Demand-Supply and Monitoring Practices, Eastin Hotel, Kuala Lumpur, 10 June 2013, organised by University of Malaya, Malaysia, and Ministry of Education, Malaysia.

3. Recently, the Ontario government introduced Regulation 274 'to prevent nepotism and favouritism in hiring practices' which stipulates that teachers must be hired on the basis of seniority. However, school boards have voiced some opposition to the regulation (Morrow and Alphonso, 2013). There is a sense that such legislation will allow for more equitable hiring practices, but that it will not necessarily prevent male teachers being actively sought after and be recruited over female teachers. The problem of an unofficial policy preference for the male gender as an under-represented population in the teaching profession needs to be understood as a broader cultural matter and one which has been motivated by post-feminist concerns about feminisation and its implications for reconstituting gender equity (Martino, forthcoming).

# References

Abraham, C. (2010a) 'Part 1: Failing boys and the powder keg of sexual politics', *Globe and Mail*, 16 October, http://www.theglobeandmail.com/news/national/time-to-lead/part-1-failing-boys-and-the-powder-keg-of-sexual-politics/article4081751/?page=all (Accessed 16 July 2013).

Abraham, C. (2010b) 'Part 2: The endangered male teacher', *Globe and Mail*, 18 October, http://www.theglobeandmail.com/news/national/time-to-lead/part-2-the-endangered-male-teacher/article4330079/ (Accessed 16 July 2013).

Abraham, C. (2010c) 'Part 3: Are we medicating a disorder or treating boyhood as a disease', *Globe and Mail*, 19 October, http://www.theglobeandmail.com/news/national/time-to-lead/part-3-are-we-medicating-a-disorder-or-treating-boyhood-as-a-disease/article4330080/?page=all (Accessed 16 July 2013).

Appadurai, A. (1990) 'Disjuncture and difference in the global cultural economy', in M. Featherstone (ed.) *Global culture: Nationalism, globalization and modernity* (London: Sage).

Bagilhole, B. and Cross, S. (2006) ' "It never struck me as female": Investigating men's entry into female dominated occupations', *Journal of Gender Studies*, 15(1), 35–48.

Ball, S. (1998) 'Big policies/small world: An introduction to international perspectives in education policy', *Comparative Education*, 34(2), 119–30.

Bernard, J., Hill, D., Falter, P. and Wilson, D. (2004) *Narrowing the gender gap: Attracting men to teaching*, Report, Ontario College of Teachers, Toronto, ON, http://www.oct.ca/publications/documents.aspx?lang=en-CA (Accessed 16 July 2013).

Blount, J. (2005) *Fit to teach: Same-sex desire, gender, and school work in the twentieth century* (Albany, NY: SUNY Press).

Britzman, D. (1993) 'Beyond rolling models: Gender and multicultural education', in S. K. Biklen and D. Pollard (eds.) *Gender and education* (Chicago: University of Chicago Press).

Brockenbrough, E. (2012a) ' "You ain't my daddy!": Black male teachers and the politics of surrogate fatherhood', *International Journal of Inclusive Education*, 16(4), 357–72.

Brockenbrough, E. (2012b) 'Emasculation blues: Black male teachers' perspectives on gender and power in the teaching profession', *Teachers College Record*, 114(5), 1–43.

Brown, A. (2012) 'On human kinds and role models: A critical discussion about the African American teacher', *Educational Studies*, 48, 296–315.

Butler, J. (1993) *Bodies that matter: On the discursive limits of sex* (New York and London: Routledge).

Carrington, B., Francis, B., Hutchings, M., Skelton, C., Read, B. and Hall, I. (2007) 'Does the gender of the teacher really matter? Seven to eight-year-olds' accounts of their interactions with their teachers', *Educational Studies*, 33(4), 397–413.

Carrington, B. and McPhee, A. (2008) 'Boys' underachievement and the feminization of teaching', *Journal of Education for Teaching*, 34(2), 109–20.

Carrington, B., Tymms, P. and Merrell, C. (2008) 'Role models, school improvement and the "gender gap" – Do men bring out the best in boys and women in girls?', *British Educational Research Journal*, 34(3), 315–27.

Darling-Hammond, L. (1997) *The right to learn: A blueprint for creating schools that work* (San Francisco: Jossey-Bass).

Drudy, S. (2008) 'Gender balance/gender bias: The teaching profession and the impact of feminisation', *Gender and Education*, 20(4), 309–23.

Drudy, S., Martin, M., Woods, M. and O'Flynn, J. (2005) *Men and the classroom: Gender imbalance in teaching* (London and New York: Routledge).

Foucault, M. (1972) *The archaeology of knowledge* (London: Tavistock).

Foucault, M. (1980) *Power/knowledge: Selected interviews and other writings 1972–1977* (New York: Pantheon Books).

Francis, B. (2008) 'Teaching manfully? Exploring gendered subjectivities and power via analysis of men teachers' gender performance', *Gender and Education*, 20(2), 109–22.

Francis, B., Skelton, C., Carrington, B., Hutchings, M., Read, B. and Hall, I. (2008) 'A perfect match? Pupils' and teachers views of the impact of matching educators and learners by gender', *Research Papers in Education*, 23(1), 21–36.

Fraser, N. (1997) *Justice interruptus* (New York: Routledge).

Gillborn, D. (2008) *Racism and education: Coincidence or conspiracy?* (London and New York: Routledge).

Griffiths, M. (2006) 'The feminization of teaching and the practice of teaching: Threat or opportunity', *Educational Theory*, 56(4), 387–405.

Hammer, K. and Alphonso, C. (2013) 'School board's hiring policy singles out men, minorities', *Globe and Mail*, 19 February, A2, A12.

Harnett, P. and Lee, J. (2003) 'Where have all the men gone? Have primary schools really been feminised?', *Journal of Educational Administration and History*, 35(2), 77–86.

Hayes, D., Mills, M., Christie, P. and Lingard, B. (2006) *Teachers and schooling making a difference* (Sydney: Allen and Unwin).

Hoque, K. E., Alam, G. M., Shamsudin, F., Akbar, S. Z. A., Moktharuddin, N. and Fong, Y. S. (2010) 'Impact of foreign teachers' recruitment on higher education: An analysis at Malaysian standpoint', *African Journal of Business Management*, 4(18), 3937–46.

Hutchings, M., Carrington, B., Francis, B., Skelton, C., Read, B. and Hall, I. (2008) 'Nice and kind, smart and funny: What children like and want to emulate in their teachers', *Oxford Review of Education*, 34(2), 135–57.

Ingersoll, R. and May, H. (2011) 'The minority teacher shortage: Fact or fable?', *Kappan Magazine*, 62–5, http://www.gse.upenn.edu/pdf/rmi/Fact_or_Fable.pdf (Accessed 16 July 2013).

Kessler, S., Ashenden, D. J., Connell, R. W. and Dowsett, G. (1985) 'Gender relations in secondary schools', *Sociology of Education*, 58, 34–48.

King, J. (2004) 'The (im)possibility of gay teachers for young children', *Theory into Practice*, 43(2), 122–7.

Lahelma, E. (2000) 'Lack of male teachers: A problem for students or teachers?', *Pedagogy, Culture and Society*, 8(2), 173–86.

Lam, Y. R., Tse, S. K., Lam, J. W. and Loh, E. K. Y. (2010) 'Does the gender of the teacher matter in the teaching of reading literacy? Teacher gender and pupil attainment in reading literacy in Hong Kong', *Teaching and Teacher Education*, 26, 754–9.

Lingard, B. and Douglas, P. (1999) *Men engaging feminisms: Profeminism, backlashes and schooling* (Buckingham, UK: Open University Press).

Lingard, B., Hayes, D, Mills, M. and Christie, P. (2003) *Leading learning: Making hope practical in schools* (Buckingham, UK: Open University Press).

Lingard, B., Martino, W., Mills, M. and Bahr, M. (2002) *Addressing the educational needs of boys* (Canberra, ACT: Department of Education Science and Training).

Lingard, B. and Rawolle, S. (2004) 'Mediatizing educational policy: The journalistic field, science policy, and cross field effects', *Journal of Education Policy*, 19(3), 361–80.

Lingard, B., Rawolle, S. and Taylor, S. (2005) 'Globalizing policy sociology in education: Working with Bourdieu', *Journal of Education Policy*, 20(6), 759–77.

Luke, A., Green, J. and Kelly, G. (2010) 'What counts as evidence and equity', *Review of Research in Education*, 34(1), vii–xvi.

Lupton, B. (2000) 'Maintaining masculinity: Men who do "women's work"', *British Journal of Management*, 11, S33–S48.

Mahony, P., Hextall, I. and Menter, I. (2004) 'Threshold assessment and performance management: Modernizing or masculinizing teaching in England', *Gender and Education*, 16(2), 132–49.

Marsh, H., Martin, A. and Cheng, J. (2008) 'A multi-level perspective on gender in classroom motivation and climate: potential benefits of male teachers for boys?', *Journal of Educational Psychology*, 100(1), 78–95.

Martin, A. and Marsh, H. (2005) 'Motivating boys and motivating girls: Does teacher gender really make a difference?', *Australian Journal of Education*, 49(3), 320–34.

Martino, W. (2008) 'Male teachers as role models: Addressing issues of masculinity, pedagogy and the re-masculinization of schooling', *Curriculum Inquiry*, 38(2), 189–223.

Martino, W. (2012) 'Queering masculinities as a basis for gender democratization: Toward embracing a transgender imaginary', in C. Greig and W. Martino (eds.) *Canadian men and masculinities: Historical and contemporary perspectives* (Toronto: Canadian Scholars' Press).

Martino, W. (forthcoming) Teaching boys in neoliberal and postfeminist times: Feminization and the question of remasculinization in the education system, Special issue of *Jahrbuch für Frauen und Geschlechterforschung in der Erziehungswissenschaft* (Yearbook of women's and gender studies in education): Masculinities – Gender construction in pedagogical institutions.

Martino, W. and Rezai-Rashti, G. (2012a) *Gender, race and the politics of role modeling: The influence of male teachers* (New York: Routledge).

Martino, W. and Rezai-Rashti, G. (2012b) 'Neo-liberal accountability and boys' underachievement: Steering education policy by numbers in the Ontario context', *International Journal of Inclusive Education*, 16(4), 423–40.

Martino, W., Rezai-Rashti, G. and Lingard, B. (2013) 'Gendering in gender research: Methodological considerations', *International Journal of Qualitative Studies in Education*, 26(4), 391–9.

Maylor, U. (2009) ' "They do not relate to Black people like us": Black teachers as role models for Black pupils', *Journal of Education Policy*, 24(1), 1–21.

McCarthy, C. (1998) *The uses of culture: Education and the limits of ethnic affiliation* (New York and London: Routledge).

Moreau, M. P., Osgood, J. and Halsall, A. (2007) 'Making sense of the glass ceiling in schools: An exploration of women teachers' discourses', *Gender and Education*, 19(2), 237–53.

Morrow, A. and Alphonso, C. (2013) 'Wynn admits practice of seniority-based hiring of teachers needs fixing', *Globe and Mail*, 25 September, http://www.theglobeandmail.com/news/national/education/wynne-admits-practice-of-seniority-based-hiring-of-teachers-needs-fixing/article14516696 (Accessed 27 October 2013).

Neugebauer, M., Helbig, M. and Landmann, A. (2011) 'Unmasking the myth of the same-sex teacher advantage', *European Sociological Review*, 27(5), 669–89.

Newmann, F. and Associates (1996) *Authentic achievement: Restructuring schools for intellectual quality* (San Francisco, CA: Jossey-Bass).

Paechter, C. (2007) *Being boys, being girls: Learning masculinities and femininities* (Maidenhead, UK: Open University Press).

Pepperell, S. and Smedley, S. (1998) 'Call for more men in primary teaching: Problematizing the issues', *International Journal of Inclusive Education*, 2(4), 341–57.

Popkewitz, T. (1997) 'A changing terrain of knowledge and power: A social epistemology of educational research', *Educational Researcher*, 26, 18–29.

Riddell, S. and Tett, L. (2010) 'Gender balance in teaching debate: Tensions between gender theory and equality policy', *International Journal of Inclusive Education*, 14(5), 463–77.

Rizvi, F. and Lingard, B. (2010) *Globalizing education policy* (London: Routledge).

Silin, J. (1997) 'The pervert in the classroom', in J. Tobin (ed.) *Making a place for pleasure in early childhood education* (New Haven, CT, and London: Yale University Press).

Skelton, C. (2002) 'The feminisation of schooling or re-masculinising primary education?', *International Studies in Sociology of Education*, 12(1), 77–96.

Skelton, C. and Francis, B. (2009) *Feminism and 'the schooling scandal'* (London and New York: Routledge).

Sokal, L., Katz, H., Chaszewski, L. and Wojcik, C. (2007) 'Good-bye, Mr. Chips: Male teachers shortage and boys' reading achievement', *Sex Roles: A Journal of Research*, 56(9/10), 651–9.

Thornton, M. and Bricheno, P. (2006) *Missing men in education* (Stoke-on-Trent, UK: Trentham).

West. C. (2005) 'The new cultural politics of difference', in C. McCarthy, W. Crichlow and G. Dimitriatis (eds.) *Race, identity and representation in education* (New York: Routledge).

Williams, C. (1993) *Doing 'women's work': Men in nontraditional occupations* (Newbury Park, CA, London and New Delhi: Sage).

# Conclusion

*Marie-Pierre Moreau*

The contributions grouped in this volume highlight the persistence in the teaching profession of inequalities based on a range of identity markers, including gender, ethnicity, sexual orientation, age, social class and nationality, and how these continue to frame individuals' chances to become a teacher and, for practising teachers, their ongoing experiences. This work, broadly informed by social constructivist, feminist and post-colonial theories (for example, Bhabha, 1990; Burr, 1995; Francis and Skelton, 2001; Hall, 2000), shows that, despite a prevailing conception of teaching as an inclusive and egalitarian profession, it can be a position difficult to access and a positional identity difficult to perform for some. Yet these contributions simultaneously acknowledge that teaching offers employment opportunities to groups which can legitimately be described as dominated and that, while teachers' experiences and discourses of teacher professionalism are, for example, gendered, raced and classed, the precise patterns of domination do vary across institutional and societal contexts. This observation has significant theoretical and political implications. The variability of (in)equality patterns across contexts questions the view that they are inevitable and, thus, opens a space to imagine alternative futures. In addition, many of the contributions in this volume highlight how teachers from dominated groups still manage to resist and subvert the dominant arrangements in place, even though this often comes at a price (for example, when one has to produce 'acceptable' accounts of their private lives which are seen by others as compatible with being a teacher).

As argued by Francis and Skelton,

> ... there has always been interest in the 'kind of people' who enter the teaching profession ... This is perhaps more true of teachers than

other professionals, because the core of their work is with children: the interface of teacher-pupil means that human relationships are a key component of the teaching-learning process.

(2008, p. 1)

Since teachers play a major role in the learning and identity formation of students and can have, under certain circumstances, some considerable power over them, interest in who they are is not surprising and, one may argue, it is even key to the success of any education system and to the well-being of children that those choosing this profession are made accountable. However, the intense level of scrutiny to which teachers are subjected (both as a profession and on an individual level) is not necessarily beneficial to anybody, as highlighted in this collection. Some teachers are also more likely to be subjected to regimes of surveillance than others (see, for example, Chapter 4, on Indigenous teachers).

In the contemporary context, the concern for the 'kind of people' teachers are has been reignited by the success of gender-, race- and class-based role-modelling 'theories', which, in many countries, inform educational practices and policies. There is in reality no evidence that the matching of learners and teachers sharing similar 'characteristics' deemed desirable by these theories increases students' performance or 'improves' their behaviour, as highlighted by the vast literature in this field (for example, Neugebauer et al., 2011; see also Chapter 11). What role-modelling theories seem to have achieved, however, is the com-modification of teachers' gender, race and social class, as these and other identity markers have been redefined as simple attributes and as the policy focus concentrates on the effects of the composition of the teaching profession, understood through rigid socio-demographic categories, on students. In line with the discourse of individualisa-tion which prevails in the context of late modern societies (Beck, 1992; Giddens, 1984), the politics of gender, race and class at play in schools and in society at large are negated and limited attention is given to the power differential which exists between some groups. For example, the disproportionate access of male White teachers to leadership and management roles has been either evacuated from pol-icy agendas or encouraged as a way to attract and retain the male teachers who are presumed to provide 'positive role models' to male students through simplistic and essentialist understandings of mas-culinity (Moreau, 2011). Similar observations have been made about teacher education programmes, which increasingly exclude the study of equality matters (Mahony, 1999).

There is a clear need for research critically engaging with the tropes underpinning dominant discourses of teachers and teacher professionalism. This volume accomplishes this goal in part, with its coverage of a range of topics, equality matters and regions of the world. However, the boundaries of this project and the positionality of those involved also need to be acknowledged. The voices of the researchers which have come to the fore come mostly from the wealthy, Western, English-speaking parts of the world. Similarly, this book covers a range of equality issues but gives limited attention to others, such as disability and religion. In many ways, this volume is also constrained by the issues it explores. As the lives of the teachers discussed in this book, processes of knowledge production remain partly shaped by the social contexts in which they emerge, which filter who becomes an academic and which research topics are seen as worthwhile. Many stories remain to be told, many voices remain to be heard.

This volume does not offer some quick solution to the issues discussed, apart maybe from reminding us that policy narratives need to be less oblivious of research narratives. It would be indeed naive to assume that inequalities in the teaching profession are a simple matter to address. These are often the result of prejudiced views and practices which are deeply embedded in national and school cultures and also have a pervasive and polymorphic nature. The facets of inequalities are many and include among other things barriers in accessing the most prestigious and rewarded segments of the teaching profession, abuse and harassment in and out of the classroom, stereotyping, social isolation and feelings of 'not belonging', and surveillance of teachers' bodies, behaviours and private lives. All of these deeply affect individuals' decision to enter and remain in the profession, as well as the formation of their identities, their well-being, their health and their relationships with colleagues, students and local communities (Day and Kingston, 2008; Zembylas, 2005).

Addressing the complexity of equality issues and bringing about social change in the teaching profession requires a multi-level intervention. As well as facilitating the engagement of education policy-makers and practitioners with recent work informed by empirical research and critical thinking, these issues could partly be addressed through a legal pathway. The effects of equal rights legislation should not be minimised and it is worth reminding here that only 80 per cent of countries in the world have equality legislation in place. However, even in the West where such legislation is usually in place, its effectiveness remains questionable (McBride Stetson and Mazur, 1995) and some schools are exempted from applying the extant legislation (see Chapter 8). Besides, subtle practices can subvert the most ambitious policies and legal frameworks (Moreau et al., 2008). Thus, legal change can only work as part of a broader, deeper cultural project aiming to produce inclusive school regimes. To echo the complexity and diversity of equality issues in the teaching profession, an intervention in this area would also need to be multifaceted. The sole focus on raising the levels of representation of groups currently under-represented, advocated in many countries, appears counterproductive. The contributions to this volume concur that there is a need for a more diverse and representative teaching workforce but also raise questions regarding this policy ambition and highlight the need to further problematise concepts of diversity and representativeness. Moreover, if diversity is a desirable aspiration, there is no reason why it should not characterise every level of the education system (that is, from nursery to higher education) and of the hierarchy of teaching jobs (from teaching assistants to headteachers). In addition, 'inclusion' and equality are not just about quantitative indicators and bringing more diverse 'bodies' into the profession. One may be a practising teacher but, as mentioned earlier, struggle in performing this positional identity. For example, increasing the presence of minority ethnic and gay teachers in the profession or of women in school leadership positions does not suffice if that means for these groups being part of a community which is hostile to them, makes them feel as if they do not 'belong' and does not value their work. In other terms, a politics of redistribution can only work if combined with a politics of recognition (Fraser, 1997). For all to be included in a wider sense, the structural features of national and school cultures which sometimes make them sexist, racist and homophobic environments to work in also need to be tackled.

## References

Bhabha, H. (1990) *Nation and narration* (London: Routledge).
Beck, U. (1992) *Risk society* (London: Sage).
Burr, V. (1995) *An introduction to social constructionism* (London: Routledge).
Day, C. and Kingston, A. (2008) 'Identity, well-being and effectiveness: The emotional contexts of teaching', *Pedagogy, Culture and Society*, 16(1), 7–23.
Francis, B. and Skelton, C. (2001) *Investigating gender: Contemporary perspectives in education* (Buckingham, UK: Open University Press).
Francis, B. and Skelton, C. (2008) 'Editorial. Introduction to special issue on teacher identities', *Pedagogy, Culture and Society*, 16(1), 1–6.
Fraser, N. (1997) *Justice interruptus* (New York: Routledge).

Giddens, A. (1984) *The constitution of society. Outline of the theory of structuration* (Cambridge: Polity).

Hall, S. (2000) 'Old and new identities, old and new ethnicities', in L. Black and J. Solomos (eds.) *Theories of race and racism* (New York: Routledge).

Mahony, P. (1999) 'Teacher education policy and gender', in J. Salisbury and S. Riddell (eds.) *Gender policy and educational change* (London: Routledge).

McBride Stetson, D. and Mazur, A. G. (eds.) (1995) *Comparative state feminism* (Thousand Oaks, CA: Sage).

Moreau, M. P. (2011) 'The societal construction of "boys' underachievement" in educational policies: A cross-national comparison', *Journal of Education Policy*, 26(2), 161–80.

Moreau, M. P., Osgood, J. and Halsall, A. (2008) 'Equal opportunities policies in English schools: Towards greater gender equality in the teaching workforce?', *Gender, Work and Organization*, 15(6), 553–78.

Neugebauer, M., Helbig, M. and Landmann, A. (2011) 'Unmasking the myth of the same-sex teacher advantage', *European Sociological Review*, 27(5), 669–89.

Zembylas, M. (2005) 'Discursive practices, genealogies, and emotional rules: A poststructuralist view on emotion and identity in teaching', *Teaching and Teacher Education*, 21, 935–48.

# Index

Note: Locators in **bold** type indicate headings.

Printed and bound by CPI Group (UK) Ltd, Croydon, CR0 4YY